D1032542

James Jones

An American Literary Orientalist Master

James Jones

AN
AMERICAN
LITERARY
ORIENTALIST
MASTER

Steven R. Carter

UNIVERSITY OF ILLINOIS PRESS

URBANA AND CHICAGO

© 1998 by the Board of Trustees of the University of Illinois
Manufactured in the United States of America
C 5 4 3 2 1

This book is printed on acid-free paper.

Library of Congress Cataloging-in-Publication Data

Carter, Steven R., 1942-
James Jones : an American literary Orientalist master / Steven R. Carter.
p.   cm.
Includes bibliographical references and index.
ISBN 0-252-02371-4 (alk. paper)
1. Jones, James, 1921-1977—Criticism and interpretation.
2. Civilization, Oriental, in literature.
1. Title.
PS3560.O49Z64   1998
813'.54—dc21
97-4887
CIP

This book is dedicated to Rita,
Louisa, Ray, and Ken;
to my parents, Ray and Eunice Carter;
to my brother, John;
and to Gloria and Kaylie Jones

CONTENTS

PREFACE

This book is the result of a fascination with James Jones and his writing spanning close to thirty years. Although I had always read Jones's fiction avidly, my scholarly interest was aroused in the late 1960s, because I believed that most critics had failed to see his attack on Hemingway's macho stance—in his December 1963 "Letter Home" for *Esquire* Jones asked what had Hemingway "done to us all with all his big masculine bullshit?" (34)—and his view that men should become more sensitive, especially with women. I had first noticed Jones's stance on manhood in *Go to the Widow-Maker* (1967), which I read soon after perusing Myron Brenton's sociological study *The American Male*, and I saw numerous links between what Jones had depicted in his novel and Brenton's insistence on replacing such traditional male values as toughness, aggressiveness, risk-taking, and "justifiable" violence with new ones, such as sensitivity, maturity, and relating well to women.

In 1973, my third close reading of Jones's earlier novel *Some Came Running* (1957) convinced me that the view I had originally taken of his work was too narrow, that his ideas about manhood and sensitivity were part of a larger vision: his concept of spiritual growth through reincarnation and karma. I had not anticipated this, especially because no review or article until that time had done more than lightly touch on Jones's belief in Oriental philosophy. For me, however, the book made sense only in terms of the metaphysical (even occult) ideas expounded by a minor character, Bob French. I therefore began to focus on Jones's portrayal of spiritual evolution.

This discovery was subsequently confirmed by Jones himself. In 1972, after learning of my interest in his work, he agreed to meet me at his home in Paris, and we spent three days discussing his work. At no time did he hint at his ideas on spiritual evolution. We talked about my analysis of his views on manhood, to which he generally agreed but with a warning against taking the kind of sociological approach I had in mind; about detective fiction, because he had just written his first (and only) detective novel and I had written my master's thesis on Ross Macdonald, whose work Jones knew well; and about the Paris student rebellion of 1968, which he discussed while taking me on a walking tour of the places where many of the events occurred that he had incorporated into *The Merry Month of May* (1971). At the end of my visit, he agreed to correspond with me and comment on my work. It was only when I sent him a letter extensively analyzing what I considered to be the spiritual underpinnings of *Some Came Running* that Jones, in a response dated July 8, 1973, avowed his belief in reincarnation, karma, image-pictures (subjective realities), and spiritual evolution. By and large, that was the way it went throughout our correspondence. I would send him analyses of his work, and he would meet me at the level I had reached through my own efforts. The more I learned, the more profound his responses became. Copies of his letters to me are included in the James Jones Archives in the Harry Ransom Humanities Research Center at the University of Texas at Austin and the Handy Writers' Colony Collection in the University of Illinois at Springfield Library Archives.

Following the publication of *Whistle* in 1978, completed by Willie Morris after Jones's death, I tried to interest publishers in my own work but was told that there was little interest in a critical study of Jones at that time. With no prospect in view, I put my manuscript away and turned to other tasks. As books about Jones's life and writings appeared, I collected them with an eye to reworking my study. Finally, after completing various other projects and finding my interest sparked by the new material that had been published, as well as by the possibility of gaining access to the valuable letters and essays in the Handy Writers' Colony Collection, I decided to return to my work on Jones.

Although the focus of my study remains on Jones's spiritual system—he believed in the unity of God or the Over-Soul, the temporary separation of egos like drops of the ocean being left on the shore, the expansion of these seeming fragments into selves, and their subsequent spiritual growth through ego-reduction until they are worn down enough (and compassionate enough) to be reabsorbed into the Over-Soul—and its embodiment in his fiction, I have added a first chapter that links his ideas to other similar systems, especially those of the theosophists and the transcendentalists. There, I also discuss the nature and limits of Lowney Handy's influence on the development of this aspect of Jones's thinking. In chapter 2, I examine the way Jones's spiritual system operates in his second published novel, *Some Came Running*, discussed out of chronological order because it contains the fullest and most explicit presentation of his spiritual beliefs. I also consider the ways in which that novel develops and enriches the tradition of American literary Orientalism as defined by Beongcheon Yu. Chapters 3 through 5 each deal with two of the novels in the order in which they were published, as well as four or five of Jones's stories, and are organized around themes representing aspects of Jones's philosophy in addition to evaluating each work individually. In chapter 6, a discussion of *Whistle*, I elaborate on Jones's final lesson on spiritual evolution—a lesson that emphasized the doubts that always accompanied his spiritual beliefs without overriding them. The Conclusion contains a discussion of the ways in which all of Jones's work, like those of the transcendentalists that had meant so much to him, helped extend and enrich the American literary Orientalist tradition.

My primary source for the concept of American literary Orientalism is Beongcheon Yu's *The Great Circle: American Writers and the Orient* (1983). At the outset of his study, Yu notes that "According to *Webster's Second International Dictionary*, Orientalism means, among other things, 'imitation or assimilation of that which is Oriental, esp. in religious or philosophical thought, or in art'" and asserts that "it is a cultural phenomenon which appears in architecture, music, painting, philosophy, religion, and other creative endeavors" (11). He also affirms that although "American literary Orientalism" is part of a "distinct, rich and enduring tradition" that has its origins in European literature, "our writers have transformed it into something uniquely American, a significant part of the American experience" (11). Yu discusses a century and a half of American writers who have incorporated Oriental cultures and visions into their lives and philosophies and thereby expanded their understanding and creativity. There is, however, a tradition of American scholarship that has focused on the impact of Asian philosophies, religions, and literatures on American literature. That tradition includes such major American literary Orientalist scholars as Yu himself, Arthur Christy, and Frederick Ives Carpenter.

Yu's concept of Orientalism and the dictionary definition on which it is based are now controversial. Edward W. Said's *Orientalism* (1978), published five years before Yu's work, offers a provocatively different definition of this key term, one that is much less restricted and far less favorable. Although noting that on one level "Orientalism is the discipline by which the Orient was (and is) approached systematically, as a topic of learning, discovery, and practice," he adds that he has also "been using the word to designate that collection of dreams, images, and vocabularies available to anyone who has tried to talk about what lies east of the dividing line" and contends that "these two aspects of Orientalism are not incongruent, since by use of them both Europe could advance securely and unmetaphorically upon the Orient" (73). Said's point is that academic studies and literary assimilations of the Orient have been largely (or almost exclusively) tools for the political and social domination of the East by the West.

As a scholar who has been immersed in the study of African, Caribbean, and African American writers and who writes about them from a postcolonial perspective, I am generally sympathetic to Said's views and find them closely related to the subjects about which I have published most. I acknowledge the immense racial and national bias and the European and American arrogance that has been directed toward all outsiders (including Asians, Africans, and Latin Americans) and a multitude of insiders (such as African Americans, Japanese Americans, and Palestinian Americans). I also recognize that a systematic approach has been developed from them and helped to develop them further. Much, although by no means all, of Said's argument is well-taken and convincing.

Having readily and willingly conceded all these points, I do not perceive the system to be as all-embracing as Said views it. A large number of Eastern-influenced writers, such as the transcendentalists, James Jones, John Steinbeck, Eugene O'Neill, T. S. Eliot, Ezra Pound, J. D. Salinger, Ursula K. LeGuin, Jack Kerouac, Gary Snyder, Allen Ginsberg, and Charles Johnson, have expanded and enriched their writings (and their readers) through personal creative involvement with Asian religions and cultures. The least convincing part of Said's thesis is his argument that "the Orient was overvalued for its pantheism, its spirituality, its stability, its longevity, its primitivity, and so forth" and that "almost without exception such overesteem was followed by a counterresponse: the Orient suddenly appeared lamentably underhumanized, antidemocratic, backward, barbaric, and so forth" (*Orientalism* 150). This seems too sweeping a generalization and does not hold true in the specific cases of many of the writers I have cited. The responses to Oriental spirituality by writers such as Emerson, Thoreau, Jones, LeGuin, Snyder, and Ginsberg were by no means overinflated and remained perennially fruitful and undiminished.

I dissociate myself from and denounce the negative, racist, domineering, and arrogant attributes of Orientalism as defined by Edward Said. I oppose both political colonialism and its close ally, cultural colonialism. Near the end of his book, however, Said cites some examples of scholarship that balances East and West without denigrating or supporting the domination of either, and I view American literary Orientalism, both in creative works and scholarship, as embodying such a balance. As Yu affirms, "The Transcendentalists, Emerson, Alcott, Thoreau, and Whitman all shared one thing in common: an openness toward the Orient," and "what was unique about their response . . . was the total absence of literary exoticism and cultural dilettantism . . . they all set a singularly American pattern of Orientalism for ensuing generations to follow" (*The Great Circle* 22). That included, eventually, the generation of James Jones, a writer whom I regard as embodying the same open spirit toward the Orient that the Transcendentalists displayed.

For these writers, Oriental religion and philosophy were not something strange, foreign, or the product of a different order of humanity. Their encounters with the concepts of reincarnation, maya, and Brahman were so fundamental that they helped shape their perception of the world. In spite of my Said-inspired misgivings, I have decided to retain the terminology "American literary Orientalism" out of respect for scholars such as Yu, Christy, and Carpenter; for writers and thinkers such as the transcendentalists, the theosophists, and the beats; and, above all, for James Jones.

ACKNOWLEDGMENTS

I would like to thank George Hendrick, who served as mentor and unofficial editor throughout most of the revisions of this work; James Giles, J. Michael Lennon, Thomas J. Wood, and Greg Randle, who read and commented on my second draft; and Morris Beja, Robert Canzonari, and John Muste. I also thank J. Michael Lennon, Judith Everson, and Thomas J. Wood, along with the rest of the staff at the Handy Writers' Colony Collection at the University of Illinois at Springfield Library Archives, for their assistance and for permission to quote from Jones's unpublished novel "They Shall Inherit the Laughter" and his unpublished letters to Lowney Handy on file there, as well as from Handy's letters to Jones and others and her notes to writers who studied with her. I am very grateful to Gloria Jones for her permission to quote from this unpublished material by James Jones. I also thank Mary Giles, who copyedited this book. Of course, the responsibility for any errors, distortions or misinterpretations in this work is mine.

An earlier version of chapter 2 appeared as "The Spiritual Growth of Dave Hirsch in James Jones's *Some Came Running*" in *Cuadernos de la Facultad de Humanidades, Universidad de Puerto Rico—Recinto de Rio Piedras* 11 (1984): 9-24. An earlier version of chapter 5 appeared as "Karmic and Social Responsibility in James Jones's *A Touch of Danger*" in *The Armchair Detective* 13 (Summer 1980): 230-36.

James Jones

An American Literary Orientalist Master

James Jones's Spiritual Evolution

When James Jones died in 1977, even though he was widely admired by other writers and still highly popular, few critics appeared to consider him more than a good minor writer, and many would not have gone that far. His tone seemed too rough, his grammar too crude, his outlook on life too simplistic, and his stance too macho in an era of feminist awareness. Moreover, in a review of *The James Jones Reader*, edited by James R. Giles and J. Michael Lennon, Michael Lydon observes that in the "decade and a half" since his death Jones had "drifted into a 'jury's out' limbo, and bringing in a favorable verdict today means bucking current critical trends. Not only is he a traditional realist in the postmodern era, he is also a White Male Author if ever there was one" ("A Voice against Anonymous Death" 120). Lydon does acknowledge his respect for Jones's war novels, the focus for the collection, and asserts that he, in apparent contrast to the book's editors and the critical majority, "would dismiss nothing by Jones" and finds "the domestic novels full of overlooked virtues" (121).

My view is that the critical accusation concerning the oversimplification—indeed, the simplemindedness and crudity in Jones's work—is itself simplistic, downplays the complexity of his philosophy, and passes over the paradoxes in his personality and writing. The accusation glaringly fails to note how often the rough surface of his fiction delineated subtle and original psychological insights; how the "clumsy," repetitious style was always rhythmically appealing and expressed emotions and ideas with remarkable precision, offering flashes of terror, perception, and unusual, intricate beauty; and how his tough, masculine voice spoke out against the insensitivity and foolhardiness of the Hemingway code of manhood and sought to replace it with restraint, compassion, and adult love. It also overlooks some of Jones's most extraordinary artistic virtues.

Responding to his powerful descriptions in *From Here to Eternity*, Joan Didion, a writer noted equally for her command of style and her acerbity in puncturing masculine (and feminine) pretension, observes that "a place belongs forever to whoever claims it hardest, . . . loves it so radically that he remakes it in his own image, and not only Schofield Barracks but a great deal of Honolulu itself has always belonged for me to James Jones" ("Goodbye, Gentleman-Ranker" 146). William Styron, a friend and fellow novelist, has remarked with acuity: "There was a certain grandeur in Jones's vision of the soldier. . . . The individuality that he gave to his people, and the stature he endowed them with, came, I believe, from a clear-eyed view of their humanness, which included their ugliness or meanness. . . . At least part of the reason he was able to pull all this off so successfully, without illusions or sentimentality, was his sense of history, along with his familiarity with the chronicles of war that were embedded in world literature" (Hendrick, ed., *To Reach Eternity* xvi-xvii). And Willie Morris, the writer and friend who completed Jones's last novel, *Whistle*, has argued that "no one has written about middle-class America . . . with the discernment and, moreover, with the love that he brought to *Some Came Running*," and that the novel "is the towering work of native social realism that American writers once dreamed of writing" (*James Jones* 78).

The scholarly evaluation of Jones's work since the early 1980s has not been as bleak as Lydon suggests. Although ignored by scholars during his lifetime (with a few exceptions such as Richard P. Adams and Edmond L. Volpe), Jones received several significant examinations after his death. Two literary biographies—*James Jones* by George Garrett and *Into Eternity: The Life of James Jones, American Writer* by Frank MacShane—have provided insight into a complex personality and offered perceptive critiques of his work. Garrett, in particular, breaks new ground with an analyses of Jones's technical achievements in language and form in *Some Came Running* and other critically slighted works. Giles's critical study, *James Jones*, also elucidates Jones's technical and moral feats in several works (notably the ambiguous cross-over relationship of Prewitt and Warden in *From Here to Eternity*); defends Jones's craftsmanship with symbol, parable, and fable in *The Pistol*; discusses the short stories in depth; and traces the theme of the evolution of a soldier throughout the World War II trilogy (*From Here to Eternity*, *The Thin Red Line*, and *Whistle*). Hendrick's collection of Jones's letters, *To Reach Eternity*, offers, as well as the editor's knowledgeable observations, the man himself, expressing a wide range of moods about many concerns, including his writing and philosophy.

Similarly, Jones the man comes through vividly in a television documentary produced in 1984 by J. Michael Lennon and Jeffrey Van Davis. The program included interviews with Jones's family and friends from all periods of his life, pictures of him, and a reading he gave of the passage in *From Here to Eternity* in which Prewitt plays Taps. Selections from the interviews, including statements by Norman Mailer, Irwin Shaw, and others, were reedited, rearranged to incorporate material not retained in the final cut of the documentary, and printed under the title "Glimpses: James Jones" in the summer 1987 issue of *The Paris Review*.

In 1989 Sangamon State University (now the University of Illinois at Springfield), which helped to support the documentary, published *James Jones in Illinois: A Guide to the Handy Writers' Colony Collection in the Sangamon State University Library Archives*, edited by Thomas J. Wood and Meredith Keating. The volume is useful for its information about that collection, for John Bowers's biographical sketch of Jones and Lowney Handy in the Preface, and for its Introduction. The collection includes not only letters by, to, and about James Jones but also his unpublished first novel, "They Shall Inherit the Laughter." Also in 1989 at Sangamon State University, Greg Randle completed his master's thesis on Jones's unpublished novel, a thesis that is also included in the school's archives. Although Randle focuses on the influence of transcendentalism on "They Shall Inherit the Laughter," he also explores the relationship of the novel, and the Emersonian philosophy underlying it, to the rest of Jones's work. Marlene M. Emmons's thesis, "*Some Came Running*: A Reappraisal of James Jones's Misjudged Masterpiece" (1996), offers not only an enthusiastic defense of the novel's structure and themes but also a highly favorable feminist assessment of Jones's ability to create complex, sympathetic female characters who are psychologically and socially credible.

Contrary to Lydon's impression, these works imply that a consensus has been reached about the classic stature of the World War II trilogy. In fact, Garrett contends that by the end of 1978 the view that "Jones had earned for himself an enduring place in the history of American literature, chiefly as the author of the trilogy of war novels" had been accepted, and that "in 1981, when James R. Giles published the first book-length treatment and assessment of Jones's work, he felt safe, almost beyond question or possible challenge, in asserting in his Preface: 'This three-volume work is our most important fictional treatment of U.S. involvement in World War II'" (*James Jones* 4). Moreover, popular demand has reinforced this viewpoint; the World War II trilogy is the part of Jones's work that remains in print.

Lydon is probably right, however, in suggesting that the jury is still out concerning Jones's domestic novels and stories. Among Jones's supporters, opinion is divided about them. Morris, Garrett, and Lydon affirm the value of nearly all of Jones's writings, whereas Giles, MacShane, and

Styron emphasize primarily the virtues of the war writings. I stand with Morris, Garrett, and Lydon.

My chief reason for returning to my study of Jones is a conviction that the systematic philosophical and religious system underlying all his work, despite these new studies, has yet to be treated fully. This system, based on the concepts of spiritual evolution, reincarnation, and karma, has been touched upon by several writers since the late 1970s, including Morris, Garrett, Hendrick (in his choice of Jones's letters and personal comments), MacShane, Giles, Emmons, and, indirectly, Randle, but their discussions are peripheral. Randle, for example, notes Jones's desire, expressed in a letter to Maxwell Perkins, "to discover an unsevered thread that will run continuously through everything I write" and asserts that "Emerson's philosophy . . . provides the conception for 'the evolution of a soldier'" and that "beginning in 'Laughter,' this concept is a 'thread' that runs through the trilogy" ("James Jones's First Romance" 16, 85).

Going beyond Randle's discussion of Emerson's ideas to the Oriental basis for them (which Arthur Christy, Frederic Ives Carpenter, and Beongcheon Yu explore) and expanding the idea of the "evolution of a soldier" in the World War II trilogy to spiritual evolution provides a vital clue to the unsevered thread that runs throughout Jones's domestic as well as war novels. Garrett takes matters a step further with his observations that the three figures in the World War II trilogy who "reappear and reenact their destinies, gifted with the same essential character and a new name" are "more like reincarnations than mere symbols of, say, the perennial enlisted man" (*James Jones* 184), and that "from the larger story of the trilogy, in which characters die or simply vanish into thin air with the ending of the particular story they inhabit, one can infer that Jones believed that there is some essential energy, some kind of continuity, a sort of resurrection of the very essence of character which transcends the limits of individual experience and even identity" (188). In contrast, Giles, although noting the mystical views in Jones's first two published novels, deems them to be "not intellectually profound" (*James Jones* 65) and disregards them in favor of other themes in these works. His lack of recognition of the manifold connections that could be made between the mystical ideas Bob French, Jones's spokesman, expresses and the various patterns of behavior of the characters and their consequences in *Some Came Running* keeps Giles from considering the novel's fundamental organizing principle and leads him to view it as disorganized and an artistic failure, although an honorable one reflecting Jones's large ambitions.

Jones's artistry cannot be appraised and appreciated without understanding the religious system that shaped his organization, characterization, symbolism, setting, and thematic development. Lacking this understanding, it is easy to misjudge him. Norman Mailer has stated that "Jones was no intellectual. . . . If you're going to keep living and working as a writer and you've got talents as huge as he had, you simply had to recognize where your shortfall is, and he didn't" (Lennon, "Glimpses" 231). Nevertheless, as an unproduced and unpublished section of the same interview reveals, Mailer admits to being influenced intellectually by Jones, to making a major change in his philosophy on the basis of a casual remark by Jones, and to failing to see the mystical element in Jones's writing:

> Interviewer: You said that when you visited Jones in 1953 that it was in your conversations with him where you really first heard about the ideas of Karma, or took them seriously at any rate. I don't find any references to any kind of mysticism, except on the battlefield, in Jones' writing. Did he hold those beliefs about Karma in a serious way . . . ?
> Mailer: I do know that I had that conversation with him about Karma. And I said, "Surely you don't believe in all that nonsense." And he said, "It's the only thing that makes sense." So I paid attention to it because he was such a tough-minded practical Midwesterner. When a Midwesterner speaks of something that mystical making sense you have to ponder it. I've been pondering Karma the rest of my life. But I'm bewildered by something you said about him being mystical about the battlefield. And I just said his ideas about war were banal. Maybe I missed something.

When one of the shrewdest easterners of our time can miss something like this, it is not surprising that so many reviewers and critics have missed it as well.

Richard P. Adams, the earliest critic who did not miss this side of Jones's writing, has rendered a very different judgment of his intellectual ability: "He penetrates to the very center of the most important cultural, political, and philosophical questions of our day" ("A Second Look" 208). Adams then notes the similarity between Walt Whitman's belief that "from any fruition of success . . . , shall come forth something to make a greater struggle necessary" with the "formulation of this common romantic idea" made by Jones's character Prewitt "in the context of the struggle and the suffering he undergoes to maintain it in action. . . . [Jones's version] stands comparison very well with Whitman's or any other" (209). Linking the "religious implications" in Whitman's ideas about struggle and suffering to Jones's, Adams observes that Jones's spokesman Malloy argues in favor of a God of growth and evolution and recognizes human failings as errors rather than sins, asking how "errors can be wrong? since they contribute to growth?" (209). For Adams, this conception was one of Jones's major achievements: "The formula resolves at once, quite simply, the nineteenth-century conflict between evolutionary 'science' and 'Biblical' religion, and also the much older paradox of the Fortunate Fall. . . . It puts the principle of growth, which always involves suffering, in place of the principle of sin and guilt followed by atonement and forgiveness" (209).

Jones responded warmly to a draft of the article Adams sent to him in 1954 and in an exchange of letters expanded on ideas that Adams had discussed. Picking up on Adams's examination of the "salutary romantic doctrines of organic wholeness and functional simplicity" and on his analysis of Malloy's important role in defining his philosophy, Jones commented:

> Theres one more thing I must go into, and that is Malloy. Malloy and the organic metaphor. I dont know where the phrase originated from, but its basic idea has been a basic tenet with me for some time. . . . It was a conviction in the doctrine of reincarnation of souls that first started me on the road to the "organic metaphor." . . . And it was the intellectual acceptance of reincarnation that started me on the way to finding a personal religion. . . . If that is so, then each new life a soul leads is only another lesson to be learned. . . . Indian philosophies have taught for centuries that God is Instability . . . , and that the universe both evolves and involves. Ive never had any occult experiences, mind you, my experience and acceptance has all been purely intellectual. And Ive developed my own lexicon and my own religion out of it, and it coincides very closely with your "organic metaphor." (Hendrick, ed., *To Reach Eternity* 212-13)

In another letter to Adams written more than a year later, while responding in part to an analysis Adams had made of *Moby-Dick*, Jones expanded upon the ideas concerning "evil" and growth:

> I take exception to your statement about the symbolism of the whale: "What it really means, as Ishmael comes to realize, is life, which is both good and evil." Do you see how one always falls into this pitfall of opposing opposites? . . .
> After all, Just what is Evil? We call evil that which hurts us, dont we? . . . But if one *truly* believes in your "organic metaphor," how can we call hurt evil since it is through pain and only through pain that we grow [?] Therefore, one might say actually that "good" is evil and "Evil" is good, because Evil makes us grow, whereas "Good" makes us stagnate, or at least not grow. (Hendrick, ed., *To Reach Eternity* 223)

These exchanges, written while Jones was writing *Some Came Running*, helped clarify his thinking, particularly about the "organic metaphor," to which he then referred in Bob French's exposition of his philosophy. French also defines "involution" and "evolution" as Jones used them in his first letter to Adams:

> If man . . . is in a state of evolutionary development, this means that he is growing, is learning. The 'organic metaphor'—the 'growing plant'—of the modern romantics comes very close to understanding this in the 'occult' way. . . . [But] before there could be *e*volution, of necessity there had to be *in*volution—going outward from God; which, unfortunately, has become the *supposedly* Evil, . . . if you take the whole process and look at it in the shape of the letter V, with God at both ends at the top and man here on Earth at the bottom, the point, you have the whole situation. We souls here on Earth, which . . . *in*volved down from God to meet our . . . material bodies as they *e*volved up to meet us and be used by us, are actually right now at the very lowest point of the V and preparing, . . . to evolve back upward whence we came. (Jones, *Some Came Running* 818)

The foundation of Jones's system is therefore a learning process, the "organic metaphor," in which each soul is forced to discern its similarity to all other souls on earth—and its isolation from them. The isolation reflects the distance each soul has fallen away from God and become immersed in self. This total immersion in self, the state of the human being at the bottom of the V, must be defeated if each soul is to be reunited with God, which is the aim of spiritual evolution. As long as a soul remains subject to the desires and illusions of its ego, it functions on the animal level, which is the lowest and most self-centered. Bob French contends that there are three levels of man—"the animal man, the mental man, and the spiritual man"—and he describes illusions as "Glamours," citing a Tibetan master's explanation that everything "is a *Glamour*. Because, after all, the world doesn't really exist. War is a *Glamour*. . . . Politics is another *Glamour*. Religion, as man knows it, is another *Glamour*. So the problem really resolves itself into one of simply getting rid of all one's *Glamours*" (*Some Came Running* 811, 820).

During the course of spiritual evolution, each individual is to be pried out of the animal level by means of a series of distressing and humiliating experiences designed to break the ego and provoke the realization that everyone is treated the same way, so no one's pride will be left intact. At a certain point in its education, therefore, each soul should reach a state of compassionate understanding in which it feels sorry about the pain in everyone's life without wishing to change or eliminate that pain. This recognition of the necessary role of suffering can come at different times for different souls, because it occurs within the context of a process of reincarnation, which spans eternity. Eventually, though, compassionate understanding will come to all souls, and they will all become one again with God at the end of time.

Giles has noted that "there is a bit of Emerson in Malloy's concept of God as 'the amalgam of [eternally evolving] individuals'" (*James Jones* 64), and Hendrick argues as well that Jones's attraction to "the theory of reincarnation and a belief in the oversoul" involved "ideas much in the American grain in the middle of the nineteenth century, for they are to be found in the works of Emerson, Thoreau, Whitman, and other Transcendentalists" (*To Reach Eternity* 52). In a letter to Maxwell Perkins, Jones indicated his awareness of Emerson's concept of God and expressed interest "in the Yogis and their various paths of attaining the Overself, as Paul Brunton and Emerson call it, which exists someplace in every man's mind, the God in every man" (Hendrick, ed., *To Reach Eternity* 94).

Despite Jones's merging of Brunton's term *Overself* with Emerson's *Over-Soul*, other passages from his writing prove that he was well acquainted with Emerson's writings. Moreover, Beongcheon Yu's description of Emerson's early fascination with ancient Greek conceptions of God and their probable influence on his conception of the Over-Soul parallels Bob French's description of the relationship between God and humans. After pointing out Emerson's fascination with the Pythagorean doctrine of anima mundi, "into which the Soul of the individual was absorbed and afterwards emanated again," Yu notes his equal enthusiasm for "the Platonic notion that the individual soul is 'but an emanation from the Abyss of Deity, and about to return whence it flowed.'" Yu then links both views to Emerson's journal entry for October 1827: "There prevailed anciently the opinion that the human mind was a portion of the Divinity, separated for a time from the infinite mind, and when life was closed, reabsorbed into the Soul of the world; or, as it was represented by a lively image, Death was but the breaking of a vial of water in the ocean" (*The Great Circle* 30).

Two passages of Emerson's essay "The Over-Soul" seem to borrow from the image in the journal, suggesting Emerson's frequent practice of recycling his own material. In discussing revelation, Emerson argued that "this communication is an influx of the Divine mind into our mind" and compared it to "an ebb of the individual rivulet before the flowing surges of the sea of life" (*Selected Essays* 189). In the other passage, he affirmed that "the heart in thee is the heart of all; not a valve, not a wall, not an intersection is there anywhere in nature, but one blood rolls uninterruptedly an endless circulation through all men, as the water of the globe is all one sea, and, truly seen, its tide is one" (186-87). Taken together, these passages imply Emerson's debt to his Pythagorean and Platonic musings. Yu also notes, however, that even though Emerson owed much to the Greeks, "He at last came close to the Hindu concept of Atman and Brahman" (*The Great Circle* 30)—that is, to the Indian versions of Over-Soul and individual soul that also influenced Paul Brunton and James Jones.

Arthur Christy, whose study of *The Orient in American Transcendentalism* (1978) remains the standard work, also notes the Greek influence but contends that Emerson was more influenced by the Hindu conception of Brahma. Moreover, Christy, although analyzing the relationship between Brahma and maya (the illusory world), cites the metaphor from the Vedanta "of the sea and its waves and the foam which comes from the sea, seeming to finite eyes different but in reality not, and eventually returning to its kindred source" (96). Like the Tibetan master whom Bob French cites, Christy also remarks on Emerson's concern with the concept of maya, which links the individual illusions of humans to the illusory nature of the world itself. Christy's discussion of maya is notable because he points out its inherent ambiguity and difficulty: "It is a quality of the Real, but in itself must be unreal, never identical with nor different from the Central Reality, else the world is dualistic. Maya cannot exist, for if it did, it would constitute a limit to Brahma. Still, if it does not exist the world cannot be accounted for. . . . Maya is accepted as the *modus operandi* of the universe, concealing the eternal Brahma under an aggregate of names and forms" (90). Christy also draws parallels between the Hindu concept of karma— a belief that all a human "suffers or enjoys is the fruit of his own deed, a harvest sprung from the actions of a previous life" (101)—and Emerson's theory of compensation.

Jones was very much drawn to Emerson's essay on "Compensation," citing it both in "They Shall Inherit the Laughter" and in a letter to editor John Hall Wheelock (Hendrick, ed., *To Reach Eternity* 116). Noting the eclecticism in Emerson's thinking, Christy is reluctant to argue that karma was the exclusive basis for Emerson's ideas about compensation, but he observes that Emerson had commented on karma in other essays and that "Karma and Compensation were the consequences of very similar attitudes toward the world and the Over Soul" (*The Orient in American Transcendentalism* 104). What links them, in Christy's view, is that "they are the laws of the conservation of moral energy as well as of physical energy in a world where there is nothing uncertain or capricious (104).

Observing that "in the Hindu mind Karma is inseparable from. . . . the doctrine of Transmigration," because "Transmigration is the method of recompensing good and bad merit," Christy is unsure how much Emerson believed in it. He concludes, however, that Emerson "was not hostile to the doctrine," because "his premises and his sympathy with the Hindus forbade that" (109). Emerson "was strong in the conviction of the eternity of the soul" while probably never being able to accept "the theological theory that God creates a new soul every time a child is born" (109), a combination of beliefs that pointed toward reincarnation. Christy also posits that Emerson added the modern concept of evolution to his other eclectic ideas, including Christian, Greek, and Indian beliefs, and that although he may never have "considered the exact manner in which the soul is reincarnated into new forms, . . . evolution probably became for him a symbol of the upward march of the soul, and the mutations of animal qualities the emanations of the Over-Soul" (112).

Finally, Emerson's stance on "evil" and its relation to growth was apparently similar to Jones's and may have helped Jones to develop his own eclectic ideas. As Christy points out:

> [Emerson] arrived eventually at a position where he could view good and evil as opposite only from the point of view of ignorance or Illusion. . . . Failings and sin belong to the unreal phenomenal world and cannot possess metaphysical significance. . . . All difficulty was overcome for Emerson by the doctrine of Compensation, as it is overcome for the Hindu by Karma. . . . The creation men live in is the result of deeds, the scene of atonement for past works. God's role is that of the Gardener who gives rain and life and the opportunity for growth. (122)

Although Emerson's philosophy may have pervaded all of Jones's writing, Greg Randle demonstrates that it was of critical importance to "They Shall Inherit the Laughter." This autobiographical novel focuses on the spiritual redemption of a young soldier named Johnny Carter (modeled on Jones himself), achieved largely through the efforts of an older married woman, Cornelia (Corny) Marion (modeled on Jones's long-time companion Lowney Handy), who employs and embodies the basic ideas of Emerson for that purpose. Embittered by war experiences that have marked his ankle and his mind and by an all-consuming rage at the hypocritical greed of civilians who became wealthy because of the war, Johnny returns to his hometown of Endymion, Indiana, only to fight with his sole remaining relative, his cousin Erskine Carter; snarl at the "respectable" people of the town, truthfully informing them that he is AWOL; and be perpetually, troublesomely drunk. After Erskine, as a lesson, allows Johnny to be jailed overnight for drunkenness (as Jones's Uncle Charles had done to him),

Johnny might easily have continued his self-destruction had he not been taken in hand by Corny and Eddie Marion (modeled on Lowney Handy's husband, Harry).

While sharing Johnny's harshest criticisms of American society and the modern world, Corny Marion exudes Emersonian optimism, living instinctively and with conscious simplicity, self-reliance, and faith in the strength of humanity, despite all its weaknesses. She is a reminder of Emerson's strictures that "society is a joint-stock company, in which the members agree, for the better securing of his bread to each shareholder, to surrender the liberty and culture of the eater," and that "whoso would be a man, must be a nonconformist" (*Selected Essays* 151), and she disregards the community's opinion of her. Yet she cares about wounded individuals such as Johnny, whose sensitivity she perceives beneath his sardonic posturing, and offers them the example of her life-style and her guidance. Corny's worst failure is with another former soldier, Al Garnnon, who, reflecting with horror and ire on the life of conformity that threatens him after the war, swerves his car "to the left to hit a *self-reliant* chicken" ("They Shall Inherit" 76, emphasis added). In contrast, her success with Johnny is signaled when he is able to tell Corny, "I've learned one thing, an important thing, since I've been back here. A man must in the last analysis depend upon himself and nobody else" (575). As Randle observes, "Johnny's realization follows closely Emerson's philosophy in 'Self-Reliance,'" wherein Emerson states, "It is only as a man puts off from himself all external support, and stands alone, that I see him to be strong and to prevail" ("James Jones's First Romance" 63).

According to Randle, "In the mid-nineteenth century, Emerson was reacting to many of the same kinds of problems and pressures that Jones himself was so upset by in the middle of the next century. Throughout his career, Jones was concerned . . . with the beleaguered place of the individual in a modern, increasingly technological and bureaucratic society. In the 1940s, Emerson also reacted to a society that increasingly encroached upon individual life" (45). Both Emerson and Jones came to view self-reliance as the answer to this problem, and Randle remarks that "Emerson's belief in the individual's creative power explains his tremendous optimism about America's future" (48).

The self that Emerson and Jones chose to rely upon, however, has to be distinguished from the ego. Near the beginning of "They Shall Inherit the Laughter," while riding on the train to Endymion, Johnny Carter has a vision of how people are bound by the illusions and petty desires of their egos:

All around him the people in the car were asleep and he felt that strange sense of fascination and of wonder that a man feels when he alone is out and the world about him sleeps. He turned away slowly from the Hollywood technique of city-life-at-a-glance and watched the sleeping people in the car. . . . The people slept because they would get their technics at the movies fresh out of the can because then it would be romantic and thrilling and not like now when in the flesh city-life-at-a-glance only bored them. . . . Their life was a can and their ego was a lid and they were shut into the ego-can by the ego-lid and the only way they could get out was to climb out into fresh-out-of-the-can. His mind felt the wonder of prodigy at being awake and looking down at the sleeping people . . . each in his ego-can while he watched the technic of city-life-at-a-glance in marquee asterisk lights. (61-62)

In opposition to this ego, what Emerson and Jones looked to was the spiritual self, the portion of divinity within, whose presence is signaled by intuition or revelation when the ego is no longer in control and people become aware of their true eternal being. As Emerson affirmed in "Self-Reliance," "What is the aboriginal Self, on which a universal reliance may be grounded? . . . The inquiry leads us to that source, at once the essence of genius, of virtue, and of life, which we call Spontaneity or Instinct. . . . For the sense of being which in calm hours rises, we know not how, in the soul, is not diverse from things, from space, from light, from time, from man, but one with them and proceeds obviously from the same source whence their life and being also proceed" (*Selected Essays* 158).

Although Emerson was surely the chief inspiration for the basic ideas behind "They Shall Inherit the Laughter," as Greg Randle has demonstrated, Jones's interest in Oriental philosophy is also indicated in an early passage in which Johnny Carter, before meeting Corny Marion, explains the yin-yang symbol to Cap Coleman, his father's old friend. After drawing a circle surrounded by an outer rim that is half dark and half white and encloses an inner part divided by a curved line, with a dark half containing a white dot and a white half containing a dark dot, Johnny explains:

This symbol is almost the whole basis for Chinese philosophy. . . . The Yin is the dark part, the evil: and the Yang is the light part, the good. . . . The good and evil are intermingled and entwined. In the good is a little spot of evil, and in the evil is a little spot of good. In the outer circle good and evil are divided into blocks of first one and then the other.

The idea is that nothing is all good or all evil. When the Chinese have a famine year, . . . they suffer through it because they know that in time the evil will go and the good will return. When they have a great harvest, they don't become exuberant and overjoyous and expect it to last forever, because they know that in time the evil will come again, too. . . .

I guess when you come down to it, that's pretty much the basis of Indian philosophy, too; although there's a lot of complications. It's the philosophy of acceptance. This symbol simplifies the whole thing more than anything I ever saw. (111-12)

Cap responds with surprise that "those Chinese are pretty smart, aren't they?" and Johnny says, "They've had thousands of years to get smart. Only people like you and me don't know they're as smart as they are, or we'd have been helping them back in 1932 instead of waiting for Japan to blow up Pearl Harbor" (112). Cap also inquires where Johnny learned "all this stuff." The intriguing reply is, "I picked it up reading and talking to people. I knew a Chinese family in Hawaii that believed the Chinese faith of ancestors and all the old Gods" (114). Finally, Johnny tells Cap about a proverb taught to him by "an old first sergeant who had been in China with the fifteenth infantry": "*He who knows not and knows not that he knows not is a fool: shun him. He who knows not and knows that he knows not is simple: teach him. He who knows and knows not that he knows is asleep: awaken him. He who knows and knows that he knows is a wise man: follow him*" (115, emphasis in the original). The proverb is, of course, suggestive in relation to Johnny's vision of the sleepers in their "ego-cans" and his own wakefulness.

The works of Plato constitute another probable influence, although a minor one, on Jones's philosophy, as *Some Came Running* demonstrates. While discussing the nature of love, the protagonist of the novel, Dave Hirsh, notes that Bob French has asked a sequence of questions that have increasingly pointed toward a particular set of ideas. "Youre pulling a Socratic dialogue on me," he finally tells Bob. "Youre making a sort of Alcibiades out of me" (812). Bob's apparent denial—"Im only asking you questions, only helping you to figure it out for yourself," because "otherwise, when you find the answer you might disagree with me"—prompts Dave to respond accurately, "Thats Socratic" (812).

The response demonstrates Jones's knowledge as well as his skilled use of the form and purpose of Socratic dialogue in the preceding passages. It also implies that although he probably did not lean much on Plato's ideas in developing his philosophy (although his character Warden also refers to Socrates during a Socratic dialogue with himself on page 180 of *From Here to Eternity*), Jones did share Emerson's tendency, as Christy notes, to divide "all men into two groups—idealists and materialists" and side "with the former unequivocally, believing that they all started with what he called the spirit, and that they all said substantially the same thing" (*The Orient in*

American Transcendentalism 50). Furthermore, as Christy observes about Emerson, and something probably true of Jones, "There can be little doubt that he found the various bodies of idealistic thought with which he came in contact stepping stones to others" so that "Platonism and Neo-Platonism were for him an introduction and corroboration of the Hindus" (50). Of course, as Frederick Ives Carpenter points out, Emerson "identified Platonism with Neoplatonism," whose doctrines represented, "historically, the fusion of Greek Platonism with a mysticism brought from the Orient by way of Alexandria" (*Emerson and Asia* 15), and Jones may have been tempted to do the same in developing his own philosophy.

In addition to Emerson and the Orientals (and, to a lesser extent, Plato), Jones was heavily influenced by the system of theosophy founded by Madame Helena Petrovna Blavatsky and carried on by William Q. Judge, Annie Besant, and others. Jones shared the theosophists' attitude toward reincarnation. As Joseph Head and S. L. Cranston, who compiled three collections composed of passages on reincarnation, explain:

> Theosophists have an approach to the reincarnation theory that is manifestly different from that commonly found in the East, or among the early Jews and Christians. In the Orient the great hope has been to escape as quickly as possible from the wheel of rebirth, and to attain Moksha or Nirvana. . . . The Theosophists, however, regard re-embodiment as the universal law of evolutionary progress, holding that in an infinite universe there must be infinite possibilities for growth and development. Hence one would never outgrow the need for fresh experience and new cycles of incarnations. (*Reincarnation: An East-West Anthology* 62)

Arthur Christy finds a similar difference in attitude between Emerson and the Orientals in their response to the experience of this world, although he does not discuss it specifically in terms of reincarnation theory: "The difference appears not in what men like Emerson and Thoreau think about the phenomenal, but in their attitude toward it. They insist on the power of the spirit to build this world. They look upon this world like the Creator of *Genesis*, and find it good. The typical Hindu, on the other hand, sees in this world the absence of good, darkness, and evil. He insists on the power of mind to get rid of it for him, to negate the phenomenal life he is obliged to live; and so he turns from it" (*The Orient in American Transcendentalism* 85). Christy believes that "up to this point the speculative journeys of the American Transcendentalists are parallel" to the Orientals, but beyond it they diverge (85). The new path they pioneer is also taken by their speculative fellow travelers, the theosophists and James Jones.

It may have been easy for the avowedly eclectic Jones to conflate transcendentalism with theosophy, because these equally eclectic philosophies draw upon many of the same sources: Pythagoras, Plato, Neoplatonism, Hinduism, Buddhism, and Christianity. Indeed, Madame Blavatsky, Annie Besant, and other theosophists frequently quoted Emerson with approval and regarded him as a kindred spirit. Bob French, responding to a question from Dave Hirsh about whether the ideas he is developing refer to "some kind of Theosophy," replies ambivalently, pointing to his eclecticism and implicitly linking theosophy with transcendentalism: "No, [it's] not exactly [theosophy]. But somewhat, too. The Great Theosophists like Madame Blavatski—like the Great Christians; or the great anything else— were not Theosophists—or Christians—They were seekers; only later, when these words acquired popularity and became creeds, were there professional 'Theosophists' and professional 'Christians'—who thereby . . . diluted and weakened and vitiated the power and truth of their own teachings. The same can be said of Emerson and the transcendentalists" (*Some Came Running* 816).

Transcendentalism and theosophy are similar in their conception of God. In Blavatsky's *The Key to Theosophy*, which takes the form of a dialogue between an enquirer and a theosophist, the theosophist's description of the universal divine principle, or universal soul, could serve as well for the Over-Soul, or the anima mundi, or Brahma:

> We believe in a Universal Divine Principle, the root of ALL, from which all proceeds, and within which all shall be absorbed at the end of the great cycle of Being. (63)

> Enq. How, then, do you account for man being endowed with a Spirit and Soul? Whence these?

> Theo. From the Universal Soul. Certainly not bestowed by a *personal* God. Whence the moist element in the jelly-fish?

> From the Ocean which surrounds it, in which it lives and breathes and has its being, and whither it returns when dissolved. (75)

Concerning maya and its relation to the portion of the Divine Spirit within humans, Blavatsky's theosophist explains in terms Emerson would likely have accepted: "Theosophy . . . holds that man, being an emanation from the . . . Divine Essence, his body and everything else is impermanent, hence an illusion; Spirit alone in him being the one enduring substance, and even that losing its separated individuality at the moment of its complete re-union with the *Universal Spirit*" (219). When the enquirer objects that "if we lose even our individuality, then it becomes simply annihilation," the theosophist counters, "I speak of *separate*, not of universal individuality. The latter becomes as a part transformed into the whole; the *dewdrop* is not evaporated, but becomes the sea" (219). This distinction implies the similar one Emerson made between the self attached to the material world and the inner portion of divinity that becomes the basis for true, creative self-reliance. It is also similar to the distinction Jones used in "They Shall Inherit the Laughter" to develop Corny Marion's and Johnny Carter's reliance on the Emersonian self.

To the extent that Emerson accepted the doctrine of transmigration with possibly a thrust toward evolution, as Christy suggests, he would have been drawn to Blavatsky's theosophist's vision of it, essentially the same vision held by Jones at his most hopeful Emersonian moments. As the theosophist proclaims, "It is a belief in a perpetual progress for each incarnating Ego, or divine soul, in an evolution from the outward into the inward, from the Material to the Spiritual, arriving at the end of each stage at absolute unity with the divine Principle. From strength to strength, . . . with accessions of new glory, of fresh knowledge and power in each cycle, such is the destiny of every Ego, which thus becomes its own Saviour in each world and incarnation" (*The Key to Theosophy* 154-55).

Of course, the theosophist also says that reincarnation's "final goal cannot be reached in any way but through life experiences, and . . . the bulk of these consist in pain and suffering," because it is only through the latter that people can learn (27). In an essay on "The Use of Evil," Annie Besant elaborates on this idea by affirming that each soul can only be led toward Brahma, the Universal Soul, after experiencing all the "pleasures" of the world and discovering how transitory they are and how much pain they bring. Besant contends, "You can never convince people that this is so unless they have followed the objects of the lower desires and found the results which flow from them" (*The Spiritual Life* 114).

This viewpoint indicates the role played not only by pain but also by apparent evil in growth and the need to experience "evil" first in order to understand it, reject it, and move on to the "good." Essentially the same viewpoint is developed in *Light on the Path*, a booklet edited by Mabel Collins and printed by the Theosophy Company, in a passage Jones modified and quoted in both novels and letters: "Remember that the sin and shame of the world are your sin and shame; for you are a part of it; your Karma is inextricably interwoven with the great Karma. And before you can attain knowledge you must have passed through all places, foul and clean alike. Therefore, remember that the *soiled garment you shrink from touching may have been yours yesterday, may be yours tomorrow. And if you turn with horror from it, when it is flung upon your shoulders, it will cling the more closely to you*" (19-20, emphasis added to indicate the part Jones quoted with variation in *From Here to Eternity* and *Some Came Running*).

Jones's fiction abounds with characters who seek to shun the "soiled garment" when it is flung upon their shoulders, only to find it clinging more firmly to them. In *Some Came Running*, for example, Edith Barclay calls her grandmother an "old whore," only to find herself becoming a whore in her own eyes because of an affair with Frank Hirsh. And in *The Thin Red Line*, Big Un Cash hates the Japanese soldiers who kill American prisoners of war so fiercely that he feels compelled to kill Japanese prisoners. These patterns in his work reveal how well Jones agreed with, and extended by example, Blavatsky's summary of the teachings concerning evil in *The Secret Doctrine:* "No Entity, whether angelic or human, can reach the state of Nirvana, or of absolute purity, except through aeons of suffering and the *knowledge* of EVIL as well as of good, as otherwise the latter remains incomprehensible" (167).

The fundamental moral agency in theosophy, as in Indian thought and, under the name *compensation* in transcendentalism, is karma, and Blavatsky even gives a nod to Emerson's law of compensation in her explanation of karma:

> Those who believe in *Karma* have to believe in *Destiny*, which, from birth to death, every man is weaving thread by thread around himself, as a spider does his cobweb; and this Destiny is guided either by the heavenly voice of the invisible *prototype* outside of us, or by our more intimate astral, or inner man, who is but too often the evil genius of the embodied entity called man. Both these lead on the outward man, but one of them must prevail; and from the very beginning of the invisible affray the stern and implacable *Law of Compensation* steps in and takes its course, faithfully following the fluctuations. When the last strand is woven, and man is seemingly enwrapped in the net-work of his own doing, he finds himself completely under the empire of this *self-made* Destiny. (*The Secret Doctrine* 146-47)

Intriguingly, Blavatsky's strong emphasis on the self-made nature of individual destiny also implies a powerful argument for self-reliance.

Although the essentials of transcendentalism and theosophy closely resemble each other, and Jones could freely have drawn from both, certain elements of his philosophy could only have been derived from theosophy. When Bob French, for example, describes the process of the separation of individuals from God and their eventual reunion with him, the process is one Emerson would have recognized. But the terms French uses, *involution* and *evolution*, are those Blavatsky employs. She explains that "in esoteric parlance, Brahma is Father-Mother-Son, or Spirit, Soul and Body at once; each personage being symbolical of an attribute, and each attribute or quality being a graduated influx of Divine Breath in its cyclic differentiation, involutionary and evolutionary" (*The Secret Doctrine* 23).

William Q. Judge uses the terms as well in a passage concerning *The Secret Doctrine* that also describes the "triple evolution of man" in a way that suggests Bob French's three stages of "the animal man, the mental man, and the spiritual man": "Nowhere else in English literature is the Law of Evolution given such sweep and swing. . . . It follows man in his triple evolution, physical, mental, and spiritual, throughout the perfect circle of his boundless life. . . . The Secret Doctrine points where the lines of evolution and involution meet: where matter and spirit clasp hands; and where the rising animal stands face to face with the fallen god; for *all natures* meet and mingle in man" (*The Ocean of Theosophy*, quoted in Head and Cranston, *Reincarnation: The Phoenix Fire Mystery* 517).

This triple evolution—physical, mental, and spiritual—forms the fundamental organizing principle of *Some Came Running*, which traces in elaborate detail Dave Hirsh's progression from animal man to mental man to spiritual man. Along with the pattern of those who unavailingly seek to shun the "soiled garment" of evil flung upon them, his evolution rightly implies that the book owes far more to theosophy—and transcendentalism—than simply the material for Bob French's lectures.

Another debt Jones's novel and philosophy owe to theosophy is the concept of the "world of bodyless souls," which Bob French outlines for Dave Hirsh: "There appears to be . . . a whole entire world of bodyless souls, spirits, complete with its own body politic, its own hierarchy of leaders and Lords and Masters and Teachers—minor Gods; Demi-Gods, if you will—surrounding the material world we inhabit; . . . this is only a very small part of the inhabited universe . . . [and] these people are apparently in constant contact with some parts of our minds, without our knowledge of course, guiding us, directing us; beneficently not malignantly" (*Some Came Running* 816).

This description is a fairly accurate summary of Blavatsky's cosmological vision in *The Secret Doctrine*, a vision having no equivalent in transcendentalism. Judge offers a similar, concise description of part of that system:

> Upon this earth and upon the whole chain of globes of which it is a part, seven races of men appeared simultaneously, coming over to it from other globes of an older chain. . . . And in respect to this earth—the fourth of this

chain—these seven races came simultaneously from another globe of this chain. . . . At the present time the seven races are mixed together, and representatives of all are in the many so-called races of men as classified by our present science. The object of this amalgamation and subsequent differentiation is to give to every race the benefit of the progress and power of the whole derived from prior progress in other planets and systems. (*The Ocean of Theosophy* 127-28)

Jones's final debt to theosophy is the master-disciple relationship that he depicted on various levels throughout his work: between Warden and Prewitt in *From Here to Eternity*, Bob French and Dave Hirsh in *Some Came Running*, Welsh and Fife in *The Thin Red Line*, and Lobo Davies and Sweet Marie in *A Touch of Danger*. This conception was not consciously a part of transcendentalism, although perhaps such relationships existed between Emerson and Thoreau and Emerson and Whitman. Theosophy, in contrast, like Hinduism and Buddhism before it, has emphasized the master-disciple relationship. Annie Besant, for example, has argued that unless he developed his psychic and spiritual elements "animal-man could not become divine, the 'perfect septenary being' whom it is the object of reincarnation to evolve," and that those in whom the triumph of the spiritual man "has been consummated . . . are spoken of as Arhats, Mahatmas, and Masters" (*Reincarnation* 48). "Those highest and mightiest embodiments of humanity" are "above us in spiritual purity, in spiritual wisdom, in perfect selflessness," although Besant also acknowledges that they were "not different from us in their essence, but in their evolution" (47). She defines disciples as "those who, being on the probationary path, are recognized by some Master as attached to himself," but warns that "the term asserts a fact, not a particular moral stage, and does not carry with it a necessary implication of the highest moral elevation" (129). *Light on the Path*, however, implies that disciples must attain a fairly high level before the masters can effectively guide, instruct, or incite them to further progress because "the voice of the Masters is always in the world; but only those hear it whose ears are no longer receptive of the sounds which affect the personal life" (Collins, ed., *Light on the Path* 47).

It might seem tempting to label the relationship between Lowney Handy and James Jones a master-disciple one, but the truth is much less clearcut, and such a generalization is dangerously misleading. It is difficult to sort out the nature and extent of her influence on Jones and Jones's influence on her. A. B. C. Whipple has written that the "biggest day" in Jones's life "was November 3, 1943 when James Jones, then a beat-up war veteran with nothing left but an urge to write, met a woman named Lowney

Handy," because "if this meeting had not taken place, *From Here to Eternity* would not have been written. . . . Far from having an intellectual inclination to be a patroness of the arts, Lowney Handy first 'adopted' Jones because he was in trouble, then grew interested in his writing, whereupon she devoted herself—even to the extent of putting her husband in debt—to helping and indeed forcing Jones to write his book." Referring to her as a "childless housewife of Robinson, Illinois, who was looking for someone to mother and who was perceptive enough to see what escaped editors, teachers and even Jones himself," Whipple records how, in the wake of her success with Jones, Handy formed a colony for other aspiring writers and "is perfectly honest with them, and makes no attempt to hide the fact that while they are in the Group she is a mother to them and an extremely possessive one at that" ("James Jones and His Angel" 143, 154).

In contrast, David Ray, a poet and former member of the Handy Writers' Colony, told George Garrett, "I cannot possibly convey to you the intensity of Lowney's power. It was charismatic and demonic. Since she used some of the same brainwashing methods to assure the loyalty of her young disciples and was from the same part of the country, I've often wondered if the James Jones of Jonesville knew of her, or perhaps visited her. . . . She was a very violent woman, and unyielding in her jealous possessiveness of her charges, of whom Jones was the chief one" (*James Jones* 85).

Agreeing with neither Whipple nor Ray, Norman Mailer, who had met Handy at the colony, argued that "like all legends, Handy's toughness was vastly exaggerated. She was terribly opinionated and, like all people from the Midwest, very proud of certain things, but a little uneasy about literary matters—probably because of that old tradition that literature started in New England and never went far away from there. So she would protect herself; she would be tentative. She handled me with kid gloves" (quoted in Lennon, "Glimpses" 217). Mailer also defended Handy's controversial use of copying literary works as a means of teaching writing, a technique that had been attacked as arbitrary, dictatorial, and mediocre on the grounds that "there are worse ways to teach that writing consists of an awful lot of dreary dull work and paying attention to small details" (Lennon, "Glimpses" 217). Angel, demon, generous mother, high-handed dictator, fanatical kook, or practical writing instructor—what can be made of Lowney Handy?

Probably the most reliable view of her is the reassessment John Bowers made in 1989. Bowers, a former colony member who stayed there longer than Ray, and his experiences, chronicled in *The Colony* (1971), left an indelible mark on his life. While noting that "her maternal instinct was overpowering" and that "one thing was apparent to all who saw [Jones and Handy] together—Lowney was the stronger in the relationship," Bowers argues that the belief, fostered by Whipple and others, "that somehow Lowney had made this ordinary man a writer, took him, polished him, and turned him out an earth-shattering writer" was a "myth" (x). Rather, "James Jones was a born writer" and "had his artistic vision" at least as early as 1942, when he wrote a review of *The Red Badge of Courage* (included in the Handy Writers' Colony Collection and published in *The James Jones Reader*), a period preceding his meeting with Handy. As Bowers further contends:

> The truth, as I've come to see it after mulling over the contents of [the Handy Writers' Colony Collection] and my own incessant rumination on the colony over the years, is that Lowney fed more off James Jones, learned and copied from him, more than the other way round. Her barracks' room talk, her actual warfare with women, her harsh unsentimental stance in public and sentimentality beneath—that wasn't the fundamental Lowney, that was James Jones. The major thing Lowney gave Jim—and at a most pivotal time in his life—was improbable understanding. . . . Others in that classic Midwest setting wrote him off as a batty drunk, or, hard-drinkers themselves, could not fathom his tender artistic side. Everywhere he turned he faced misunderstanding and repression—except in the arms and care and psyche of Lowney Handy. (x-xi)

Bowers's implication that Jones found comfort "in the arms" of Lowney Handy is not entirely accurate, because she refused to have sex with him during a portion of their fourteen years together, and that became a source of intense contention that indicated shifting patterns of dominance between them. The Handy Writers' Colony Collection include a letter postmarked September 26, 1948, from Handy to her sister, Fay, in which she admits, "I hate and dislike and have always hated and disliked sex. If you think I am holding Jim through sex you are silly. I slept with him at first, but quite frankly I used to grit my teeth to go through with it. He was half crazed by the army and he thought you showed love that way. But he didn't want sex. He wanted someone to believe in him. I had to go through that to make my stand, and to thwart the women who wanted husbands." Blunt and unambiguous as that statement appears, it cannot be taken as the whole truth. Although Handy's marriage "seemed ideal," she had "contracted gonorrhea from her husband" shortly after the marriage began. Her consequent "hysterectomy made her suspicious of sex from then on." Although "she liked men," she "was reluctant to have much to do with them sexually, except as an act of charity" (MacShane, *Into Eternity* 76). Jones's letters also reflect his view that Handy had turned away from him largely because of his involvement with other women.

Jones's remembrances of their early sexual encounters bear little relation to Handy's, suggesting the kind of situation he portrayed so well in his fiction in which individuals perceive the same experience from such vastly different perspectives that they seem almost to be living in different worlds (the phenomenon he referred to as "Glamour" or illusion). In a diary entry for November 8, 1943, he wrote "that he spent the day in bed with [Handy], that she liked his writing, and that 'she subjected herself to me; she made herself my disciple in everything from writing to love'" (Hendrick, ed., *To Reach Eternity* 37). Similarly, in a letter dated January 25, 1949, a time when he was making a determined effort to convince Handy to resume having sex with him, Jones wrote:

> I know that you say I never had you, at least not the sexual love that I have looked for. I cannot believe that. I have been thinking hard lately. In the first place, I have for me at least to make a distinction between "sexual love" and "sex." Maybe you misunderstood that from my last letter. Maybe not. Whatever you think, for me there is a difference. And I am honestly convinced, without wishful thinking, that you loved me that way once. I remember too well the first day I came down here, and you met me in the door of the kitchen into the living room and the light that was all over your whole face, and how you said that one thing I could always count on, you would never do anything to hurt me. Then you led me upstairs, as warm and trembling and excited as I was. (Handy Writers' Colony Collection)

At one point, Handy convinced Jones to follow a strict regimen of yoga exercises and meditations according to instructions in Paul Brunton's *The Secret Path*. In doing so, she was "trying to reduce his sexual life not only for the future but because she thought that too much sex would be bad for him" (MacShane, *Into Eternity* 89). In a letter to Handy postmarked November 16, 1947, Jones recounted a conversation with editor John Hall Wheelock about "the Yoga breathing exercises I had fooled with; . . . how I put myself to sleep with rhythmic breathing" and "how I kept a glass of water on the desk, after learning how the Yogis kept a vessel of water by them" (Hendrick, ed., *To Reach Eternity* 109).

Jones, however, came to suspect that Handy was manipulating his sex drive through yoga, and that may have formed part of his motive for rejecting both yoga and Brunton. In a January 27, 1949, letter, he first described the shift in control in Handy's marriage, with Harry Handy being firmly "the dominator" until Jones's "love saved [Lowney Handy] from that" by inducing him to become "a dominated man . . . it has become the same battle between you and me," Jones shrewdly observed, "you using Yoga, me using sex (there are millions of ways besides sex)" (Hendrick, ed., *To Reach Eternity* 129). Jones's success in persuading Handy to pursue a sexual relationship with him suggests that for a while he was in charge of their relationship, but the struggle between them surely continued until he left her to marry Gloria Mosolino, who by all accounts made his remaining years the most fulfilling and stable ones he ever knew.

The issue of control, dominance, or influence in their relationship is not only significant but also unavoidable because of the numerous beliefs and values Jones and Handy held in common. David Ray has described her "philosophy" as "culled primarily from Madame Blavatsky, Paul Brunton, W. Somerset Maugham and the unassailable Ralph Waldo" ("Mrs. Handy's Writing Mill" 25), a comprehensive list of her basic sources if we add only Annie Besant and some handbooks on yoga. Emerson, Blavatsky, and Besant were primary sources for Jones's philosophy as well. As MacShane observes, "to aid the release of his artistic energy, Lowney introduced Jones to her considerable library of Eastern philosophy, especially books from India and Japan and including Madame Blavatsky's theosophical works." Paul Brunton was "another contemporary philosopher of the East . . . to whom he was introduced by Lowney" (*Into Eternity* 87).

At the same time, in "They Shall Inherit the Laughter," the knowledge Johnny Carter displays of the yin-yang symbol (and of Chinese and Indian philosophy) predates his meeting with Corny Marion, a circumstance that suggests a similar predating of Jones's awareness, although only limited reliance can be placed on a work of fiction. There is also Jones's response to Richard P. Adams's criticism that he was insufficiently familiar with certain Romantic writers, including Emerson, a criticism Adams might not have made had he the opportunity to read "They Shall Inherit the Laughter" attentively. "Generally, . . . I think Id agree that I do have an insufficient familiarity with them, and with the tradition in which Im working. But then, Ive not known I was working in any tradition, but have always just been figuring these things out for myself.—And, I might add, intend to continue to do, for two reasons: one, so that my processes may remain largely subconscious and therefore closer to their roots, and two, so that I may not be *bound* by any tradition, or school" (Hendrick, ed., *To Reach Eternity* 211).

This refusal to be boxed in by any tradition or philosophy provided the underpinnings for Bob French's refusal to identify the philosophy he was describing to Dave Hirsh as theosophy, because "the great Theosophists like Madame Blavatski . . . were not Theosophists . . . they were seekers."

This passage and others in *Some Came Running* demonstrate through their detailed accounts of theosophy, Indian philosophy, and transcendentalism that Jones had read works on those topics with care. His ideas were not derived from anyone else, including Lowney Handy, even though she may have introduced him to some (or many) books.

As John Bowers remarks, the Handy Writers' Colony Collection is indeed vast and sheds as much light on Handy's influence on Jones as is possible. Although it does not provide a definitive, unambiguous solution to their complex relationship, it offers abundant information about Handy and Jones (and also Handy and her husband, sisters, brothers, and the writers in the colony) and about Handy's ideas. The collection also helps establish the parameters of Handy's influence.

One matter the collection resolves beyond any doubt is the extent of Handy's belief in her Emersonian-Bruntonian-theosophical-yoga philosophy: It was fundamental and obsessive. It guided her daily activities; permeated her casual as well as her intimate personal letters; became inextricably blended with her advice on craft to aspiring colony writers; and determined most of her attitudes toward her environment, money, other people, and herself. Her letters to Harry Handy, for example, all in the Handy Writers' Colony Collection, were peppered with advice:

> In the beginning—the Chela—the student, the beginner employs his Yogic Exercise only fourteen to twenty-eight times a day. These won't be too many for you. . . . The copying of Annie Besant will serve as meditation for this winter. Meditation is nothing more or less than a concentration on spiritual thoughts. Annie Besant *Meditation* . . . or *Spiritual Life* are taken almost exactly from the *Bhagavad-Gita* and *Upanishad* (the Hindu Bible). (August 30, 1948)

> If you get a good foundation in Besant—you've just about learned all there is to know. (September 18, 1948)

> In the old days the last stage an initiate went through was—equivalent to a deep trance stage, where the student finds the silent, inscrutable, god within himself. He knows that all people are part of himself, that as he travels the WAY OF THE CROSS, the road of sacrifice (where you think of world good, brotherhood, helping one another). (October 14, 1948)

> Knowing My Yogi as I do—I now know that I have given all I need to and that any more would be detrimental. There comes a time to turn loose of your children—your pupils—even your husband. . . .

It seems that everyone is given problems. Mine has been to conquer the love for overeating. . . . Yours is drink. Jim's is sex. The battle is always there to be made. We must always understand and be kind and patient but never Judging and—you can't do it for them. (January 21, 1949)

Sometimes I feel that I have been your worst enemy. That perhaps I have held you back by an old picture much like a snake is bound inside its old skin until it sheds it. . . . I HAVE TO FIGHT HARD TO CHANGE MY SKIN NOW AS JONES AND THESE OTHER STUDENTS WANT TO KEEP ME TO A PATTERN THEY HAVE MADE IN THEIR MINDS, A PATTERN THAT IS VERY SERVICE-ABLE TO THEM. Sometimes I think the real reason I get sick is that it gives me a chance to break the old pattern and shed my outworn skin.
     Remember always you can be anything you see.
THOUGHTS ARE THE KEY. (April 16, 1955)

Other advice to Harry emphasized the major connection between her views on yoga and her belief in the value of copying, the central tenet of her colony:

When you are up here I insist that you copy. It makes you hold your mind IN CONCENTRATION. The Yogas prove that the key to growth, the key to God, or an ultimate state of goodness is VIA CONCENTRATION. When the earth was formed The Logos MEDITATED. He saw all of it in his thinking, and out of his seeing the earth materialized. It is thus with writing a book, building a Colony here, or a Refinery, or birthing a baby, making a house, a planet, people. IT IS THE DREAM. I never see these people who come in here as they are. I try to see them as they will become. (April 16, 1955)

Her loudly proclaimed (and often ridiculed) belief that she could take any man on the street and turn him into a writer—Handy had little faith that women could become writers—was rooted in her conviction, like Emerson's, in the presence of a divine self. As she wrote to a colony writer named Judd, "The whole basis of my teaching is that GOD IS IN EVERY MAN and I can teach him to speak. Make of the writer a kind of channel so that GENIUS can come through." In another undated note (all of Handy's notes to her students were undated) to "Eve" (probably Eve Olstad), one of the few women she agreed to help become a writer, Handy explained, "There is a plane of mind power that supersedes the REASONING MIND—the intellect—and that is the intuitive mind—the perceptive—the OVERSOUL as Emerson called it." That "is what we call GENIUS, the illumined mind." The methods Handy used to instill this self-reliance in students, particularly her insistence that their faith in her be unquestioning and that they follow all directions without complaint, would likely have horrified Emerson, who might have been tempted to separate his droplet of self temporarily from the Over-Soul to chastise her had he known what she was doing with his doctrines.

Because the mystical and the practical are so fully mixed in the foundations of Lowney Handy's approach to teaching writing, it is to be expected that they would be just as mixed in her comments about her students' writing—and they were. Consider Handy's advice to her sister, Fay, who studied with her, about the importance of always knowing well "each and every character in your story." It begins with a practical discussion of how Jones approached his characters:

> HERE IS THE KEY TO EACH CHARACTER IN JAMES JONES' WRITING. He knows them as well or better than he knows his best friends. He knows what they will do under each and every given circumstance. How they vote . . . how strongly they feel about politics . . . about any question currently popular. He knows if they have religion or not and if they take it seriously or not. He knows how they felt on the first day of school and the last day if they are through school. He knows how they feel at the first death in a family and how they feel about their own dying. (Handy Writers' Colony Collection)

Then, she moves on to the less tangible, and in her view infinitely greater, benefits to be gained from such omniscience:

> A hidden kind of fascination over and above the story itself will keep the reader coming. He is absorbed by the gradual exposure, or withdrawal of veil after veil from the past. Because the author seems to be rushing the reader inevitably toward a close . . . that comes in obedience to a series of long-drawn-out precedent impulses. If this is visualized correctly and the author knows his character well . . . he can even get across a kind of effect as though the reader had been the character (as though the author is really laughing at himself . . . a kind of sardonic humor that is hard to achieve) and you will feel as you read it (the reader) that he has gone back even farther into the past lives and the inevitableness of Karma (LAW OF CAUSE AND EFFECT . . . AS YOU SOW SO SHALL YOU REAP) in lives that have even preceded this reincarnation. . . . GREATER ART no author can achieve. (Handy Writers' Colony Collection)

Similarly, in an extended discussion of a work in progress by a student named Charlie (probably Charles Wright), Handy observes:

So Earl is a man in strife . . . torn by his guilts and his desires . . . this is du-
ality. Conscience. . . . (the still small voice of God, so-called) . . . or Soul-
force AND THE LOWER ANIMAL MAN operating under the five senses, his
desire-emotional nature. . . . the animal (Old Adam) instincts . . . self-
preservation, sex, and all the appetites that come under the GUT MIND or
Solar plexus of the animal man.

Only when a man has transmuted (PSYCHOLOGY CALLS IT SUBLIMA-
TION) his lower energies up into the heart center . . . is Christ born in a cave
of the heart—or manger . . . ALL RELIGION IS SYMBOLICAL. . . . and per-
tains to every man. . . . An Initiation . . . is a growth . . . IN CONSCIOUS-
NESS. . . . and when the Christ Child is born in a manger of the heart this
means that a man is developing and can use influences, in conjunction with
several planets or Constellations . . . and his sensitive apparatus is higher . . .
vibrates on a higher frequency . . . is less the SELF-CENTERED INDIVID-
UAL . . . which is involutionary. . . . or of the last Solar System. (Handy
Writers' Colony Collection)

Such a critique bears little relation to traditional literary criticism, and it is
clear from these and similar remarks that Handy expected (or hoped) that
her more advanced students would come to share the spiritual beliefs that,
for her, could never be separated from literary theory.

She frequently referred to her mystical philosophy in letters to Jones,
even citing it in the midst of their most intimate arguments and treating it
as a commonly accepted or mutually understood basis for disputation. In a
letter of January 20, 1949, responding to Jones's plea to resume their sexual relationship, she contended: "If you will believe me there's this trait in
you that is a carry over from many lives. . . . You are gluttonous for sex. You
indulge—over-indulge in your sleeping hours. You've got to make your first
fight and conquer there then the daylight will take care of itself. If you will
go on a diet if the wildness comes it will relieve it—eat less meat—also force
your thoughts away from sex when going to sleep—and tell yourself in the
astral world you'll do anything else but what will carry over into your fight"
(Handy Writers' Colony Collection). Continuing the same argument
months later, Handy asserted on November 30, 1949:

You can make your life—re-make it. It takes time and the thought groove
will be difficult to press into your mind to begin with—but if you want to
change and grow you've got to make the effort. When you go to sleep you
enter the astral world. The emotional world. According to Annie Besant
and other Yogi writers—there are seven planes that they know about—although two of them man will not reach while evolving on this plane—but

five he travels through. The Physical—the Astral—the mental—then the Buddhic (spiritual) and finally the Nirvanic or union or peace.

I'm sure that at night you enter into some fine sexual affairs. You have more wet dreams than most anyone I ever heard of—and then I remember you telling me about when you were still only a baby and having very odd dreams for a child that young. You couldn't have known what you were dreaming about.

Anyway if you want to change—you'll have to begin there. Paul Brunton has it down in black and white. Annie Besant also says the same thing. She says you have to make up your mind to resist the Astral world when you go to sleep. (Handy Writers' Colony Collection)

Jones's style of disputation was different, tending to be more direct, personal, and literary, with little of the mystical that so obsessed Handy. On January 25, 1949, responding to her criticism that he was a "romantic" like Hemingway, Jones pointed to the "romanticism" in Handy's own personality and behavior and affirmed:

All men must have ideals, to go on living. An ideal, "the blue hills in the distance," is basically romantic. It is romanticism. To be absolutely realistic is to be absolutely cynical—take James T. Farrell, a realist. On the other side, there is Hemingway—a modern Byron. In between there is the romantic who is still sane enough to know that he has not reached his "blue hills." When the time comes to either you or me that we believe we have reached our "blue hills," then we will be Hemingway. However, if we do not believe in "blue hills," we will become James T. Farrell, or Zola, neither of whom either one of us can read because they are so depressing to us.

In that sense, then, we are both "romantics." And must continue to be. It is in the conflict of wanting the "blue hills," and never getting them, that the art we are both capable of comes out. Still, we must believe in the "blue hills."

You have acquired a new interpretation of your "blue hills" in the last five years, a yearning for Yoga. My "blue hills" are still the same they always were—a yearning for love, "sexual love" if you will, that I always had and found partially for a while in you, and then lost, saw going away from me bit by bit while apparently there was nothing I could do to regain it, or save it. Love of a woman, a mate, a comrade, an equal, a meeting in body, a meeting in mind, a meeting in spirit. . . . I know I will never reach my "blue hills," as you will never reach yours, whatever they are. But I *must* have them to strive for. (Handy Writers' Colony Collection)

Although the words "a meeting in body, a meeting in mind, a meeting in spirit" suggest the three levels Jones learned about from theosophy (animal man, mental man, and spiritual man), a division Handy knew well and to which she would have responded, his subsequent phrase, "whatever they are," implies some distancing from her "blue hills" of yoga. In another section of the letter Jones insightfully analyzed a fundamental difference in their modes of self-expression and therefore in their basic approaches to life.

> You never say things directly, always cover them under a camouflage, its as if you are putting out a sign or something, its there for them to see and if they see it you know them then, you were testing to see if it was there. . . . I dont work like you do. I cant stick in a signpost and watch and see if it is recognized, I just dont seem to have the faculty. I wish I had. That way, you can save your pride either way, if they recognize it you can welcome them proudly, and if they dont you can slyly chuckle proudly to yourself. (Handy Writers' Colony Collection)

The different approaches to self-expression and life were reflected in Jones's and Handy's attitudes toward the mystical. Although they shared an interest—and even a belief—in many of the same mystical concepts, such as reincarnation, karma, the Over-Soul, spiritual involution and evolution, and a world of bodyless souls or spirits of leaders, lords, masters, and teachers (almost all concepts that could be traced to theosophy and transcendentalism), they valued these concepts differently and gave them vastly different roles in their lives.

For Handy, such beliefs, coupled with the yoga exercises and added to the ideas of Paul Brunton and Annie Besant, were all-consuming. They dominated her life in a way that they never dominated Jones's, although he accepted and lived by them a while. As Handy wrote to a colony member named Al (either Albert Nash or Alvin Pevehouse), there was a time when "Jim went on fast—did exercises in the rising sun—read PAUL BRUNTON— I can show you books he has marked and written in the margin" (Handy Writers' Colony Collection).

Ultimately, however, the exercises failed to work for Jones. They never produced the god-consciousness at which they were aimed, and his honesty would not allow pretending to a feeling he did not have. As he wrote to Richard P. Adams on July 16, 1954, he had never had "any occult experiences"; his "experience and acceptance" of reincarnation had "all been purely intellectual" (Hendrick, ed., *To Reach Eternity* 213). He made the same disavowal of certainty, with the same stress on the intellectual nature of his belief, in a final letter to me on July 21, 1975, twenty-one years after his statement to Adams and less than two years before his death: "As I told you in the beginning, I have never been able fully to espouse a religious philosophy that embraces reincarnation and various mystical ESP, largely because I have never had any personal experiences which I could point to as valid in any of these realms. Still, the idea of reincarnation has always intrigued me and interested me" (Hendrick, ed., *To Reach Eternity* 366). Clearly, such reservations kept Jones from having the same level of involvement with the concept of reincarnation that Handy maintained.

Although Jones eventually expressed his disillusionment with two of the sources of Handy's opinions identified by David Ray—Brunton and W. Somerset Maugham's *The Razor's Edge*—he never dismissed Madame Blavatsky or theosophy. Blavatsky's approach to mystical philosophy was primarily intellectual, as was Jones's, and much of her appeal has been to other intellectuals intrigued by mysticism, including James Joyce, William Butler Yeats, D. H. Lawrence, Jack London, Henry Miller, Maurice Maeterlinck, George W. Russell (AE), and Albert Einstein.

That Handy would attempt—and be permitted—to intervene in Jones's work, affecting his literary techniques as well as his content, was inevitable despite their differences in temperament and level of involvement with mysticism, the intensity of their relationship, the emotional support and belief that she gave so overwhelmingly and he needed so much, her near fanatical conviction of her ability to teach writing and yoga (a conviction Jones shared for a long while), and her extraordinary aggressiveness. During much of the time Jones was writing, "They would eat together, and Jones would tell her about the morning's work. He confided in her about everything, and she would go over his typescript and comment on it. . . . She was not a stylist, nor was she competent to discuss the nuances of writing, but she could tell if he fudged or misrepresented what she knew to be true" (MacShane, *Into Eternity* 135).

John Bowers has recorded two claims Handy made to having influenced the writing of *From Here to Eternity*. The first involved Prewitt's death: "I said, 'Jim, Prewitt's going to get killed. That's what ultimately happens to anyone who bucks the system the way he does'" (*The Colony* 122). The second concerned her solution to Jones's writer's block: "Lowney had told us every day, like a litany, how Jim had once got bogged down in writing *Eternity* and how she had got a large swatch of butcher paper from the meat market and the two of them had outlined the rest of the book" (124). Handy's description of the fight she and Jones had over whether Prewitt should die was vivid and violent—"We were literally on opposite ends of the room throwing anything we could lay our hands on at each other"—but apparently Jones disputed her version, because she admitted to Bowers that "now he thinks he thought up killing Prewitt off all along" (122). Handy also acknowledged a notable failure: She had hated the title *From Here to Eternity* but had never been able to persuade Jones to abandon it.

She was much more satisfied with the title of Jones's next book, *Some Came Running*, which she may have suggested because, as Bowers dryly observes, providing titles was "Lowney's bailiwick" (*The Colony* 123). Calling it "perfect," she explained that the title came from the biblical passage concerning "the man running up to Jesus and asking what he has to do for eternal life" and being "told to give up all of his possessions to the poor" (123). That interpretation accurately points to one of the themes in the novel, one developed through Dave Hirsh's experiences and growth, the spiritual advancement for which it is necessary to abandon material possessions, including one's attachment to the material world and the desires of matter-bound ego.

Handy, however, also had an occult interpretation of the title that is more problematic. That Jones was aware of the occult version of Christianity upon which Handy drew and in which she believed is shown when Bob French argues that "Christ himself taught reincarnation" and that "all but the most veiled allusions to it" were excised by Saint Paul and the First Council of Nicaea (*Some Came Running* 815-16), a reflection of Blavatsky's view that, as "every well-informed Occultist and even Kabalist" could tell you, "Christ, or the fourth Gospel at any rate, teaches re-incarnation as also the annihilation of the personality, if you forget the dead letter and hold to the esoteric Spirit" (*The Key to Theosophy* 186). What is in question is whether Jones accepted the whole of Handy's occultist Christianity or only part of it, particularly as she applied it to his novel.

In an October 24, 1954, letter to Harry Handy, she argued with some validity that "in Jim's book they are all afraid, and they wait for another reincarnation to try it," because "NATURE DOTH MAKE COWARDS OF US ALL" (Handy Writers' Colony Collection). She then contended that the secret meaning of the title was that Christ had come "to found a New Kingdom on EARTH" for those "who have fined their vibrations by suffering—or have made an AT-ONE-MENT—or have made an intelligent union of spirit and matter." Proclaiming that "the GATES OF GOLD only answer to each person when his vibrations are right," she exhorted Harry to change his vibrations, informing him that "this is done—BY CONSCIOUS WILL POWER DEVELOPMENT. . . . You and you alone can overcome whatever your cross is." Again, much of Handy's interpretation reflects themes that were consciously developed in the book: reincarnation, growth through suffering, and each soul's responsibility for its own "crucifixion." But the shrillness exemplified by her capitalization of words and punctuation as well as the references to

Christ's "New Kingdom on EARTH," "vibrations," and the "Gates of God" indicates ways in which she and Jones may have diverged.

In one undated note, Handy suggests that perhaps Jones had once tried to include occult material that went beyond Bob French's brief references to the world of bodyless souls and spirits. Because the note is only addressed to "Jim," and there were two students at the colony by that name, it is not definite that the note was intended for Jones. "Jim," it begins, "I think your gal holds forth too long on the Fire-Fourth Dimension and you the author prolong the things she sees into meaning too much—symbolisms (your theory isn't as important as it sounds to you, in fact I can disprove the theory completely)" (Handy Writers' Colony Collection). If she was discussing *Some Came Running*, the "gal" is surely Gwen French, the writing teacher modeled largely on Handy, but the published novel includes no discussion of the "Fire-Fourth Dimension." If Jones had considered using the occult in this way, he finally rejected doing so.

The Handy Writers' Colony Collection also includes a three-page, undated piece of correspondence by Handy to "Jim" that begins, "Maybe you can use the gist of this or something of this idea for SOME CAME RUNNING." The statement includes many ideas that were familiar to Jones and had become part of the thematic focus of his works, such as Handy's definition of sensitivity as "a forgetting of self . . . and awareness of others" and her explanation that "most people want to dominate everyone, and make everyone notice them," which "is the opposite pole of being sensitive" and "the very thing we are trying to escape . . . animalism . . . self-centered, physical, lower body, personality . . . ego." *Some Came Running* also exemplifies Handy's description of disciples as "ordinary men like all of us . . . but men who have sacrificed the personal goal for an evolutionary one" and her assertion that "every person who makes a path cuts it through the jungle for another . . . and a road is made by many following that same pathway." Dave Hirsh undergoes a pattern of spiritual progress that prepares him by the novel's end to become a disciple in his next incarnation, studying under the direction of a great master. Among the side effects of his progress are Bob and Gwen French's decision after his death to make themselves vulnerable to the kind of pain they had earlier tried to evade, which will almost certainly speed their spiritual progress.

A large portion of Handy's statement, however, is not embodied in Jones's novel, and that he may or may not have accepted. He always had more reservations and doubts about reincarnation, karma, and other key concepts than she did. She argued, for example, that "man must transmute" the "lower energies" of the "sex, liver (spleen), and solar plexis" (which she deemed to be "the highest mind level of the animal state") into "higher centers" (Handy Writers' Colony Collection). She also claimed that "when he moves the sex energy up to the throat he becomes creative, when he moves solar energy up to the heart . . . THE CHRIST IS BORN IN A MANGER OR CAVE OF THE HEART." As a result of this process, man would become "a superman . . . or genius . . . and the intuitions are his guide instead of the lower animal instincts." Christ had come to found a new kingdom on earth, and Handy defined this kingdom as "SUPERMAN," explaining that "there were already four kingdoms on earth . . . mineral, vegetable, animal and the human kingdom . . . so the new kingdom, the fifth is to be superman . . . or he who has learned to connect with his soul . . . or the last outpost of the stars . . . all of his centers are vibrating and he is the recipient of solar and planetary and cosmic energy."

Most of what Handy wrote belongs to the occult part of Blavatsky's *The Secret Doctrine*, and there is nothing in Jones's novel to indicate that he dismissed such ideas. But the fact that he did not make use of them also indicates the limits on his work of the influence of Lowney Handy, theosophy, and any other source. He was willing to accept any advice or idea that appeared reasonable and that he felt he could portray honestly, but it had to strike a chord within him.

Ironically, Handy herself may have provided the best insight into why a dedicated writer such as Jones would forever evade the control of even the most dictatorial writing teacher, editor, and would-be world savior. In a note to "Tom" (probably Tom Chamales, author of *Never so Few*), she warned that although "everyone steals—THERE IS NOTHING NEW UNDER THE SUN . . . you can't use any of it until you make it your own" and explained that "you have to become what you took—before you can give it part of yourself and that NEW—ORIGINAL—that fresh outlook—that makes for good creative work" (Handy Writers' Colony Collection).

At its best, Handy's system of copying aimed at inspiration, not slavish imitation or obedience to Lowney Handy. In this, she resembled her idol, "the unassailable Ralph Waldo." As Arthur Christy notes, "The key to Emerson's workshop was the essay 'Quotation and Originality,'" in which he defends his borrowings with the quotation "it is no more according to Plato than according to me" (*The Orient in American Transcendentalism* 3). As one of his journal entries indicates, Emerson contended that one's experience is what determines the choice of quotations, and "for good quotation . . . there must be originality in the quoter,—bent, bias, delight in the truth, and only valuing the author in the measure of his agreement with the truth, which we see, and which he had the luck to see first" (*Selected Essays* 4).

Jones made his borrowings from Christianity (occult or otherwise), transcendentalism, Orientalism, Platonism, theosophy, and Lowney Handy his own when he shaped his philosophy and sharpened his creative writing. He filtered what he had learned through his experience; subjected it to the test of his compulsive honesty; and embodied, expanded, modified, and elaborated on it through the skilled use of such basic fiction writer's tools as organization, characterization, setting, theme, symbolism, irony, and sometimes, as in his unpublished novel and the first two published ones, long, didactic speeches by designated spokespersons. He became a literary alchemist, transforming everything that came his way into a vision and style that could never be mistaken for that of any other writer. Moreover, his eclectic philosophy, composed from borrowings and given vitality and originality by the experiences, character, and highly personal revision of its creator, much as Emerson absorbed his borrowings and gave the world transcendentalism, became the "unsevered thread" that Jones wanted to hold his work together. The image of the unsevered thread strikingly recalls Blavatsky's description of the reincarnating portion of the human being as "the golden thread on which, like beads, the various personalities of this higher *Ego* are strung" (*The Secret Doctrine* 166).

Jones's commitment to the artistic representation of his reincarnationist philosophy may paradoxically be revealed in his decision to stop expressing that philosophy didactically after *Some Came Running*, his fullest exploration of the topic. Although his philosophy made sense to him and helped him overcome the anger and self-pity that had occurred when he went AWOL from the army in 1943 and became involved with Lowney Handy, it was not something he sought to impose on others. A key aspect of that philosophy, which Handy preached but violated daily through her attempts to remake others in her own yoga image, was that each individual creates his or her own karma, including the conditions for learning in each new life. Moreover, Jones believed that spiritual evolution took place at every moment and did not depend on whether any soul in any incarnation understood it at the time. Understanding would come later, when the soul was ready. Finally, like Dave Hirsh, Jones felt that writers can never succeed in imposing their illusory world on others but may be able to break out of it "partially" by making "other people's illusory world more real" to himself or herself "through the writing" (*Some Came Running* 1230). As he phrased the idea, "If there is any one comment about life which is not disputable, it is that life is not teachable. . . . But life is certainly re-creatable, in fiction. And that is how fiction, if it is good enough, serves us. We can each of us become another, see through his eyes, live through his life. If only enough good fiction were written, we could each of us become all men" (Hills, ed., *Writer's Choice* 225).

Jones's concern with what he saw as excessive didacticism in his writing emerged while he was writing *Some Came Running*. As he admitted on July 31, 1953, to editor Burroughs Mitchell, "I think that one of my own general problems—one thats always with me—is this tendency I have to try and tell or show everything, to get down exactly every nuance and subtlety of a scene so that it is easily understood. . . . That is the main thing wrong with *Running* right now, I think. I should be leaving more unsaid, to be handled by the imagination" (Hendrick, ed., *To Reach Eternity* 193-94). That concern grew over the years. Willie Morris came to view it as a trait defining Jones as a writer and concluded his memoir, *James Jones: A Friendship*, with a notable example. His final memory of Jones emphasizes Jones's hesitation over including several paragraphs in *Whistle* that would explain why Sgt. Marion Landers keeps yelling "Pay!" throughout a fight in a bar, because "maybe they're too spelt out. They hurt a lot" (254).

Landers reflects on the anguish, hate, and love he felt during the fight that had fueled his demand for payment for everything he had experienced during the war:

> The anguish was for himself. And every poor slob like him, who had ever suffered fear, and terror, and injury at the hands of other men. The love, he didn't know who the love was for. For himself and everybody. For all the sad members of this flawed, misbegotten, miscreated race of valuable creatures, which was trying and failing with such ruptured effort to haul itself up out of the mud and dross and drouth of its crippled heritage. And the hate, implacable, unyielding, was for himself and every other who had ever, in the name of whatever good, maimed or injured or killed another man. (Jones, *Whistle* 255)

Surely Morris left this paragraph for the end of his memoir because it sums up much of Jones's perspective about war, humanity, and life. But although it offers cogent psychological and philosophical analysis, the paragraph is a far cry from the explicit enunciation of a philosophy that Jones had made through Bob French.

It is possible that other factors contributed to Jones's lack of directness about his philosophy after the publication of *Some Came Running*. Hendrick has suggested that perhaps he was less open because of the association between the formation of his philosophy and Lowney Handy, who may have helped to shape it. Timing supports this theory, because Jones's breakup with Handy and her violent attack on his new wife, Gloria, occurred after *Some Came Running* was published. Moreover, according to Hendrick, I was the only person who corresponded with Jones about his philosophy in his later years, and we did so only after I had discovered his views in *Some Came Running*. He may also have become less overt because of incomprehension and a lack of sympathy for his views, even among many critics who supported his work. Although both factors may have contributed to Jones being less vocal about his mystical beliefs, the plotting, characterization, and patterns of symbolism in his later work demonstrate that he never abandoned them entirely, although his doubts about them continued. He finally mastered the technique he ascribed to Handy: leaving signs for attentive readers. Although he had once thought doing so was beyond him, it now added to his power and skill.

Perhaps the best example of the power Jones gained by indirection comes at the end of his final novel, *Whistle:* the image of Mess Sgt. John Strange, waiting alone in the ocean to meet eternity. As Hendrick affirms, "The poetic passage is mysterious, as were the mystic passages of Emerson, Thoreau, and Whitman" (*To Reach Eternity* 368). Yet one interpretation suggests that the passage may be a clear, final expression of Jones's ideas about the separation of humans from God, their subsequent immersion in self, the reduction of their egos through pain coupled with the compassionate understanding it eventually brings, and their ultimate reunion with God.

The image of Strange begins with his presence in the ocean, which has often provided the representation for the anima mundi, Brahma, and Emerson's Over-Soul. While in the ocean, Strange starts "in a sort of semi-hallucination" to feel himself swelling, swelling, it may be argued, into the separated and isolated self "until he's bigger than the ocean, bigger than the planet, bigger than the solar system, bigger than the galaxy out in the universe." As he "grows this picture of a fully clothed soldier with his helmet, his boots, and his GI woolen gloves seems to be taking into himself all of the pain and anguish and sorrow and misery that is the lot of all soldiers" (and, by extension, all of reincarnating humanity) and taking it "into the universe as well" (*Whistle* 576). Afterward, "he begins to shrink back to normal, and shrinks down through the other stages—the galaxy, the solar system, the planet, the ocean—back to Strange in the water. And then continues shrinking until he seems to be only the size of a seahorse, and then an amoeba, then finally an atom" (576). And then a droplet in the ocean of the Over-Soul? But although this fascinating and forceful image of Strange in the ocean and his "semihallucination," spoken into a tape recorder by a dying man committed to his art until his final moment, may have been inspired by the ideas of Madame Blavatsky, transcendentalism, and Lowney Handy (as well as the mushroom-induced expansion-contraction of Alice in Lewis Carroll's *Alice's Adventures in Wonderland*), its spiritual and artistic resonance ultimately belong only to that American literary Orientalist master, James Jones.

2

_____

The Basic Philosophy:
Everyone Comes Running

When *Some Came Running* was published, reviewers denounced it roundly. As Jones's biographer Frank MacShane reports, Granville Hicks termed the book a "monstrosity"; Edmund Fuller fulminated that "if you like bad grammar, the grossest promiscuity, the most callous adultery, aggressive vulgarity, shoddy and befuddled philosophy, *Some Came Running* is your book"; the *Time* reviewer snidely remarked that "Choctaw rather than English would appear to be his first language"; and "J. Donald Adams twice devoted his weekly column, 'Speaking of Books,' to attacking the publisher for bringing out the novel in the first place" and criticized Jones "for reveling 'in a fatuous pride in being illiterate, standardless and faithless'" (*Into Eternity* 162).

Since Jones's death, however, the novel has been treated with greater understanding and respect, and even critics such as MacShane and James Giles, who decided that the book was ultimately unsuccessful in achieving its artistic aims, have deemed it an ambitious and honorable failure. And some critics (and even reviewers) have taken a much more positive stand. Willie Morris calls it "a majestic, encompassing book" and notes that after the ferocious reviews it became "subsequently the most neglected . . . great novel of twentieth-century American literature" (*James Jones* 76-77). Tom Carson argues that it "emerges as the crucial book in Jones's career" and exclaims, "What a fucking great book" ("To Hell with Literature" 19). Moreover, in response to the nearly universal condemnation of Jones's prose by its early reviewers, Carson contends that "at its crowded, methodical, vernacular best, [the prose] does just what he wanted it to do—involve you in the events, and put you inside the characters' heads with striking veracity and conviction" (19). Michael Lydon has written that Jones's domestic novels were "full of overlooked virtues," and that "*Some Came Running* may be the best of these, a bleak tale of hate between two brothers and one of the earliest and sharpest pictures of the postwar boom" ("A Voice against Anonymous Death" 121).

George Garrett, who felt that "in years of studying the critical receptions of books" he had "never seen anything quite to match the harsh treatment accorded Jones and *Some Came Running*" (*James Jones* 9), may have put his finger on an important part of the problem when he noted that the book was "enormously complex and demanding. . . . What was original was easy to miss," and "what was admirable was easy to ignore" (122, 123). He also offers the most sympathetic and convincing defense of the Jonesian approach to language: "Jones, as he wrote *Running*, was involved in an experiment with language, a kind of discovery. . . . he calls it working with 'colloquial forms,' by which he means not merely the free and easy use of the living, *spoken* American idiom in dialogue or in first-person narration, but the attempt to carry it into the narrative itself, into third-person narrative" (116). Garrett further points out that "many of the best American writers during the same period," such as Faulkner and John O'Hara, shared "this experimental concern of what to do with the rapidly changing American vernacular" (116). Garrett might well have added the names of Saul Bellow, John Updike, and so many folk-inspired African American writers that Houston Baker, Jr., and Henry Louis Gates, Jr., found it necessary to create "vernacular theories" to expound their literature and culture.

Whatever else is said about *Some Came Running*, the novel remains the fundamental testament of Jones's philosophy. In no other work does he explain so thoroughly his ideas concerning karmic relationships, Glamours (illusions), spiritual discipleship, the subjectivity of everyone's "image-picture" of the world, and the involution-evolution process. Although he never explicitly referred to these ideas again in his fiction, Jones continued to use them as the basis for characterization, plotting, and overall meaning. *Some Came Running* provides a key to all his other work, including *From Here to Eternity* and even "They Shall Inherit the Laughter," which both preceded it. It is because of its central role in explaining and illustrating Jones's philosophy that I have taken the novel out of order, placing my discussion of it ahead of my analysis of *From Here to Eternity*, which also approaches the belief system didactically through Malloy, Warden, and Prewitt but without covering it as fully or directly as *Some Came Running*.

The novel concerns Dave Hirsh's development from a self-centered slob intent on avenging ancient pinpricks to his ego by inflicting similarly small-minded hurts on others, notably his brother Frank (who, like Erskine Carter in "They Shall Inherit the Laughter," seems an incarnation of Jones's self-righteous Uncle Charles and equally a target for literary revenge), into a compassionate human being capable of comprehending and acting upon the full spiritual significance of his transformation. Similar patterns, although not as full-blown, are displayed by Prewitt, Warden, and Karen Holmes in *From Here to Eternity*; Stein, Fife, and Welsh in *The Thin Red Line*; and Landers and Strange in *Whistle*, among many other characters.

Dave evolves through the animal, mental, and spiritual levels. When he arrives in Parkman, Illinois, his emotions and actions are animalistic and primitive. In addition, he fits Jones's definition of a slob: "someone who has an inordinate ego which makes him close his mind down around his small beliefs and prejudices" (Interview 245). Relishing the "furor" his return to his hometown "was going to create" and "the malices he would activate" (Jones, *Some Came Running* 4), Dave pointedly rejects the bank in which Frank Hirsh has part interest—a calculated, petty revenge against his brother for having self-righteously ordered him out of town nineteen years earlier. Even though he is thirty-six and the veteran of a horrifying war, Dave lives ever in the moment of his boyhood shame. Could anything signal his continuing childishness more clearly than his long-treasured grudge?

In spite of the war's and his brother's embittering influence, the most probable reason Dave has turned himself into a drunken, lustful, spiteful clown and abandoned the writing he once valued is that his unrequited love, Harriet Bowman, married someone else. As a result, when he meets Gwen French, a local Parkman College English teacher, his first thoughts are not about the possibility of loving her but only about his desire to have sex with her and gain the ego satisfaction of having her love him. Nevertheless, he may unconsciously realize that his ill-fated attempt to seduce the unyielding Gwen will push him out of an animal existence toward intellectual and spiritual development. Her father, Bob French, theorizes that the only way humans can develop is through experiencing pain—"Physical pain, mental anguish, spiritual suffering" (819). Because people can never be induced to search out unalloyed pain, he argues, it comes to them in the form of something they would seek, such as love. Hence, in running after unrequited loves like Harriet and Gwen, Dave is opening himself to enormous pain, to sensitization toward the longings and feelings of other people as well as to a growth-inducing revelation of his own inadequacies. As Bob also contends, love on the animal level means only the desire for sex. Love on the mental level, however, means the desire to be loved by someone else to gain justification for self-love, and love on the spiritual level means the need to move beyond yourself toward God, who is also in motion and therefore cannot be pinned down, limited, or understood. God is impersonal, without humanly assignable attributes—anima mundi, Brahma, the Over-Soul. It is Dave's love for Gwen on the mental level that turns him into a writer again, as his love for Harriet Bowman had done before. Because his entanglement with Gwen is more powerful than his previous one-sided relationship, however, his writing under her influence is more painful, sensitive, and honest than anything he had created while chasing after Harriet.

Dave is the prime example of Gwen's theory that writing is not an end in itself but only a "by-product of the near psychotic love-hunger of the individual; . . . A by-product that the individual willingly gave up himself, when he reached the Love climax and either got or did not get the Love-object" (568). Gwen also speculates that there is an "almost mathematical clinical progression from the beginning sense of unlove up through the height . . . of talent to the Love climax . . . thence almost immediately into the decline of talent and on down to the inevitable destruction of talent, or the individual, one" (567), and Dave's involvement with Gwen bears that out.

He begins writing again as a means of keeping Gwen interested while he is trying to seduce her, and he constantly expresses the hope that she will be pleased with what he has done, with the underlying longing for her to transfer her admiration for his fiction to his person. Nevertheless, even though he writes to win Gwen's love, he doesn't try to idealize his life or romanticize other people. As Bob French would explain, using his concept of love on the mental level, Dave cannot justify his love for himself if he induces Gwen to love a falsified, unflawed image of himself.

Gwen's view is that an artist is also driven toward self-exposure by the combination of a "desire for unbridled license" coupled with "this higher-than-normal, stronger-than-was-customary-in-humans sense of high integrity and great morality, forming that perpetually balanced and forever insoluable conflict within that made you the artist" (566). That motive ties in with the previous one, because both are based on the equally powerful holds on the artist's nature exerted by his or her ego and the vulnerability of an artist's ego. Dave acts again and again on the needs of his ego, only to find that his actions seem designed to puncture his pride. That realization forces him to reevaluate the behavior as well as his reasons for it. When he returns from a trip to Florida that was prompted by outrage at not having been invited by the Frenches for Christmas, for example, he discovers that Gwen and Bob had expected him to come over, and he has to admit to himself that he has acted childishly. The trip was productive, however, because he had written a fine short novel, "The Confederate," while he was away and been able to expand his sympathy by learning to understand the way of life of Southerners, a group he had feared were alien to him.

The incident is typical of Dave and suggests the way in which ego and his desires are inextricably valuable and damaging. Gwen addresses this idea when she remembers the "drinking and sexing" of the writers she has known and reflects that "they were all like runners" (thus giving an interpretation to the title), "runners with huge enormous feet. They were dependent upon their feet to run, and needed them. But those same feet were always tangling them up and tripping them. And if they ever win a race it was both because of their feet and in spite of them, simultaneously" (305).

Dave's writing can be viewed both as a result of his imperfections—that is, of his captivity to his desires and illusions—and as a means to free himself from them. He could not have become a writer without his ego and his desires, but he cannot move on to discipleship, the next spiritual stage, until he is ready to leave them behind. Only when he has fulfilled himself at the artist stage will he perceive the need to serve as a disciple "working consciously and specifically with some Great Master" (830). Although the artist stage at its peak is the preliminary step to the lowliest disciple stage, artists who can carry their attempts at self-exposure to the utmost limit then move beyond those selves toward God. Bob French implies the ways in which art is founded on imperfection and in which disciples—and, above all, leaders, lords, masters, and teachers—supersede artists when he asserts to Dave that "the way of the artist . . . is never to *know*. . . . If he *knew* what God was, he would be too sure. And the very nature of an artist, a great artist, is that he must never *know*; must never be *sure*. That is why he works so hard, and so painfully. If he *knew*. . . . Well, I dont suppose he would ever produce anything, would he? He wouldnt *need* to" (1182-83). This spiritually informed conception of artists needing to be ever pursuing their visions and never attaining certainty about them is the one Jones expressed to Lowney Handy in his letter of January 25, 1949: Struggling artists must neither reach nor lose sight of Romanticism and the "blue hills in the distance." Moreover, it reflects the creative tension that undergirded Jones's spiritual "system" and fiction throughout his life, keeping him an artist rather than a "knower" to the end.

Even though Dave's head is filled with ideas for future novels after the moment of revelation in which he frees himself from most of his illusions, he senses that he is approaching death and will never be able to write about any of them. It can be argued, however, that the reason he dies at this point, apart from the plot complications involving his relationship with Ginnie Moorehead, a promiscuous factory worker, is that he has learned all that he needs to know to become a disciple and is ready to begin—literally—a new life, either in the "world of bodyless souls" and "spirits . . . surrounding the material world we inhabit" (816) or in a new body on earth.

Perhaps the most significant change in Dave's artistry during the time he is bound by his love for Gwen is his shift from "unconscious writing," which depends on the author's emotions, to "fully conscious writing," which has a "preconceived effect" toward which the author is working (695). This type of art is far from that of the lumberjack who tried to put "everything he ever felt about life and beauty and frustration" into making the skillets hanging in Gwen French's kitchen (270) and the folk art of Prewitt and his friends in composing "The Re-enlistment Blues" in *From Here to Eternity*, not to mention the kind of writing early reviewers of *Some Came Running* were certain Jones advocated as well as practiced. Nevertheless, this "fully conscious writing" is presented as an advance over Dave's former, more spontaneous writing, although it has a potential drawback that authors need to know and guard against. As Gwen points out, in fully conscious writing, "It's no longer enough to just *feel* something and then write it. You have to construct. And then you have a tendency to lose all the fresh originality of your emotions, which came out of your innocent unconsciousness of them, because now you know what they are" (695-96).

The most important implication here is that Dave has grown in both his awareness of his emotions and his control (at least artistically) over them, although he still has a long way to go before reaching the understanding necessary to free himself from them. The book Gwen views as an example of fully conscious writing is Dave's "comic combat novel," in which he attempts to show that the lives of men in combat are "no more brave or fine, or possessed of any other human virtue, than their life at home would have been" and recognizes that each one of the "laughable (but unpitiable) fools" about whom he writes is "DAVID HERSCHMIDT, who could look back on one of the most foolish lives of any of them, but who would no more admit it than they would, if accused of it" (650). Dave's movement toward self-knowledge, self-acceptance, and self-transcendence is further confirmed by the slightly earlier decision to change his writing name from the pretentious "D. Hirsh" to the more legitimate "David Herschmidt."

Dave is almost finished with his combat novel when the crisis comes in his relationship with Gwen, and, true to her theory, he is unable to write anything for a long time. When he resumes writing, its quality is inferior to what he has done earlier. After he has given up Gwen and become attached to Ginnie Moorehead, the best he can do is a sentimental love story, which nearly destroys the overall effect of his combat novel, followed by a vicious but equally unsuccessful depiction of his deteriorating relationship with Ginnie. At the end of the book, even though Dave seems eager to write again, his writing is no longer important. He is beyond the attachment to the world that had necessitated his fiction.

Dave's self-entrapment with Ginnie provides a fitting conclusion to his development in this incarnation. It forces him to confront his strongest illusions, which form the basis for his decision to marry Ginnie. First, he feels that he needs a woman but is "too old" and "too fat and ugly and too broke" to appeal to anyone other than the unattractive Ginnie (1187), although his gambler friend Bama Dillert points out that Dave's fortunes could change at any moment and money from selling his book (or any other source) would greatly improve Dave's chances with women. Dave ensnares himself in the trap of self-pity that Gwen warns her writing student, Wally Dennis, about when he decides to enlist in the army and escape his suffering over Dave's niece Dawn's marriage. Gwen makes the dangers of any form of pity clear when she tells Wally, "All the chains, and limitations, and prisons we build around ourselves resolve themselves into that one word Pity. . . . It's the opposite way from Freedom. Just as much as Ego, and Vanity. And it doesn't matter a damn whether you Pity yourself or Pity someone else, Pity always binds you closer to the imperfection you see—that you *hunger* after" (1022).

Dave's self-pity binds him to his sense of the imperfection of his body and its "needs," yet ironically, when he marries Ginnie to obtain continuous sexual pleasure, he finds that she no longer wants to have sex with him because she believes that respectable married women do not like sex. Worse still, his sexual desire and longing for companionship make him dependent on someone else when he should be seeking salvation. When Dave was tormented by Gwen's abandonment, Bob had cautioned him that "every man must find his own salvation. . . . it's not to be found outside. In another person. Not in friendship; but most particularly not in love" (1084). Dave had considered this advice useless then, however, and refused to guide himself by it, allowing himself later to be caught by the "married man's settled panic at the thought of being without his wife" (1207). Nevertheless, Dave finally has to admit that he and Ginnie can never make contact with each other because "each of them had in them a sort of superimposed picture, like a celluloid overlay on a map, of life—and of what life was, or was not, and also what it should be; or, rather, what they wanted it to be," and these separate pictures "could not be made to coincide" (1229). Fortunately, though, that realization frees Dave from his dependence on Ginnie and enables him know that he, like all other humans, must be forever alone. It also liberates him from the demands of his body so he may be able to "make the crossover" from the material world to the world of bodyless souls (820).

This concept of "image-pictures," the collision of subjective realities, may be Jones's most original contribution to the philosophy he derived from theosophy and transcendentalism and the greatest element of complexity in his art. At the least, it allowed him to bring a variety of philosophies and social views to his work, thoughtfully linking their interactions and resistances. As he wrote to me on July 21, 1975, "I have never deliberately, concisely structured any of my novels [around my philosophy]. Instead, it is more as though I were trying to examine various philosophies in contradistinction to each other" (Hendrick, ed., *To Reach Eternity* 366). It is this aspect of *Some Came Running*, and of Jones's work in general, that George Garrett captures so well:

> It is by and through the gradual revelations of character and of their conceptions and misconceptions of each other that the story is told. These people are only, at best, partly successful at understanding each other. And they are even less able to comprehend honestly their own motives. Such a story needs space to develop, because all of the characters are so mixed, deeply ambivalent, and self-deceiving even as they seek to deceive others . . .
>
> The result of all this is an enormously complex and demanding book, one which requires patient and intense concentration for the reader not to fall into some of the misconceptions that bedevil the characters. It would be a mistake, at any point, to attribute any of the characters' opinions, theories, prejudices, and follies to the author. (*James Jones* 122-23)

I do not consider Garrett's last assertion to be entirely valid, because Bob French and, at times near the end of the book, Gwen and Dave, all voice Jones's philosophy, even though, as Garrett notes, they are all filled with self-deception and frequently fail to approach their ideals. Bob French, for example, clearly delineates the same philosophical system that Jones discussed in letters to Richard P. Adams and me, and when French speaks in general terms his ideas are not only sound but also well supported by the rest of the novel. Yet Bob French seriously misapplies the philosophy to his own life. By refusing to give Dave some desperately needed advice because he seeks to avoid karmic entanglements, Bob becomes partly responsible for Dave's death and takes on a greater karmic debt than would have been the case had he helped Dave. He even labels himself "the villain of the piece" because he "refused to be a *part* of God's will" by withholding advice (Jones, *Some Came Running* 1253). This is a misjudgment, of course, but one that will lead him to a higher level of understanding. Although wise in the ways of Jones's system, Bob is still subject to its operations. Choosing not to act is itself an act that has karmic consequences, and Bob's error-filled interpretation of the system in terms of his own life leads him into fruitful collisions with other consciousnesses. Like those unaware of or hostile to the system, Bob, too, has to act, make mistakes, suffer, and grow.

Even though Garrett may be partly mistaken about the presence of spokespersons for Jones in the novel (although not about their fallibilities and frailties), he provides a useful exposition of the role of "image-pictures," or colliding subjective realities. He has also thoughtfully observed that role in helping emphasize such collisions. Reflecting that "not only are the thoughts and words of the characters presented appropriately in the vernacular, but also much of the narrative itself, as if the author-narrator were speaking almost in a composite language of the characters, within the context of the characters' own verbal capacities and limitations" (*James Jones* 116), Garrett emphasizes the ways in which this handling of language contributes to the confusions and conflicts between them: "Much of the story is told through dialogue, a direct form of dramatization virtually necessitated by the split between theory and practice in the lives of all the characters. If the theory is false, then the theory must be fully expounded to make that point. Distinction between narration and dialogue is minimalized by the use of 'colloquial forms'" (122).

Of course, nowhere is the split between theory and practice more evident in *Some Came Running* than in Dave Hirsh's misbegotten decisions and their consequences, and nowhere is he more mistaken than in his reasons for marrying Ginnie. Like his first reason for marrying, Dave's second—his pity for Ginnie and his desire to offer her an opportunity to make a better life for herself—is seriously flawed in conception and execution. In trying to improve her life, he binds himself to Ginnie's imperfections and becomes subject to her because he can understand much of her point of view, even regretting his failure to provide what she had expected from him. She, however, comprehends neither his outlook on life nor his expectations. He is therefore caught in a vicious circle: His sensitivity, acquired through his involvement with Gwen, makes him weak in relation to Ginnie, and his weakness with Ginnie renders him even more sensitive. The situation exemplifies the point of Bob French's poem "The King Is Helpless," which argues that the power given to the queen in chess is an "astonishing foresight—of the power women would someday come to wield in modern society," and that this new power has a "definite evolutionary purpose: namely, to make the men more *sensitive*" (933). Moreover, Bob's poem, like the chess symbolism it employs, is symbolic of the evolutionary critique underlying Jones's attitude toward Dave's sensitization, as well as Jones's sociological views on male masochism and the popular notions of he-man masculinity in "Just Like the Girl," "The Tennis Game," *The Thin Red Line*, and *Go to the Widow-Maker.*

Dave's sensitivity is a flaw as long as it remains tied to pity, but it prepares the way for a final, compassionate understanding that allows him to lament the suffering of others without believing he can do something to eliminate it or that it would benefit any individual to be spared a single moment of pain. In the end, he can even feel compassion for the man who fires the bullet that terminates this life, as well as a sad but unpitying compassion for Ginnie, his fellow countrymen, and all the men involved in the Korean War. He realizes that he has caused Ginnie pain just as she has caused him pain but finally learns that we are not "responsible for the pain we cause in others," only for the pain *that others cause in us*" (1231, emphasis in the original). Even though he regrets the suffering he has brought to Ginnie, he recognizes that, as Bob has said, "Each man must find his salvation in himself alone" and "nothing anyone did *to* you, or *for* you, made one damn bit of difference, in the end." What Ginnie does is "her problem, not his" (1231).

Dave's realization about his inability to "help" anyone on the personal level also applies to the social, political, and military levels. Before his revelation about individual salvation and responsibility, Dave's democratic ideals were similar to Prewitt's: "If he had ever believed in anything, Dave Hirsh believed fervently in the rights of the free individual. . . . Every human being had the right to some measure of dignity—no matter how unbeautiful that human being might be physically, or how low and undeveloped mentally. That human being still had the right to be treated optimistically and believingly. . . . Everybody ought to be given their chance" (1168). Because Dave has held this viewpoint and witnessed daily violations of individual rights by governments, groups, and others, he begins to see decadence everywhere and notice parallels between his country and the Roman Empire on the brink of its decline and fall. From his provincial perspective, such an event seems a disaster no less solemn than Armageddon. Fortunately, or inevitably, he also develops doubts about this idea just before his death: "Was it really the Decline and Fall of the Roman Empire, after all? being enacted over again? . . . perhaps that was only another of his illusions. God, he had so many. . . . He loved this country—and this town, too. . . . But perhaps that was an illusion, too? Why should a man love one country—or one town—or one person—more than he loved another?" (1233-34).

These reflections indicate an extension of Dave's sympathies, because he had once hated Parkman and has only come to feel part of it upon his return from Florida. They also suggest that his compassion has come to embrace all of suffering humanity. They imply how close he is to believing that every soul is of equal importance. We all were put here to learn, and we all have eternity in which to complete this spiritual education. That would mean, of course, that everyone has a chance, although it is not the chance Dave envisioned when asserting his views about the rights of free individuals. Flagrant injustices, such as murder, corruption, sadism, colonialism, and war, should therefore be regarded not as horrible anomalies that reasonable people ought to eliminate in their quest for a sane and comfortable utopia, but rather as distressing yet ultimately beneficial instruments for helping each soul evolve to a higher state of being. Dave's vision resembles Blavatsky's:

> It is only the knowledge of the constant re-births of one and the same individuality throughout the life-cycle; the assurance that the same MONADS— among whom are . . . the "Gods" themselves—have to pass through the "Circle of Necessity," rewarded or punished by such rebirth for the suffering endured or crimes committed in the former life; . . . that can . . . reconcile man to the terrible and *apparent* injustice of life. . . . For, when one unacquainted with the noble doctrine looks around him, and observes the inequalities of birth and fortune, of intellect and capacities; when one sees honour paid fools and profligates, . . . and their nearest neighbor, with all his intellect and noble virtues . . . perishing of want and for lack of sympathy; . . . that blessed knowledge of Karma alone prevents him from cursing life and men, as well as their supposed Creator. (*The Secret Doctrine* 222)

This reconciling, Blavatskian vision of the necessary and spiritually progressive role of suffering underlines the mistake implicit in Dave's third reason for marrying Ginnie: his desire for a happy, contented relationship modeled on the principles his friend Bama enunciates when he marries Ruth. Because Dave is running away from the pain of his failure with Gwen, a happy relationship with Ginnie threatens to negate all the spiritual growth he has attained. Bob French had previously pointed out the dangers of a happy love relationship to Dave with his inquiry, "Did you ever notice how disgusting, how really idiotic . . . re*quit*ed lovers are?" (1085). If Dave would have witnessed *Weight* magazine's interviewer with his newly married niece, Dawnie, and her fawning husband, Shotridge, he would have had to agree. Dave, however, runs no risk of falling prey to a stultifying happiness like Dawnie's, because he has made serious miscalculations about Bama's principles and Ginnie's ability to fit them. Whereas Bama requires achieving enough control over a woman and a situation to gain the benefits of wife and family while being free to live as he chooses when apart from them, Dave plans to enjoy marriage for its own sake without living freely outside of it.

More significantly, Dave is incapable of Bama's uncaring treatment of women and his unsentimental recognition that Ruth wants only money, a home, a farm to run, and children. Thus, he refuses to face the implications of Bama's question, "What if I was to sell that farm and move her up here, to live the kind of life you and me live? . . . shed take off and leave me so goddamned quick itd make yore head swim, thats what" (1188-89). Dave does not understand, Bama argues, that what Ginnie wants most is to be respectable and that he will therefore be unprepared to handle her as Bama would. Dave has always hero-worshipped Bama for the worst of reasons, his life-style and his growth-impeding ability to dominate women, yet the folly of such unreflecting adoration has never been more evident than when Dave follows his hero's example without listening to his advice or comprehending the causes behind Bama's apparent success.

Dave's worst misjudgment, however, is the assumption that Ginnie could become like Ruth. As Bama explains the attributes of an ideal wife, "First, they got to be dumb. . . . And second, they got to be very very respectable; and its better if theyre real religious too. Then theres another third thing: They got to be used to takin orders from the menfolks, so that they believe thats the right way of things and the way they ought to be" (772). When Dave tells a sympathetic Bob French about Bama's concept, Bob warns that one must "be quite sure that they *are* dumb; and that they *are* goodnatured" (1182), to which Dave responds, "Those are two things I *am* sure of" (1182). But he is wrong again on both counts. Ginnie shows her cunning self-centeredness during a visit to Gwen French, whose disgust she deliberately arouses to turn her away from Dave, and in the way she tricks her angry, gun-toting, former husband Rick into leaving the house where she and Dave live by claiming that Dave is visiting the Frenches. Dave's misreading of Ginnie's character is perhaps the main reason he is so vulnerable to her manipulation, although that vulnerability will also lead him to understand her later—and eventually to his salvation.

Dave's final reason for marrying Ginnie—his belief that a stable, peaceful relationship with her will be more productive for his writing than his tormented relationship with Gwen had been—is not only based on the same misreading of Ginnie's character as his previous reasons but also on a misconception—or maybe a convenient overlooking—of the nature of the writing process. As a result, the work he does accomplish is greatly inferior to his work while he suffered from unrequited love. He agrees to abandon his unremunerative writing for a job that will enable him to support Ginnie and himself. Appropriately, the weighty and deftly symbolic end of their relationship is reached when Ginnie hits Dave's typewriter with a saucepan.

Considering the number of illusions and blunders in each of Dave's reasons for marrying Ginnie, it is amazing that the outcome is so fruitful for his spiritual development, yet that is the heart of the vital paradoxes in the book: pain brings growth, evil brings good, the clash of powerfully held illusions brings the end of those illusions, and the worst worldly choices bring the best spiritual results. Dave's final meditation reveals not only how such paradoxes operate but also how they apply to nations as well as to individuals:

> Undoubtedly no two humans on earth ever lived in identical worlds. . . . Because each had his own private world, and what was more wanted to if possible impose it upon everyone else that he possibly could, in order to prove to himself that it did in fact exist. And that was always where the trouble came. Because the other man—or woman—or nation, for that matter—was doing the same identical thing. Consequently, only clash resulted—and with the clash, trouble.
>
> And from the trouble came the pain: the pain of defeat, the pain of victory and the hate it brought, but most of all the pain of being forced to relinquish part or all of that illusory world each has built up for himself. (1229)

And along with the pain and loss of one's illusory world come selflessness, sensitivity, sad, unpitying compassion, and freedom not only from illusion but also from desire, vanity, possessiveness, and dependence on others. That means that the state of war with which *Some Came Running* begins and ends is not a special visitation of evil to bring about the doom of the human race, but it is an intensification—and maybe not even that—of the human condition, with the same conflicts between the illusory worlds of each individual as in "civilian" life and the same opportunities for experiencing pain, individual growth, and salvation. Earlier, Dave sums this up in relation to his writing, although he was not yet prepared to accept it in relation to his life:

> The upshot, the lump, of what he wanted to get said was that each man was a Sacred Universe in himself and at the same time, inextricably, a noisome garbage pail whose bottom had rotted out and was poisoning the garden air and needed to be got rid of posthaste, forthwith and forsooth. That these two were not only inextricable, but were actually one and the same. And that therefore there was no Evil; and probably no Good; only Growth;—or if there were, they were so inextricably involved, like man himself, that no man-brain or -system, no Philosophy of Meaning, would ever separate them without automatically perverting both. And that therefore there was only growth, only change, and the pain of change, and the ecstasies of that pain, to embrace; because that was all there was, to embrace. (756)

The only viable attitude an individual holding such a viewpoint can take toward life, struggle, injustice, and anguish is one of acceptance rather than rebellion or judgment. Yet, paradoxically, such acceptance frees individuals from the very things they are accepting and moves them toward a more spiritually advanced way of life and thought.

The many paradoxes of the novel are of critical importance, because the religious system developed in *Some Came Running* is founded on the greatest paradox of all, the concept of *felix culpa* (fortunate fall). Because this concept is also critical in Nathaniel Hawthorne's "My Kinsman, Major Molineux" and *The Marble Faun*, it is appropriate that Gwen decides to study Hawthorne's work (and Walt Whitman's, too) when she returns from the desert after having tried to burn out the pain of her relationship with Dave. It is even more appropriate when, at the end of the novel, Bob remarks to Gwen about Dave's death, "We *all* are guilty. You, me, that girl, everyone. And yet at the same time we all are also *unguilty*. We suffer, and we learn; and then we grow.—Though growth may often seem like 'Sin' to others; to the ignorant. Do you remember the end of Hawthorne's *Marble Faun?*" (1256). The most significant elaboration of the fortunate fall as it applies to the related concepts of growth and the nonexistence of evil, however, is Bob French's discussion of the "involution-evolution" process. He argues that the process's beginning, the "going outward" of each soul from God, inspired the unfortunate and misleading "symbol of Satan and his Dark Angels being kicked out of Heaven," whereas "the *in*volution can no more be Evil than the evolution; since without the one the other would be impossible" (818). This viewpoint suggests both Walt Whitman's "Santa Spirita . . . including God, including Saviour and Satan, / Etherial, pervading all" ("Chanting the Square Deific," *Complete Poetry* 560-61) and Blavatsky's depiction of Satan, supposed evil, and spiritual evolution throughout *The Secret Doctrine*.

Given Bob's assumptions, as Jones's spokesman, that human souls are at the farthest point in their involution and just setting out toward their reunion with God, it is not surprising that spiritual evolution, as Dave and other characters experience it, includes the act of leaving nearly everything they started out with. Or, to put matters another way, they are leaving everything they had accumulated during their immersion in self throughout the vast process of involution. That is why the epigraph from the tenth chapter of the book of Mark, about the man who came running to Christ to ask how to gain eternal life, is apt. It suggests that spiritual advancement requires abandoning possessions. Accordingly, Dave's illusions are not the only things he leaves behind during his final moments of life. Almost as a preparation for leaving his material body, he sets out to leave his home (both house and town), nearly all material goods except his typewriter, and the wife upon whom he has become so dependent. In doing this, he resembles Christian in *Pilgrim's Progress*, who has to abandon wife, friends, and material possessions for his spiritual journey. Dave packs "only one bag—and, after looking at all his clothes in the closet, wondered why he even packed that much" (Jones, *Some Came Running* 1232). Thoreau might have considered the same thing as he prepared to go to Walden Pond.

The most important "possession" Dave leaves is his ego. He is able to escape from his desire to seem important to other people because he has learned that his worldview is an illusion; there is no way for him to make anyone else see the world from his perspective. Thus, he no longer regards writing as a way to compel others to look at him, but rather as a means of making "other people's illusory world more real—to [himself]" (1230). That realization frees Dave from his previous reason for writing, which was founded on the needs of his ego, and from the prison of his ego itself. His ego is a figurative prison that resembles a federal prison that "always disturbed" Dave when he looks at it from the shell factory where he works (1201). Having shed his ego, he passes out of the range of the ego-bound perceptions of others.

What he leaves behind as he moves out of this life is his legacy to others, including not only his material bequests of property to Ginnie and the manuscript to Bob and Gwen but also, more significantly, his spiritual bequest of the karma he had made "with and also *in* everyone he had come in contact with since he first came back to Parkman." The karma, he recognizes, "would stay with all of them . . . until the day they died. And perhaps, as Bob maintained, would stay with them afterwards, too" (1231). As usual, Bob French provides the explanation: "Whenever we meet people and create *desires* in them; whenever we cause them to love us or to hate us,—or perhaps both, . . . in so doing we are making Karmic attachments between them and us, all of which must be worked out in future lives. . . . Their original desires toward us come into it too; and almost always our meetings with people in our lives are holdovers and in one way or another the working out of meetings in past lives. . . . The purpose always being . . . to eventually free ourselves of all Karma" (932). Bob also tells Dave that he is "convinced you and Gwen have that type of a karmic attachment; and a very powerful one" (933), and there can be little doubt this is true.

Gwen's attachment to Dave seems almost as strong as his to her, even though her ego will not allow her to confess that and thus alter their relationship. To protect her virginity, she has imprisoned herself by an extraordinary combination of pride in her virginity and pride in maintaining an image of an experienced, worldly woman grown weary of sex. The image of a supposedly sophisticated woman who eschews sexual attachments irresistibly suggests Lowney Handy, the primary model for Gwen French although Jones took care to mix her traits with those of Emily Dickinson, whose biography he had studied. Even when Gwen realizes that she loves Dave and wants him to see through her lies and overcome her resistance, sending out "signs" like those Jones found in Handy's letters, she cannot break through the crust of her ego and false self-image, which she both hates and loves, to indicate directly that she might be willing to have sex. Her pride is again evident during Ginnie Moorehead's visit, when Gwen is violently agitated by the idea that Dave's desire places her on the same level as fat, disgusting Ginnie. It is only after Dave's death that she can admit to herself that in the midst of "all her champings and cageshakings and miseries and wild outcries, she had nevertheless been proud of [her virginity]" (1256).

Ironically, Gwen has always wanted to avoid being "a silly, lying, vain, preening woman: playing spiritual, playing at being the Pedestal: the universal 'Conscience'—and all the time being sly and deceitful underneath the thin veneer of sweet and soulful respectability" (1248). Yet she has become exactly like that despised image by trying to be the opposite. A large part of the reason she chooses the role of a woman of the world who once had numerous lovers is that she does not want to seem respectable and spiritual. Yet Gwen's misleading counter-image provides a more eminent position than the image of an innocent virgin would have given and lends added authority to her role of spiritual advisor to her students of creative writing. Moreover, her willingness to advise students about personal matters reflects the scorned role of universal conscience and is equally based on a lie. (It is hard not to read into this an implied criticism of Handy and her relationships with the Writers' Colony students, and it seems only too likely that Jones did this consciously.) Gwen has good reason to be struck by a phrase from the occult book *Light on the Path*, which warns, according to Jones's artistically modified version, *"Shun not the cloak of evil, for if you do it will be yours to wear. . . . And if you turn with horror from it, when it is flung upon your shoulders, it will cling the more closely to you"* (1249, emphasis in the original). She has done everything she had not wanted to do and has become what she condemns, but out of that experience she has supposedly learned how to free herself. She becomes what she has only pretended to be and opens herself to the pain that comes from the sexual relationships she has feared so much.

Dave's karmic legacy to Gwen is the guilt that leads her first to reveal her inexperience and past lies to her father and then to have her hymen punctured as an act of penance and intended self-liberation. Through Gwen's response to her guilt, Jones implies that such karmic legacies force people to face something about themselves they had been trying to hide and compel them to move beyond the obsessions and mistakes that have trapped them. Gwen's decision about her hymen, however, affords only limited proof of her growth, because she is building her future on a new lie. In addition, she still feels that "physical contact . . . was just too—too intimate a thing to do—without love" (1255). A man would have to be "sensitive, and kind, and gentle, and intelligent . . . and be all of those things, and be them damned plainly and clearly" before she would consider a relationship with him (1258). Such thoughts reveal the large amount of pride she retains. Even though she seems to follow in Dave's footsteps by choosing to forsake Bob French, her home, her virginity, her sheltered existence, and her previous false image of herself, she has obviously not evolved to his level.

The conflicting signals concerning the extent of Gwen's growth may reflect a clash between Jones's desire to assert that she is now fit to carry on Dave's projected novel about his sister "Francine and the group in Hollywood" (1232, 1256-57) and his realization that she is still far from ready for such a task. It is possible, moreover, that he was torn between an idea he wished to convey about Dave's spiritual legacy to Gwen and a characterization that could not be altered easily or sufficiently to support this idea. It is equally possible that he deliberately portrayed Gwen as clinging to self-deceptions that could only be removed by considerable future experience. That portrayal perhaps constitutes a judgment about his primary source of inspiration for her: Lowney Handy.

For whatever reasons, Jones was much more convincing in suggesting the large, probably lasting, spiritual gains of Edith Barclay, which spring from her karmic relationship with her grandmother, Old Jane Staley, even though she and Gwen work out their karmic bonds through the same basic patterns of guilt, self-exposure, penance, and self-liberation. Edith even follows the pattern of shunning the cloak of evil, only to have it wrap itself around her more tightly. Her shame over her grandmother's open, publicly witnessed sexuality finds a lesson-provoking parallel in her own publicly exposed sexual entanglements. Edith comes to regret calling Janie an "old whore" when she realizes that she made her grandmother feel too ashamed to seek treatment for a severe illness that she feared was venereal disease. The stages in Edith's expiation are explicitly outlined in the text:

> It was all . . . Old Jane, really. Old Jane and her diverticulitis and her dis-
> charge she had so desperately tried to hide. That was . . . what had made
> (Edith) take the house [that her lover Frank Hirsh had bought her] in the
> first place. It was . . . a sort of penance to old Janie. . . . She had been Frank
> Hirsh's "mistress"; Frank Hirsh's kept whore; and that was what she had
> wanted to be—because of Janie. . . . And now with the humiliation of being
> kicked out forcibly by her lover's wife, she had, in some obscure way, she
> felt, paid her debt to Janie. (1158-59)

Because, as Bob points out to Gwen at the end of the novel, no one is "ever *really* responsible for another's death" but only for one's own (1252), guilt in the context of *Some Came Running* means accepting responsibility for something you will later discover you are not truly responsible for. Nevertheless, it is necessary to experience this guilt in order to evolve to the level of a higher understanding: genuine responsibility resides only in the individual and his or her actions. Thus, Edith's acceptance of guilt for Janie's death is, in a sense, a mistake, but it is an error that is more fruitful from a spiritual standpoint than an accurate judgment of her responsibility would have been.

Edith Barclay had begun as an intelligent but puritanical, possessive, and self-contained young woman. Her ability and independence are shown by her handling of the secretarial work at Frank Hirsh's jewelry store, where she must "create for herself out of whole cloth a practical system," an act she regards as a "triumph" in "a battle fought and won against not only or-der and system but against herself and her own misgivings" (77). As a result of this sense of triumph, she liked to stay late, alone in the store, savoring her past struggle and accomplishment and enjoying her sole occupancy be-cause she felt "it was her store then. It belonged to her" (76). Edith's pos-sessiveness is further illustrated by her anger at Janie for having dared to try on Edith's jewelry in front of the mirror. Her incessant desire for privacy at the store and at home makes it evident how self-contained she is, and her horror at her second lover's attempt "to teach her some of the more unusual ways of making love" (83)—her later sexual education by Frank implies that these ways were fellatio and cunnilingus—reveals how conventional she is in her sexual outlook.

The first changes in Edith occur as a result of her affair with Frank, which breaks through her self-containment and makes her vulnerable. Much of her love for him is "pity for him and his childish ways" (1053), however, and that pity binds her to him long after she has realized that he is "about as petty, and jealous, and totally selfcentered a man as probably existed anywhere" (1052). Edith chains herself to Frank through womanly pride, which makes her, once she has given "her love to a man, . . . unable to admit that she had been wrong" (1052). Pride also leads her to refuse presents from Frank, making the decision to accept a house (along with her desire to be exposed as Frank's mistress) a signal of her decrease in pride.

In yet another sign of diminished pride and possessiveness, Edith places the jewels on Janie's corpse that she had denied Jane while she was alive. Moreover, she acquires many of Janie's personality traits, such as the "native" psychological acuteness that enables her to see, as Janie did, that "Frank and Agnes Hirsh owed their 'second honeymoon,' their new closeness and warmth, to her: Edith Barclay." She also acquires "Jane's old harsh raucous gravelly laugh" (1054). Edith then surrenders her job, her reputation, her pride, her aloofness (both personal and sexual), her dependence on Frank, her past images of herself, her property (the jewelry and the house), and her security. She also leaves everything and everyone she has known. Her final reflections bear out the concept of growth and the way such learning operates: "She had no regrets at all, and no fears. She had no sense of loss. If she had it all to do over again, probably she would not have done it—knowing what she knew now. But then, how could she know now what she knew, if she had not done it?" (1160). Significantly, her final thought before leaving is one of compassion for both Frank and Agnes.

The similarity in the patterns of growth followed by Dave, Gwen, and Edith reveals the most notable way in which Jones unified his gigantic novel. All of its characters are like the man who came running to Christ to ask how to attain eternal life. They grow or fail to grow according to their willingness to give up their possessions. The characters who make the largest spiritual advances are Dave, Gwen, Edith, and Bob French, who abandons his confidence in his wisdom, his unwillingness to take part in human squabbles for fear of creating karma (a decision inevitably snaring him more firmly in the karmic web), and his close contact with his daughter. Among those who hold themselves back are Frank Hirsh, who clings to his wealth, status, and imaginary control over women through peeping-tomism; Agnes Hirsh, who prefers sacrificing her gall bladder to sacrificing her partial control over Frank; Bama Dillert, who would rather be shot than surrender his macho vanity; and Wally Dennis, who clings to his pride in his virility and the false security of his Randall Number 1 combat knife, which a North Korean soldier later uses to slit Wally's throat.

In addition, Jones used the mythical town of Parkman as a microcosm to point out how the activities of its inhabitants represent the human condition. He did so by selecting characters from all levels of society, with a lively working class represented by Jane Staley, a servant; Ginnie Moorehead, a factory worker; and Bama Dillert, a small-time gambler. The middle class makes its impact through Bob and Gwen French, who are professional intellectuals; the established upper class appears in the character of Anton Wernz III; and upward mobility is exemplified through Frank and Agnes Hirsh's rise to the wealthy elite. At the same time, Jones skillfully demonstrated that the surface divisions of society conceal the isolation of each soul and the harsh reality that salvation comes to individuals, never to groups. As Christ did, he argued that class structure is spiritually valueless and that the rich take an especially rough path to their salvation. Above all, Jones painstakingly demonstrated that people from all backgrounds face the same choices between egotism and selflessness, ruthlessness and sensitivity, rebellion and acceptance, binding pity and unattached compassion, and temporary escape into happiness and painful growth. In his eyes, the basic human condition of spiritual evolution toward reunion with God supersedes all social views and all material aims.

Jones maintained a fine balance between his seemingly opposed yet inextricable goals of portraying a multilevel society and picturing the individual human condition. He realized that any form of society, but perhaps that of a small town most of all, is founded on the interrelatedness of its members, and he indicated various ways in which the social and economic structure of Parkman affect his characters. Old Janie earns her small income by working as a maid for Frank Hirsh and others like him; the promiscuous, low-life Ginnie absorbs middle-class notions about respectability; and the seemingly independent Bama resents and envies Frank, whom he has never met. These social connections are ultimately illusory, however, and individuals who lack illusions will find they have no need for society. The small town Jones constructed so laboriously finally splinters into a loose assortment of individual souls working out their individual salvation in quasi-isolation, although ever subject to the effects of karma.

Jones's spiritualist vision of life comes close at times, although it never crosses, that thin red line to being antisocial and antiliterary. Dave must die, for example, because he is at the point of ceasing to exist as a social being and as a novelistic creation. Without his ego and illusions (including his imaginary social connections with other souls), Dave can no longer be identified and analyzed as an individual. It was a novelistic limitation that Jones apparently recognized, and it may explain why he neglected to deal

with the spiritual level in his work. He chose instead to fill his fiction exclusively with characters on the levels of animal man and mental man, individuals who are still convinced that their subjective "image-pictures" of
the world are real and can be set on a collision course with other characters
equally certain about their own subjective realities.

Jones's balancing of social surfaces and subjective realities, of a structured community and spiritually isolated individuals, is his novelistic solution to the dilemma of maya posed by Arthur Christy in his comparison of
Emerson and the Hindus. As Christy pointed out, maya (the operant force
behind our images of the world and all phenomenal life) "cannot exist, for
if it did, it would constitute a limit to Brahma" (the Universal Soul), yet "if
it does not exist the world cannot be accounted for" (*The Orient in American Transcendentalism* 90). That means that maya must be just "real enough
to produce a world, but not real enough to limit Brahma" (90), an enormously difficult feat. As Emerson did, Jones passionately immersed himself
in all the brouhahas, glittering brilliance, and balderdash of American culture and all the contemporary social problems of his day. Yet the fact that
he also saw through the deceptive allures of such immersion and the possible deceptiveness of the world itself provided a double edge to his social
and philosophical vision.

In maintaining this ultrafine, ultrademanding balance, Jones produced,
simultaneously and inextricably, in Willie Morris's words, a "towering work
of native social realism" and a "majestic, encompassing" cosmic vision. That
blend marks *Some Came Running* as a major contribution to a tradition
Beongcheon Yu has called American literary Orientalism. Yu, who has analyzed the work of the American transcendentalists along with that of Eugene
O'Neill, T. S. Eliot, J. D. Salinger, and others, cogently argues that "American Orientalism has been no mere exoticism, no mere escapism, no mere
dilettantism, but has constituted an authentic part of the American experience" and that "as a literary tradition it has inspired many of our writers
and has, in turn, been enriched by them" (*The Great Circle* 227-28), It is
long past time to affirm James Jones's vital and enriching role in developing this tradition.

3

Individual Salvation and Growth

This chapter and the two following it are, in the wonderfully weird phrase Henry James used to describe a certain type of novel, "loose and baggy monsters" because they have resulted from an uneasy compromise between two opposing approaches I considered and rejected. One approach would have been to focus exclusively on the reincarnationist philosophy running through all of Jones's writings, providing procrustean discussions that ignore any autobiographical elements, social commentaries, artistic techniques, or other material that did not quite fit my thesis. The other approach would have been to ignore or downplay the philosophy by devoting a chapter to each novel and another chapter to the short stories, concentrating on the attributes and achievements of each work. Borrowing from the analogy by Madame Blavatsky that I used in the first chapter, the first approach would have meant emphasizing the unsevered golden thread of the spiritual entity that reincarnates, in this case the core of Jones's reincarnationist system. The second approach would require pointing out the threaded multishaped beads of the new and varied personalities formed each time the spiritual entity takes on a new body, in this case each new novel or short story. What I want to show, however, are both the thread and the beads, the vital link between all of the works and the special qualities of each.

In making this compromise, I believe I am following in the footsteps of Jones, who wrote to me on July 21, 1975, that he had never "deliberately, concisely structured" any of his novels around his ideas (Hendrick, ed., *To Reach Eternity* 366), although in my view *Some Came Running* comes close to being structured in that way. Probably Jones's best description of the way he approached ideas in his work was in a September 3, 1955, letter to Robert Cantwell: "Im working totally consciously and I know it. But Ive taught myself a trick which is to do all my *thinking* when I am not *working.* . . . when actually writing, I let intuition and instinct say for me what Ive already decided I want to say, but have deliberately and with malice aforethought made myself forget" (Hendrick, ed., *To Reach Eternity* 230). That careful cultivation of conscious thought (which surely included reference to his reincarnationist system) and intuition (which might have come from his extraordinary personal experience that provoked thesis-defying jolts from the unconscious or a subliminal response to the day's news or any of a thousand sources) developed the balance needed to make his creative work profound and vital.

I have emphasized Jones's conscious thought, the unsevered golden thread, by organizing this chapter and the two following ones according to themes emerging from Jones's reincarnationist perspective: the paths people follow, at varying times and in varying ways, to salvation and growth; the role of sexuality and popular conceptions of manhood and womanhood in aiding or hindering growth; and the question of responsibility to ourselves and others as reflected in the karmic bonds that shape and are shaped by social contacts within every step toward salvation. Excluding *Some Came Running*, which I discuss first because of its role as key to Jones's entire philosophy, this chapter and the two following all contain discussions of two novels in the order in which they were published, as well as four or five stories loosely discussed in terms of one of the themes.

The thematic emphasis is somewhat arbitrary. For example, although *From Here to Eternity* and *The Pistol*, because of their portrayal of the attack on Pearl Harbor, seem to be the novels most concerned with the unexpected strokes that cut the ground from underneath people and leave them gasping at their unprotected, unprotectable nakedness (a major development in the growth toward salvation through reunion with God), such moments occur in the other novels, too. Similarly, questions about bravery, manhood, and responsibility abound in these two early novels and in the later ones.

Even more difficult and maybe more whimsical is the placement of the stories. Some were easy to locate in my discussion, such as "The Way It Is," another story reflecting the impact of Pearl Harbor and linked historically and thematically to *From Here to Eternity* and *The Pistol* so that it belonged in the same chapter with them. Others, however, might have been analyzed in more than one chapter. "None Sing so Wildly," for example, comments on the Protestant link between salvation and security and the park policeman's attempt to impose salvation from outside, themes that would enable it to fit comfortably in this chapter, but the story also deals with the effects of a strong karmic bond between the a male and a female character and their struggle over responsibility. The greater depth of the latter theme leads me to place my discussion of "None Sing so Wildly" in chapter 5.

To balance the emphasis on the thread of conscious thought, I have tried to give due consideration to the beads of individual, embodied, quirky, and creative character in the novels by including evaluations of each that emphasize their wholeness and specialness while continuing to note the thread that runs through them. For both novels and short stories I have also tried to develop holistic interpretations that attempt to capture size, shape, color, and heft. In examining *Go to the Widow-Maker,* for example, I consider the novel's autobiographical underpinning and the social and personal consequences of American popular conceptions of manhood and womanhood that likely had as much to do with the organization and meaning of the work as the thread of reincarnationist thought that also permeates it. Stories such as "The Ice-Cream Headache" and "Just Like the Girl" similarly reflect Jones's family history and provide the same personal, social, and spiritual commentary. Yet in analyzing his gleeful manipulation of the traditional hard-boiled detective novel format in *A Touch of Danger,* which is not autobiographical, it is necessary to consider Jones's knowledge and transformation of the genre's conventions, which he knew well from the days Lowney Handy assigned the work of Dashiell Hammett and Raymond Chandler to her Writers' Colony students.

The threaded beads in this chapter are related to the most basic element of Jones's philosophy: an individual's painfully illuminating growth toward ultimate reabsorption into God. Such growth for Jones entailed a movement from selfishness to selfless compassion and from a life bound by illusions and desires to one marked by inner freedom and an acceptance of the world as it is. Spiritually advanced souls assume full responsibility for their lives, having learned that salvation cannot be found outside—in a pistol, a great love, a supreme status, a fortresslike pile of material possessions, a book of army regulations, a rigidly enforced set of laws, a socially prescribed code of manhood and womanhood, or any church or Bible—but must be worked out from within. Experience, as has been almost universally recognized, is the great teacher but only when its lessons cannot be evaded and are—at long last—faced unflinchingly. The hardest lesson is that personal love solves nothing, although unattached love offered to all helps penetrate our awesome isolation and leads toward peace. A sign of such learning is that once spiritually advanced souls recognize the inevitability of isolation, they generally go off by themselves, yet with a sorrowful awareness of the agony of others. Flight from pain results in backsliding, although it can never hold back for long, certainly not from here to eternity, the suffering that leads to growth. Neither can it hold back the surrender to a desire for an impossible security for whatever reason, as is the case for the band members in "The King" who allow themselves to be co-opted by their free-dom-fearing, middle-class relatives.

The paradox of growth that Jones cited most was that people come to resemble what they despise. Although Karen Holmes in *From Here to Eternity* and Gwen French in *Some Came Running* read the warning in *The Light on the Path* about the futility of attempting to shun the soiled garment or cloak of evil when it is flung upon one's shoulders, the same caution should also have been issued to Big Un Cash in *The Thin Red Line*, Harry, Hill, and Louisa Gallagher in *The Merry Month of May*, Sonny Duval and Chuck in *A Touch of Danger*, Bobby Prell and John Strange in *Whistle*, and many others. Such transformations compel people to empathize with others and thus learn directly how it feels to be "evil." To consider whores evil, for example, requires experiences that teach the inner reality of being sexually promiscuous, although we do not have to become precisely what we loathe. Edith Barclay learns all she needs to know about whores from a single affair. The upshot of such experiences is that people transcend the state of mind they believe to be evil by passing through it. Becoming what we hate is only a stage in development rather than a goal or destination.

A related and equally significant paradox in Jones's system is that the meaning of errors only emerges and becomes spiritually fruitful after those errors are made. That paradox hints that even estrangement from God and total immersion in our egos is not wrong in any final sense. Through such immersion people begin the spiritual evolution that will lead to selflessness and reunion with God. Isaac Bloom in *From Here to Eternity*, for example, learns to value life while killing himself, and Richard Mast in *The Pistol* is taught the necessity of looking for salvation within himself through seeking it in an external object. Because everyone is subject to the "original sin" of beginning evolution at the animal level, there is no disgrace in making mistakes. The point of those mistakes, however, is to teach ways to master the areas of life that have caused difficulty and then move toward a more spiritual level.

James Jones's first novel, *From Here to Eternity*, justly lauded by review-ers and critics as well as widely loved by the public, introduces nearly all of his main ideas about growth. Through his spokesman Jack Malloy, Jones links his views on growth to his conception of a God who is also evolving. As Malloy's term "God of Acceptance" suggests, the development of hu-manity and God involves increasing empathy and affinity between them. Milt Warden and Karen Holmes, reflecting Jones's stress on reducing the ego and developing compassion, come to recognize the role that pride has played in their love. Both learn how to express their feelings without being possessive or making personal demands, and Karen also learns that self-contempt can hinder growth as much as vanity. When Warden and Karen have reached a high level of self-acceptance and unpitying concern for others, they find the strength to separate and face the prospect of aloneness, even though both will form temporary associations with others in the future. The novel's other major character, Robert E. Lee Prewitt, similarly learns that his fight against the unjust decisions of army authorities is motivated by pride. He must acknowledge and embrace what the injustices teach, knowing finally that confronting them has helped him move beyond them.

Jones's emphasis, however, is on the disconcerting unpredictability of life and the consequent need to adjust rapidly and flexibly to change. Carefully structuring his work around two protagonists subjected to a lengthy series of unexpected events, Jones has Warden repeatedly bend without betraying his integrity, regarding each setback as a goad to a newer, more devious pursuit of his goals, and Prewitt refuse to compromise, preferring death to dishonor although he begins to learn to be less rigid and judgmental near the end of the book. Although both men move far beyond the animal level and gain considerable insight into themselves and life, Warden manages to combine material survival with spiritual advancement. Prewitt, however, will likely take another lifetime or more to attain Warden's endurance and adaptability.

Warden and Prewitt, as well as many of the other characters in *From Here to Eternity*, are romanticized, larger-than-life figures. Jones regarded their idealization as a flaw and sought to eliminate it in subsequent novels. As he told Maurice Dolbier, "I look back at 'Eternity' and I think it was a very romantic book, . . . the same kind of people . . . are in the new novel [*The Thin Red Line*], but I try to show them behaving more the way they would, and did, in real life" ("Writing" 5).

Jones had reason to be disturbed about mythologizing Prewitt. Such romanticizing likely does interfere with the theme of spiritual evolution, because it has led many people to view Prewitt as a tragic hero rather than a too-proud man needing to learn humility and compassion. Moreover, as Ben W. Griffith, Jr., demonstrates, Jones built up Prewitt as a "folk hero circumscribed within the limits of a vocation or profession" ("Rear Rank Robin Hood" 41). Certainly, Prewitt's proficiency in soldierly skills and bugling is as extraordinary as John Henry's steel-driving or Paul Bunyan's ax-swinging. He seems so superior to the forces leagued against him that it is only too easy to see him as the "good guy" and Capt. Dana Holmes, Maj.

Gerald Thompson, and Sgt. James R. "Fatso" Judson as bad. The injustices Prewitt fights are such blatant ones that most readers see him as right and his defeat as undeserved, even though that emotional judgment runs counter to the ideas Jones wanted to convey.

Yet the romantic elements of the plot and characterization may well be the source of the book's continuing strong appeal. Unlike *Some Came Running*, which seems to reflect more accurately both daily life and Jones's philosophy as a whole, *From Here to Eternity* is packed with many tense and thrilling incidents: Prewitt's struggle against "the Treatment," Angelo Maggio's violent arrest, the investigation of homosexuals, Isaac Bloom's suicide, the beatings in the stockade, Fatso's murder of Blues Berry, Prewitt's murder of Fatso, and the attack on Pearl Harbor. The characters are also exciting: an army private at odds with his superiors, a top sergeant who maneuvers for control of his company, a captain's wife who has an affair with her husband's subordinate, a prostitute who loves a client and shelters him from the law, a general who rules through fear, and a prisoner who may be a new messiah. Even though the book's excitement veers toward the melodramatic, it is well controlled and gives the novel great power.

More significantly for his philosophy, Jones's creation of a romantic myth undercuts the realistic surface of his novel and enables him to convey highly mystical conceptions. In all his writings before *Whistle*, Prewitt and Warden are Jones's only characters who have experienced astral projection, and Prewitt is the only one who remembers past incarnations and recognizes at the moment of his death that he is moving on to a new incarnation. In *Whistle*, not only does Marion Landers undergo an astral projection experience similar to Prewitt's, but each of the three other major characters also experiences overtly mystical revelations.

Apart from *Whistle*, however, Jones's later mystical scenes are muted and limited. John Bell's vision of the universe through the eyes of the dead soldier Kral in *The Thin Red Line* and Ron Grant's experience in the underwater cavern in *Go to the Widow-Maker*, for example, do not approach the extravagance of Prewitt's experiences. Yet Prewitt's memory of his past lives and his vision of the soul's existence outside the body powerfully and accurately reflect Jones's fascination with what Madame Blavatsky termed the "noble doctrine." Because such experiences lie well outside the range of normal, everyday life, perhaps it helps skeptical readers to have them represented in a romantic setting, although Jones's technique in creating a thoroughly realistic setting and then exposing its underlying spiritual realities is also effective in *Some Came Running*.

Another element of romanticization that lends support to Jones's mystical viewpoint in *From Here to Eternity* is exemplified by Jack Malloy. Jones prepares readers to listen to his spokesman by demonstrating Maggio's idealization of Malloy and Prewitt's grudging discovery that this idolization is deserved. Moreover, Prewitt's initiation into astral projection through following Malloy's advice about mind control trumpets Malloy's role as a man of spiritual wisdom. In addition, Malloy's unfailing compassion, his ability to endure great pain without wanting to inflict it on others, and his unegotistical refusal to barter his soul proclaim him a saint. Even the inability to feel possessive love, which Malloy sees as a flaw, may be a sign that he exists on a higher plane and has passed beyond the stage where such love could teach him anything further. Although his view that passive resistance can reveal mistaken ways of life is proved by the effect of Prewitt's death on the man who shot him (and in modern history by Gandhi's and Martin Luther King, Jr.'s applications of Thoreau's "Civil Disobedience"), Malloy recognizes that the purpose of saintly behavior is personal spiritual advancement rather than social revolution. Judged on this basis, he merits Prewitt's description as the "new Messiah of the new faith Malloy had also prophesied. A Messiah who refused a following and preferred to work alone" (Jones, *From Here to Eternity* 665).

Jones's most intriguing spokesman, however, is not Jack Malloy but rather the wily manipulator Milton Anthony Warden. Warden establishes that role during his first visit to Karen Holmes, when he claims that he has been "forced by irrefutable logic to accept the weird outlandish idea of reincarnation" and that he has "decided to not believe in mortal sin, since obviously no Creator who was Just would condemn His creations to eternal hellfire and brimstone for possessing hungers He created in them. He might penalize them fifteen yards for clipping, but He wouldnt stop the ball game" (118). Warden understands that the "punishment" meted out for "mistakes" is a part of each soul's education rather than a harsh, permanent condemnation for wrong-doing. It is, he admits, as far as he has been able to develop his views on God and salvation. He has not yet seen the role of ego-reduction in the process of reincarnation or considered the directions that his spiritual growth might take.

Warden's chief characteristics are flexibility and a strong bent toward deviousness, allowing him to maintain integrity not by hurling it against all available objects as Prewitt does but by easing it gently around these objects. Although he is contemptuous of brownnosing, he sees nothing to be gained by provocation and views life as a game in which he sets many of the goals and rules. If an officer plans something Warden resents, he does not defy him but will strive indirectly to change the officer's mind. Moreover, Warden regards obstacles that officers place in the way of his goals as challenges to his ingenuity, and he sometimes adds a few to increase the difficulty of a self-appointed task.

Yet Warden places what he considers to be the good of his company above his personal desires and employs his manipulative techniques less for his own benefit than for that of the company and various individuals within it, although he places the company before any individual. Warden displays little longing for the authoritarian control that General Slater deems essential and desirable and welcomes the presence of efficient individuals capable of making their own decisions so the functioning of the company will not depend only on him. He is relieved, for example, when he realizes that the new appointee, Maylon Stark, is able to run the kitchen without assistance.

Nevertheless, Warden does believe in discipline and occasionally metes out punishment, although most of the time he strives to circumvent punishments that officers intend to order. When Prewitt reaches the front half of the work detail line, for example, Warden is ready to place him on the worst details. He also bestows sanctuary when Prewitt is in the second half of the line, exemplifying not only Warden's sly and arbitrary gamesmanship but also his determination to help Prewitt learn how to take care of himself. In this instance and others, Warden acts as master to an unwilling or unready disciple. When Pete Karelsen asks why he does not place Prewitt in Pete's platoon, where he would have a chance to get ahead, Warden significantly responds, "Maybe I'm trying to educate him first" (163).

What Warden tries to help Prewitt learn is how to be flexible and react toward obstacles as Warden does. Yet he knows that the self-made private will have to discover that view for himself. Considering Warden's seeming ability to get along under any conditions, we must ask why becoming an officer would damage his integrity. What makes the maneuvering he would have to do as an officer so different from the maneuvering he does under Holmes to keep his outfit running? One explanation concerns the natural hostility that Warden, an enlisted man, has toward officers, but his feeling must be based on something more solid or it undermines readers' faith in his integrity. A more satisfying explanation is that Warden, like Prewitt, views officers as top dogs who must treat their "inferiors" as underdogs. He realizes that he, too, might acquire some of those corrupting traits if he becomes an officer.

Several other events occur just before Warden's decision not to accept his commission that disturb him and add dignity and justification to his stance. First, Prewitt dies and Warden inherits *The Re-enlistment Blues* and Prewitt's list of books to read. The fact that he has read most of the works on the list reminds Warden of his philosophical links with Prewitt and the grudging respect he always felt toward Prewitt. As James Giles notes, "Prewitt represents to Warden the doomed idealist and is, then, the embodiment of his own troublesome 'backward romanticism'" (*James Jones* 52). Warden's renewed sense of affinity with Prewitt and his troubled reflections about him (particularly concerning how he and Prewitt are alike) make him resent the military police officer, who is interested solely in erasing any black mark for Prewitt's death. It is fitting that Warden receives *The Re-enlistment Blues*, because he is the only character with authority who has shown any understanding of ordinary soldiers.

The second event that affects Warden at the time of his decision is the announcement of a compulsory withdrawal to safe duty stateside of enlisted men around Pete Karelsen's age below the rank of master sergeant. The announcement outrages Warden because he is aware of the physical and mental decay that semiretirement will bring to Pete. Stagnation, as always, is the greatest threat to growth, and when Warden witnesses Lieutenant Ross's fear-inspired reluctance to speak to his superior about keeping Pete, and Colonel Delbert's refusal to consider such a proposal, he becomes justifiably alarmed about Pete's future—and his own.

The third significant event is Warden's observation of how officers around him behave when he receives notice of his impending commission. Their way of welcoming him into their closed society makes him realize that he, too, will be expected to cultivate a snobbish attitude. In yet another event, Warden notes anew, in telling Stark about Captain Holmes infecting Karen with a venereal disease, the devastating effect of the casual corruption that seems to be bred into officers. Finally, he sees how much his men need him during the Japanese attack. Had he been an officer, he might have been too far away to help in time. His sense of responsibility and concern might have been enough in themselves to make him continue to prefer his present rank.

The most difficult aspect of Warden's decision is that he must choose between, as Jones told me, "the man's world and the woman's world." That choice resembles the one that will confront Ron Grant in *Go to the Widow-Maker*, wherein the path of spiritual growth clearly lies in the direction of the "womanly" traits of sensitivity, concern for a significant other, and avoidance of excessive risk-taking. Grant, however, does not risk being separated from his work and sense of responsibility by his decision to stand by his woman, whereas Warden would be forced to surrender both to attain a lasting union with Karen. Moreover, if Warden did make such a sacrifice, he would lose his self-respect as well as Karen's respect and thus would have gained nothing. Spiritual growth is always individual, and even minute differences in circumstances may dictate vastly different decisions to attain the same goal of salvation.

Paradoxically, even though Warden "loses" Karen, or perhaps because of that "loss," his relationship with her greatly aids his growth. He began their affair to get revenge on Captain Holmes, although his motives soon change when Karen tells him what her husband has done to her and he is moved by compassion. Nevertheless, his sexual feelings remain "savage" and self-centered, and he is prepared to sacrifice a possible long-range relationship for the short-term delights of a few afternoons. It is only during their final time together, after Warden has learned that Karen knows he turned down the commission and still wants to be with him, that he overcomes the selfish part of his love for her and becomes concerned about her feelings. Instead of making love for his own gratification, he touches her tenderly without trying for consummation and finds he is making more potent love than before, a situation that probably reflects Lowney Handy's version of yoga and occult attitudes toward sex. Even though Warden later adds Karen to the list of women he has loved and wonders how many more the future may bring, his concern while he is with her is strictly for her rather than himself.

The equally selfless concern Warden now displays toward Pete Karelsen indicates how much he has changed, because he had once used Pete as his "punching bag" (159) to relieve frustrations. During the Japanese attack, Warden sees how well Pete handles himself in combat and gains a respect for him that provides the basis for his outrage over the decision to send Pete stateside. He may also reflect that the same fate would eventually be his, and in fighting for Pete he is fighting for himself. Whatever Warden's reasons for deploring Pete's situation, his sympathy and regard for Pete are greater than ever before, and that marks an advance in his feelings.

Another sign of the change in Warden is the tenderness he displays while telling Stark about the source of Karen's venereal infection and the infection's influence on her affair with Stark, although the incident is ambiguous because Warden realizes that the information will hurt Stark and has been looking forward to this moment with relish. Nevertheless, Warden's gentleness with Stark is stressed again and again, and he shows concern by saving Stark from the consequences of Stark's subsequent cleaver-swinging rampage. Moreover, Stark is the last person seen in Warden's company, and the two of them seem to be friends again.

The final sequence with Warden and Stark also indicates Warden's difficulty in adjusting to the loss of Karen, as well as his ability to cope with that loss. When he and Stark go to town together, Warden provokes a fight to release his pent-up frustrations and afterward laughs "witlessly" while fleeing from the military police. During their escape from the MPs, he and Stark observe Karen's boat slide out to sea, "silently and pitilessly" (845). After that, Warden treats Stark and himself to two of the prostitutes at Mrs. Kipfer's. Because an earlier conflict with Karen had made Warden stay away from Mrs. Kipfer's out of fear of "ruining his reputation with a fiasco" (710), his presence now implies that he has come to terms with his suffering and will be able to face the future with confidence.

Karen Holmes also gains strength from her affair with Warden, similarly beginning with ego-bound motives and later discovering that inner freedom comes through moving beyond such desires. Like Warden, Karen enters the affair to strike back at her husband and assert her independence from the "lord and master" with whom she remains for security. She and Warden are filled with the self-pity that traps Johnny Carter and Al Garnon in *They Shall Inherit the Laughter*, Dave Hirsh and Wally Dennis in *Some Came Running*, George and Sandy Thomas in "Two Legs for the Two of Us," Mona and Larry Patterson in "Secondhand Man," Hill Gallagher in *The Merry Month of May*, Sonny Duval in *A Touch of Danger*, and Bobby Prell in *Whistle*.

Karen has an additional motive for the affair, however, that sets her apart from Warden and involves her even further in self-pity. Her husband's marital gift of venereal disease that makes her sterile (an event suggested to Jones by Harry Handy's similar infliction of the disease on Lowney Handy), has led her to regard her body as evil and sex as ugly (as did Lowney). Shortly after her return from the hospital, therefore, she attempts to use Stark as an "instrument" to "clean" herself (334). Karen still considers herself dirty when Warden makes his pass, however, prompting her, until falling in love with him, to regard him as another instrument to be used.

Later, Karen discusses the quality that attracted her to Warden: "You were honest, and if you thought it by god you said it, and to hell with the consequences. I admired that" (619). Warden had looked for a woman able to respond to sexual declarations honestly. It is therefore significant that Karen matter-of-factly agrees the first time he asks her to have sex, although she pretends no enthusiasm. Her mood alters abruptly, however, when her son comes home and she and Warden face the danger of discovery. Although she is most concerned about the threat to herself, she knows that Warden could be severely punished under military law. After her son has departed, she meets Warden on a more human level, especially because his amusement at having been forced to hide in a closet for the first time, even though he was once a traveling salesman, provokes her own. Karen's laughter, and the tears that follow it, prompt Warden to show her "the great gentleness that was in him, that he was always wanting to bring forward, but never could" (126). It is her appreciation of this gentleness that leads her to respond, "I never knew it could be like this" (126).

Karen's main problem is timidity and self-distrust. She has been estranged from her husband since he gave her gonorrhea, but she fears having to earn her own living and has found no other man to take care of her. Thus, when she becomes involved with Warden, she prods him to become an officer like her husband so she can keep her benefits when she transfers her loyalty. Like Warden, however, she discovers the folly and futility of planning.

When confronted by her inability to control life as she had hoped, Karen follows the path trodden by other spiritual pilgrims, Dave Hirsh, Gwen French, and Edith Barclay, for example, and casts away her last holds on security. After learning about Warden's rejection of the commission that was to undergird their new life together, she nevertheless openly defies her husband to be with Warden one last time, although she knows he cannot marry her or even help if Holmes should divorce her. She tells Warden that the greatest gift he has given her is her "freedom. Dana can never touch me any more. You've made me loved" (825). She had suspected for a long time that "there must be another reason, above, beyond, somewhere another Equation beside this virgin + marriage + motherhood + grandmotherhood = honor, justification, death," and that "there must be another language, forgotten unheard unspoken, than the owning of an American's Homey Kitchen complete with dinette, breakfast nook, and fluorescent lighting" (66). But she has never found the strength to discard these goals until her final meeting with Warden. Paradoxically, the love that has led Karen to look outside herself and become concerned about the feelings of another person has also made her self-directed and self-reliant. She has accomplished the difficult task of ridding her love of selfishness and possessiveness, and that accomplishment has enabled her to face her mistakes in loving and communicate her awareness of them to Warden: "I've hated you bitterly, at times. All love has hate in it. Because you are tied to anyone you love, and it takes away part of your freedom and you resent it, you cant help it. And while you are resenting the loss of your own freedom, you are trying to force the other to give up to you every last little bit of his own. . . .

Love will always have hate in it. Maybe thats the reason we're on this earth, to learn to love without hating" (624).

As a result of this new vision of love, Karen is able to give herself freely to Warden and then return to her husband the next day without remorse or fear. The prospect of having to fend for herself is no longer intimidating. She admits to her husband that she has spent the night with another man, whom she refuses to name, and indicates that she intends to live as she chooses, regardless of Holmes's wishes. Significantly, after that conversation she goes for a walk by herself and finds that she enjoys being alone, a discovery that will later be shared by Capt. James Stein and Geoffrey Fife in *The Thin Red Line*, Jack Hartley in *The Merry Month of May*, and others. Karen then meditates on Stendhal's philosophy of happiness. "The good thing about that Stendhal," she reflects, is that "he understood the very important place that misery and tragedy played in the making of a full happiness" (835).

On the boat that takes her away from Hawaii, Karen almost succumbs to her longing for the old existence when she sees a girl whose appearance of "flawless simplicity" reminds her of the "painstaking hours of hard work" she used to spend in making herself attractive. She sees, however, that "a woman with a small child could not compete in the league this girl played in" (854). Her final lesson about the social attitudes she once held comes with the realization that the "girl" must be a prostitute, Lorene, whom Warden had told her about. That insight frees Karen to act without regard to social restrictions or other pressures to conform. She is obviously attracted to a young lieutenant colonel in the Air Force, even though she has asserted to herself that love is over for her. He has sought her company on the ship, and it is also apparent that she will consider having an affair with him.

It is notable that Jones's one serious disagreement with critic Richard P. Adams concerned Adams's interpretation of Karen. His comments in a letter to Adams on July 16, 1954, reflect a greater sensitivity about women than most critics have acknowledged in his writing:

> Perhaps the only thing I positively *did* not like was your passing reference to Karen "making up to a young Lt Col" on the boat. . . . Ive had Karen called nymphomaniacal by so many goddamned people—usually men!—that I see red where she is concerned. You are a sensitive enough person to know, Im sure, that Karen was anything except nymphomaniacal. She was desperately lonely and unhappy living in a man's world, and she didnt give a damn if she broke some of their rules. Anyway, she was *not* making up to the Lt Col; he was making up to her. And she withheld judgment and decision about sleeping with him until she could be more sure if he

was worth giving all that love that she needed to give, to. (Hendrick, ed., *To Reach Eternity* 211-12)

As her attitude toward the young officer implies, one of the most important advances Karen has made by the end of the novel is overcoming abhorrence for her body and life. Like Gwen French, she was warned that it is impossible to avoid the "cloak" of "evil" (Jones, *From Here to Eternity* 60). But in spite of this warning, she has condemned her husband for his sexual appetite and herself for the adultery she committed in revenge. After bidding Warden farewell, though, she can sit down with Stark's new mistress, talk to her as one "happily adulterous" wife to another (830), and tell her husband honestly that she feels no shame over her affair. Moreover, when her son asks whether he can enlist, she can reply sardonically that he'll "be just the right age for the next one" (858). Karen knows that nothing is truly or irrevocably evil, including war, and that her son will have to learn about life through his own experiences and mistakes.

Like Karen, the novel's other major character, Prewitt, often considered book's protagonist, discovers that he cannot thrust aside evil through an act of will. His promise to his dying mother not to hurt anyone ironically leads him, through a series of unforeseen events, to murder a man. Along the way, he directly and indirectly damages a number of lives, including his own, by rigid adherence to a set of absolute ideals. He also gains insight into the process of spiritual evolution through reincarnation and into the meaning of love, making the same spiritual journey from selfishness to fellow-feeling that Warden and Karen make but attaining a more explicit revelation of its direction and purpose.

Prewitt has a dim memory of past incarnations in his "wild visions . . . of having once played a herald's trumpet for the coronations and of having called the legions to bed down around the smoking campfires in the long blue evenings of old Palestine" (14). The visions help explain the "call" he feels to play the bugle in this incarnation. In his early boyhood, he was drawn to music because he discovered that the songs to which he listened gave him a "first hint that pain might not be pointless if you could only turn it into something" (13). As an adult, he finds that even a simple lament like his friend Sal Clark's version of "Truckdriver's Blues" can conjure up a meaningful vision such as a half-glimpsed image of each soul's separation and return to God:

> In the simple meaningless words he saw himself, and Chief Choate, and
> Pop Karelsen, and Clark, and Anderson, and Warden, each struggling with
> a different medium, each man's path running by its own secret route from

the same source to the same inevitable end. And each man knowing as the long line moved as skirmishers through the night woodsey jungle down the hill that all the others were there with him, . . . each man wanting to reach out and share, . . . but each unable, . . . to make known he was there, and so each forced to face alone whatever it was up ahead. (130)

Hence, Prewitt uses his bugle as a medium to attempt communication with those souls whose isolated paths come close to his own. The night he plays Taps, which he regards as the "song of the Great Loneliness," he forges a bond with his fellow soldiers that could not exist otherwise and touches their souls with the bugle's lament-filled paean to their common situation. Once the bugle is silenced, however, he is unable to sustain the vision, either for himself or his briefly shaken listeners.

Prewitt's worst fault, like Witt's in *The Thin Red Line* and Prell's in *Whistle*, is being so proud that he is willing to make a multitude of sacrifices rather than surrender the minutest particle of his pride. After all, pride has driven him out of the Bugle Corps, thereby increasing his isolation by removing his chief means of communication. His pride is allied to a powerful idealism, but both pride and idealism are aimed at holding on to a mental status quo that proves impossible to maintain. Moreover, Prewitt is keenly aware of what he feels due him, but only intermittently aware of what he owes others. He displays little concern for what would happen to Violet Ogure if she would forsake her parents and community to live with him until he is transferred. He also pays scant attention to Lorene once he has decided to return to his unit. In addition, Prewitt's refusal to accept any kind of compromise often drives others away from deals they have made with life into a dangerous realm from which there may be no return—or at least none in this incarnation. Thus, Prewitt realizes too late that it was his contemptuous presence on the "date" with two homosexuals, Hal and Tommy, that made Maggio wild with guilt. As evidence of his cold-bloodedness, Prewitt solicits money from Hal before pursuing Maggio (although he intends to split this money with his runaway friend) and subsequently decides to employ the money for a passionless seduction of Lorene. Although Hal and Lorene seem legitimate targets, and Prewitt's later affection interferes with the seduction, such actions imply selfishness and even callousness.

Only during his last moment in this incarnation, when confronted with the choice between killing once more or letting himself be killed without fighting back, does Prewitt begin to demonstrate the growth that has resulted from his experience, especially from his contact with the teachings of Jack Malloy, whose views on reincarnation he has come to regard as logical "when he was drunk" (723); his awareness of the futility of his murder of Fatso; and his reading books by Jack London and others. The fact that Prewitt takes a gun with him when he tries to return to his company after having gone AWOL implies that he considered killing in self-defense when he started out but decides not to "become a Disciple of the Word" kill when faced with the choice of doing so (789). His thoughts reflect comprehension of his attackers' fear and appreciation of the way they are handling the threat they think he represents.

When Prewitt's mother died while he was a boy and still a Christian, he expected to see angels over her bed or some other sign of her encounter with God and immortality. He discovered, however, that the single spiritually uplifting aspect of her death was "the fact that in this last great period of fear her thought had been upon his future, rather than her own. . . . it was there, he felt, that the immortality he had not seen was hidden" (17). Neither the Christian concept of death, with its emphasis on an eternity of joy or torment earned during an absurdly brief span of time, nor the atheistic view of death as an absolute cessation of life fits his circumstances. His last reflections before moving on to his next incarnation concern the process he is going through: "As if in a way he was seeing double, he realized it wasnt really going to end after all, that it would never end. . . . What he had thought a long time ago . . . that day in Choy's with old Red. How that there was always an endless chain of new decidings. It was right after all" (791).

One of the things Malloy tries hardest to teach Prewitt is the doctrine of passive resistance, which is not merely opposing injustice without hitting back but also without mentally attacking the perpetrators of the injustice. This doctrine owes much to both Thoreau and Gandhi reinforcing Arthur Christy's argument that "Mahatma Gandhi's adoption of Thoreau's principles is in itself the most definite proof that can be found of the latter's Oriental temper" (*The Orient in American Transcendentalism* 211) and demonstrates once again Jones's American Orientalism. Such resistance is aimed at change not destruction and based on a feeling of love that demands nothing in return. As Malloy explains, "A guy named Spinoza. . . . said: *Because a man loves God he must not expect God to love him in return.* . . . I dont use passive resistance for what I expect it will get me. I dont expect it to pay me back any more than it ever has" (659-60, emphasis in the original). That statement applies as well to Prewitt's love for the army, and he reflects that the men who shot him "were the Army too. . . . it was not true that all men killed the things they loved. What was true was that all things killed the men who loved them. Which, after all, was as it should be" (789). Soon he notes the impact of his approaching death on the man, Harry, who fired at him. When

Harry says to his fellow military police, "You know I didnt mean to shoot him. . . . It makes you feel pretty shitty," Prewitt remarks to himself, "Thats what they call passive resistance, soldier. Aint that right, Jack?" (790).

Another lesson Prewitt learns concerns the folly of never bending when pressured by the unpredictability of life. It is a lesson that Mazzioli in "The Way It Is," Norma Fry in "None Sing so Wildly," Louisa Gallagher in *The Merry Month of May*, and many other Jonesian characters should also have noted. Even though he had anticipated being sent to the stockade, Prewitt could not have envisioned the sequence of events that put him there. Like everyone else, he assumes he will be court-martialed for resisting the Treatment, but instead he initiates his downfall by rejecting Bloom's gratitude for rescuing his dog. When Ike Galovitch attacks him because of the fight with Bloom, Prewitt believes he has at last found a "common enemy." He realizes at the moment he knocks Ike out, however, that Ike is only a drunken old Slav who needs a hero to worship and thinks he has found one in Captain Holmes.

Once Prewitt is imprisoned, he is again compelled to acknowledge the unexpected through Maggio's change from a naively cynical boy to a tough, anguished wild man. After he becomes outraged by Fatso's savagery toward Maggio and Berry, even though he realizes that his friends invited their beatings, Prewitt becomes fixed on Fatso's destruction. When he returns to active duty, his thoughts prevent him from adjusting to the radically altered circumstances in the company or responding to the friendly gestures of everyone except Ike. His only reality, the only image-picture he can see, remains the stockade. The company can no longer meaningfully exist for Prewitt until he confronts Fatso, shatters subjective reality, and replaces it with another that includes the company.

Later, when Prewitt talks to Warden about killing Fatso and wanting to return to the company, the top sergeant tries to think of the most unlikely possibility he can and says that the only way Prewitt can come back without penalty is if the Japanese attack Pearl Harbor and the army releases stockade prisoners to fight. When that incredible event happens and salutarily wreaks havoc on virtually all the characters', and all Americans', image-pictures and stability, Prewitt attempts to return to his unit. He is then killed by military police, who take him by surprise.

Apart from the sneak attack on Pearl Harbor, perhaps the most astonishing event in the novel (although not really surprising when Jones's views about shunning the cloak of evil are considered) is Prewitt's murder of Fatso. Because Prewitt's deathbed promise to his mother not to hurt anyone has been both compounded by his regret over blinding the fighter

Dixie Wells and stoutly affirmed in the face of the Treatment, he should be horrified at the thought of killing a fellow enlisted man. He has been prepared for that action, however, by the atmosphere of the stockade as well as his simplistic picture of the world as divided into absolutes to be won and lost, with no conceivable ground between. The Number Two barracks of rebels and "fuckups" provides a womb because it temporarily frees Prewitt from questioning the presence of injustice in the universe by narrowing his focus to a local injustice that seems more comprehensible. Even that impression, however, is proved false by Fatso's failure to understand why Prewitt wants to kill him. Although Prewitt's view of life is often too self-confined to allow him to cope adequately with the world, his fate hints at the complexity of the world and leads him to recognize that complexity during his final minutes.

While Prewitt is in solitary confinement, he tries Malloy's system of mind control, which separates his soul from his body and makes him feel "as if there were two of him, and one of him went out of and away from the other of him" (579). He notices that the connection between these two images is "a kind of cord that looked like it was made out of jism . . . and he knew from somewhere . . . that if that cord ever got broken he was dead" (579). His experience at the end of the cord "was as if for the first time he had gone off the world like a spaceship and could really see all of it, and grasp the reason for all of it, and realize . . . that more than anything else it was like a small boy going to school every day . . . and if he does not learn one lesson one day . . . the wasted day helps him learn it that much quicker the next day" (579).

When Prewitt lies waiting for his death, he can "feel himself beginning to go clear out of himself," and he encounters again "the cord he had seen that time in the Stockade that looked like it was made of come" (790). The return of this experience at such a time naturally brings back memories of the vision of the complexity and meaningfulness of the world. Because he leaves this incarnation in the midst of the renewed lesson, he should be able to build on it, knowingly or unknowingly, in his next life.

Perhaps the best of Prewitt's earlier perceptions, and one that accords well with his final view of the world as highly complex, is that a person or group may be an underdog in one place or situation and an oppressor in another. For example, in *Go to the Widow-Maker*, Letta Bonham is long the victim of her husband Al's Victorian attitude requiring sexless "purity" for wives, but when she learns about his affair with Cathie Finer she victimizes him by having him arrested and taking away his control of the schooner company. In *From Here to Eternity*, Isaac Bloom is both underdog and oppressor. Suggestively, he shares the same last name as James Joyce's coarsely sensitive, blunderingly insightful, Jewish common-man hero in *Ulysses* who is intrigued by what his wife, Molly, stumblingly terms "met him pike hoses" (reincarnation). Bloom's personality reflects that of one of the most obnoxious Jews in literature: the whiny, cry-baby, blindly self-centered, and uncomprehending Romantic Robert Cohn in Ernest Hemingway's *The Sun also Rises.* Cohn, like Bloom, learns pugilism to defend himself against racial prejudice only to discover that his knowledge makes no difference. The juxtaposition—and implied blending—of these two memorable literary images of the Jew suggests an intertextual approach to character aimed at revising Hemingway's narrower, more vicious depiction in the direction of Joyce's humane and holistic vision.

In *From Here to Eternity*, Bloom-Cohn's consciousness has been shaped by his sense that Jews are despised and that because he is a Jew he can do nothing to prevent being despised. He has become a victim of the general attitude toward Jews although he is also personally responsible for much of his alienation. Bloom's defensiveness about being a Jew has made him act in ways that are offensive to many men who would not have been put off by his religion. When Jimmy Kaliponi remarks that "Jewboys" lack the "heart" to be fighters (497-98), he reveals the validity of Bloom's belief in the injustice directed against his religion (and also implies the relativity of prejudice through Kaliponi's case). Bloom, like Prewitt, can choose how he responds to that injustice. Just as Stark's example of waiting until he has a good job lined up before quitting his old outfit shows how Prewitt could have safely escaped from the Corps, where the "punk" bugler was appointed over him, Sussman's example of ingratiating himself while retaining awareness of his Jewishness, as Leopold Bloom does in *Ulysses*, points out what Bloom could have accomplished. The matter is complicated, as Jones intends, by readers' awareness of how prejudice against Native Americans affects the wasteful limits set on—and accepted by—Chief Choate. Thus, Bloom, like Prewitt, is both a victim of circumstances and a self-made victim.

Bloom is as much victimizer as victim, however, and it is fascinating to watch him swing dizzily back and forth between those roles in the time preceding his suicide. One minute he is lamenting that his rise to a corporalcy and victories as a fighter can never overcome the prejudice against him, and the next he is asserting his new authority abusively toward Sal Clark, whom he absurdly denounces as one of the "Wop Fascisti" (567). Next he reflects on the injustice of the reputation he thinks he has acquired for homosexuality (a reputation he fears may be justified) and then remembers how his report against Prewitt had launched the investigation of homosexuals that proved so embarrassing to Bloom himself. It is as clear a mixture of good and evil as could be found in such short compass. Yet Bloom must be judged as a whole rather than as separate actions, especially considering that his largest error lies in trying to deny parts of himself, particularly his Jewishness and his involvement with homosexuals. That denial leads directly to the attempt at suicide that he seeks to call off too late.

Bloom's suicide appears to be Jones's first literary attempt to come to terms with the suicide of his father, Ramon Jones. In a letter of March 22, 1942, to his brother Jeff about the death, he observed that "in that last split-second before the blackness hit him, he probably grinned and told himself what a Goddam fool he is" (Hendrick, ed., *To Reach Eternity* 20), essentially the same remark Bloom makes at the end of the novel. "I loved my father," Jones later affirmed, "and I hated to see it end like that" (*Viet Journal* 2). In "The Ice-Cream Headache," a story based on three generations of Jones's family, Tom Dylan, who seems modeled on Jones, speculates that his father will commit suicide in five years. At least two of the central characters, in *Whistle*, Landers and Strange, kill themselves, and Bobby Prell's death in a bar fight also seems a form of suicide.

The sequence with Bloom strongly supports Jack Malloy's philosophy about the need to replace the Old Testament "God of perpetual punishment and vengeance," and even the New Testament "God of perpetual love and forgiveness that only punished evil when He absolutely had to" (Jones, *From Here to Eternity* 645-46), with the Malloy-conceived "God of Love-That-Surpasseth-Forgiveness, the God who saw heard and spoke no evil simply because there was none" (647). The past conceptions of God, with their fixed rules and desire for humans to follow carefully laid out, fully defined paths, are superseded by that of the "God of Growth and Evolution," whose only demand is that humans profit from their mistakes. Hence, if Bloom is to be judged, it must be on the grounds that he failed to develop beyond his sense of the limitations placed on him and sought to avoid learning from his errors. Like the small boy going to school in Prewitt's vision, he is forced to work out his lesson, whether he wishes to or not.

Although Bloom's suicide is a blunder, it teaches him in a new life to place a higher value on life. He foolishly believed he would be committing an act that has irreversibly bad consequences, and he regrets those consequences at the very moment he can no longer prevent them. But Jones's view of reincarnation, like those of the theosophists, Hindus, Buddhists, and perhaps Emerson, implies that no act can have eternally "bad" results. Malloy argues that the ability to commit suicide is the only freedom humans have, but that it is a cowardly action. Death provides a safety valve in the evolutionary process, a break between one incarnation and the next. Yet it never offers more than a temporary release from pain and no lessening of the opportunities to glean knowledge from life. Whether he wants to or not, Bloom has no choice but to carry the consequences of his mistakes and whatever insights they have provided into the next incarnation—and the next and the next—until all his lessons are learned. Bloom-Cohn merges with the God who goes beyond—yet includes—Jews, Christians, Moslems, voodooists, Hindus, Buddhists, Platonists, and theosophists.

Jones's third published novel, *The Pistol*, carries over not only the Pearl Harbor setting from *From Here to Eternity* but also the twin themes of the unpredictability of material life and the absence of material security it occasions, two key realizations needed for spiritual growth. *The Pistol*'s brevity, however, indicates a much smaller compass and implies that the level of achievement may be smaller as well. Often his own best critic, Jones treated the book slightingly, although he may have done so in part because of his desire to defend the much maligned *Some Came Running* as his "best novel": "[*The Pistol* is] okay, for an easy job, an easy out. But human beings themselves are never that easy to symbolize; they're never all black or all white like that; they aren't really any longer human at all" (Interview 242).

Elsewhere, I have followed Jones's lead and argued that in making things "easy" for himself in *The Pistol* he restricts not only his characters by reducing them to traits (Mast is the brainy one, O'Brien the brawny one, and Corporal Winstock the misuser of authority) but also his plot and his dialogue by confining the plot to the attempts of several characters to get Richard Mast's pistol and the dialogue to their similarly worded justifications for these attempts (Carter, "James Jones: An American Master" 129-30). Although Jones managed to hold readers' attention by introducing such threats to Mast's possession of the pistol as trickery, bribery, and physical force, he sacrificed too many vital elements of fiction for the sake of his ideas.

James Giles's analysis of *The Pistol* has led me to reconsider my earlier evaluation, however, and see that Jones's skilled handling of the book's deliberately restricted format demands greater appreciation than I—or even Jones—was willing to grant it. Giles argues that the pistol is "clearly a symbol imposed from outside," depending not "upon the personality of a single character for meaning" but rather speaking "to the needs of all the major characters in the novel" and thereby dominating "Jones's novella in a way that Prewitt's bugle never could" (*James Jones* 92), The pistol becomes a talisman and is the story's true protagonist. Moreover, as an "experimental fable or parable," *The Pistol* should be judged by criteria other than those used to judge realistic novels; the proper criteria include the qualities I used to condemn the book: tight control, conscious restriction of plot and character, and careful focusing of theme. Giles further points out that "given Jones's vision that Pearl Harbor resulted in a historical epoch in which warfare became the normal circumstance of humanity, it is not surprising that his symbols of salvation are weapons of destruction . . . the exemplum of the parable is complex and debatable, but this ambiguity is not a sign of failure, but of success" (93).

Part of the ambiguity, as Giles emphasizes, concerns the role of authority, which in *The Pistol* is "inconsistent, often bungling, but always threatening" so that "one of the main reasons that it is impossible to fight successfully against 'authority' is that its power is so erratic and unpredictable" (94). Balancing Prewitt's realization of the folly of always bucking authority in *From Here to Eternity*, Richard Mast, the central character of *The Pistol* although not the protagonist if we accept Giles's viewpoint, discovers that it is a mistake to bow to authority on all occasions, although there may be times when it is impossible to evade doing so. Even though Mast cannot resist the impersonal operations of the authority who snatches away his security and leaves him defenseless in the wake of the spiritual evolution process, he can dispute the claims of many individuals who declare they have a right to dominate him. Moreover, he is taught to rely on the knowledge he gleans from experience rather than on the projections of his imagination or the impressions of other people.

In a sense, *The Pistol* begins where *From Here to Eternity* leaves off, because it opens with the Japanese attack on Pearl Harbor. As Jones indicated to me in a letter dated January 25, 1974, he had vacillated between including it with the earlier novels, *The Thin Red Line* and *Whistle*, for an "army quartet" and leaving *The Pistol* to stand on its own.

The terrifying unexpectedness of the attack is stressed by the description of Mast tranquilly having breakfast when the bombing starts. Significantly, the contrast to peaceful activities and the unexpectedness recur in the attempts to take away the pistol that he and the other characters regard as the only protection against such frightening events. For example, O'Brien takes the pistol when Mast is feeling closer to him because they have mutually challenged an apparent danger. Similarly, it is when Mast feels most secure in his possession of the pistol that the supply clerk arrives to take it back. Ironically, Mast has retained the pistol for so long only because of the confusion caused by the attack on Pearl Harbor, which was also the reason he had wanted the gun in the first place.

The link between Mast's view of the pistol as a means of ensuring his safety in battle and Wally Dennis's belief in the protective qualities of his Randall Number 1 combat knife implies that Mast's reliance on a weapon may be as foolish as Wally's. The sole evidence that supports Mast's conviction about the saving properties of the weapon is Sergeant Pender's statement that his own pistol had saved his life twice. Yet the fact that Pender took his weapon from a dead soldier indicates that a pistol, although it may help to protect, cannot guarantee survival.

Mast's folly in depending on an external means of salvation is further shown by the way he structures his life around protecting the pistol. The need for constant vigilance and distrust converts the pistol into a perilous burden like the American demolition trap, which becomes potentially useful to the Japanese and so necessitates increasing measures to prevent them from reaching it. Mast is compelled to stay alert constantly to keep anyone from taking his weapon. Moreover, his fight with Grace on a steep, mountainous incline means that he is risking his life to protect the object that is supposed to safeguard his life.

Mast's self-deluded, continued belief in the pistol as a means of salvation is matched by his self-deception about the way he obtained it. When he first invents the story of purchasing the handgun from a man in the Eighth Field Artillery he knows the reality of his situation, but after a while he half-recalls being issued the pistol for guard duty and half-believes that he bought it. After Sergeant Pender allows him to keep the pistol, Mast blinds himself to the truth until Musso the supply clerk reclaims the missing weapon. By then, Musso's action is the only thing that can free Mast from his image-picture of being the true owner of the pistol.

Mast's combination of self-delusion with disguised self-interest paves the way for his destructive sense of righteousness, because the most vicious act in the novel is Mast's kick in Grace's face. The kick comes from Mast's bitterness at the supposed violations of morality that Grace and everyone else who has tried to get his pistol commit. Even though Grace brings the injury on himself by taking precautions against being kicked when Mast would not have thought of doing so and by trying to kick Mast first, it is Mast's accumulated feeling of outraged righteousness that gives his kick such force. His cruelty demonstrates the way his quest for an external means of salvation has temporarily impeded his inner growth.

Mast has also obstructed growth by his self-imposed ideal of masculine toughness. He wants the pistol partly because it enables him to appear like his idealized conception of a soldier, which is based on Wild West cavalrymen. Like Prewitt and Maggio, he admires cowboys. As Frank MacShane notes, "Jones wanted [his novel] to contain some of the flavor of the 'mythological history of the Old West,' because he was interested in the lengths to which people would go 'in killing, injuring, lying, cheating, hurting' to attain salvation of any kind, personal or otherwise" (*Into Eternity* 170).

MacShane also records how Jones loved the western films *The Wild Bunch* and *High Noon* and how Rose Styron found him once with his young son, Jamie, "sitting on the edge of the round fur-covered bed in full American cowboy outfits, both of them, with matching hats and boots, holsters, the works" (240). Clearly, Jones distinguished between what appealed to him emotionally and what he believed in intellectually, although his attitude toward bravery always seemed somewhat mixed. As Gloria Jones recalled, "He was born gentle. He had the most terrible war for a young man to have gone off to. He had to kill a young man his own age. . . . He became such a pacifist after that. He wrote somewhere that bravery was the most pernicious of virtues because it forced men to do things that they might not do under other circumstances" (Lennon, "Glimpses" 208). At the same time, MacShane observes that "the matter was not simple" for Jones, and that "certainly cowardice is not preferable to bravery, and individual development is important. Jones wrote of his son, Jamie, 'I want to teach my boy to be brave and strong, not to run away, to fight back when he has to. Yet I must admit that there is a paradox in my thinking. I also want my boy to be gentle. That's the goal I'm really striving for'" (*Into Eternity* 224). Such conflicting attitudes and aims were not to be easily resolved, and they provided Jones with a creative tension akin to that he experienced from trying to reconcile his doubts with his reincarnationist beliefs.

Mast's tough-guy vision of himself, pistol on hip, leads him to risk walking slowly across an open square when the Japanese are attacking. Furthermore, he is willing to put his life in jeopardy again while on guard duty because he wants to show off and is flattered that "big, tough O'Brien whom he had seen engaged in so many heroic-sized fistfights" asks him what to do about a noise (Jones, *The Pistol* 38). His satisfaction at the relatively safe and easy establishment of his toughness is the main reason he feels so warm toward this treacherous comrade-in-arms on his return and why he is then so vulnerable to O'Brien's ruse. When Mast regains the pistol, he slaps it into his holster "toughly, confidently" (48), thus indicating that he has learned little about the absurd and destructive effects of acting tough.

When Mast finally loses the pistol for good, he asks himself whether it had "all been for nothing? all the worries? all the effort?" (157). The answer can only be negative if his experiences have helped him evolve beyond his former illusions and the self-love that prompted his desire for a means of personal protection. It is unclear whether he is ready to make this self-transformation, but he has taken two steps toward it by admitting his self-love to Sergeant Pender and recognizing that his self-delusion about the way he acquired the pistol was "silly" (157). In contrast, O'Brien, who never had even Mast's illusory claim to the pistol, rails at the weapons carrier bearing the representative of impersonal army authority away with the pistol and "upward at the sky" (158). Such self-pity could trap Mast as well if he has not gained the wisdom from his experience to accept that the world never offers an assured means to material salvation.

Mast never seems to acknowledge the extent to which his ordeal has been self-chosen. As everyone points out, he could attain relative safety at any time by becoming a clerk and working in the rear echelon. It is his decision to take part in combat and risk facing the Japanese officer whom he fears so greatly. All his striving to secure a personal shield against disaster amounts to hedging his bet. He wants the "glory" of having proven his manhood in battle without seriously risking anything. The walk across the square during the attack is trifling because he does not believe he can be hit; the presence of the pistol on his hip has convinced him of his invulnerability. Yet he believes that without a pistol he can be killed by a Japanese major with a samurai saber. Perhaps Mast's loss of the gun, coupled with his continued fear of the Japanese officer, will make his risk real to him. One of the results of any growth stemming from this fear, however, will be to move him beyond such fears to a stronger, less self-concerned state of mind.

A similar change that has already occurred in Mast is the way he has learned to handle his fear of authority. The only reason he tries to turn in his guard duty pistol after the Japanese attack concerns "some inherent nervousness at the idea of going against authority" (21), and he later surrenders it to Corporal Winstock out of this same fear. When he discovers that Winstock abused his authority, however, Mast challenges him as an individual, although he fights out of anyone's sight to avoid being court-martialed for striking a superior. Because of this incident, he later rejoices at the absence of authority during the Marconi Pass detail. Mast's feelings change again, though, after the fight with Grace that occurs because Corporal Fondriere refuses to exert his authority to stop it, and Mast returns to Makapuu Point with a sense of relief that "there, there was Authority. And with Authority there were rules" (139). It is even more ironic therefore that the first attempt made against his pistol after he has acquired a more favorable attitude toward authority comes from a representative of that authority.

The change in Mast between the way he acted toward Winstock's order and the way he responds to Sergeant Paoli is obvious; he refuses to obey the direct command of a superior even though he is warned that Paoli is prepared to have him court-martialed for disobedience. Mast is not totally defiant, though, because he obeys Paoli's order to accompany him to Pender and gives Pender the final decision about the pistol. In persuading Pender to bend the rules and allow him to keep the pistol until a superior orders Pender to confiscate it, Mast not only wins a victory over "the Book says" morality of Paoli (another untrustworthy form of external salvation) but also makes a Warden-like compromise with authority. He is enabled to act with some measure of free will within the confines of a determined situation. Even though he surrenders the pistol to the same authority that had given it to him when an unusual set of circumstances brought about a temporary disruption of the rules, Mast can still retain the confidence and skill he gained while defending the pistol and whatever amount of wisdom and self-transcendence his experiences have taught him—not a bad trade for one little weapon.

❖

Affirming that "Jones's success with *The Pistol* indicates a considerable talent for writing short fiction," Giles observes that "his only collection of short stories, *The Ice-Cream Headache and Other Stories* is a major addition to his canon" (*James Jones* 100), and I believe that he is right. He cites "the volume's thematic variety and technical versatility" in its favor while noting that the "two main groups of stories in *The Ice-Cream Headache* are army stories and tales of midwestern childhood fiction" that are "closely related to his major novels" (100). These stories not only develop and extend many themes that are central to the longer works but also are highly interesting in themselves.

The four story-beads on this portion of the unsevered golden thread of Jones's reincarnationist philosophy all pertain to the conflict between security and salvation so powerfully developed in *From Here to Eternity* and *The Pistol* and prominently displayed throughout his other writings. In "The Way It Is," the constant pressure toward spiritual growth that denies men and women the illusory comfort of a permanent belief in their security is represented by the incessant pummelling of the wind. John Slade's acceptance of the wind at the end of the story indicates his progress toward the painfully benevolent goal of compassionate understanding and reabsorption into God. In "The King," jazzman Willy Jefferson's comeback from poverty and misery is followed by his loss of talent in the midst of some fame and ease. The pattern is paralleled on a lower level by the band members, who try to emulate him but then allow themselves to be "protected" by middle-class relatives, implying that suffering develops an expressiveness linked to spiritual growth and security breeds mediocrity and stagnation.

In "The Valentine," the boy John Slade is spiritually educated through being stripped of his defenses against humiliation. His ability to confront, no matter how reluctantly, the ridicule he has brought on himself is the surest sign that he has grown. Finally, in "The Ice-Cream Headache," the worldly decline of a family over three generations is accompanied by an increasing humility and perceptiveness about life. The grandfather's combination of self-assurance and self-righteousness is replaced by the grandson's self-questioning and sympathy for others. In Jones's work, pain is always the chief instrument of growth, and it pierces through everyone's feebly erected security in the service of salvation.

As in *From Here to Eternity* and *The Pistol*, the complete lack of protection in wartime is a major theme of Jones's early story "The Way It Is." Moreover, as in the shorter novel, Jones again focuses on the panicky period following the attack on Pearl Harbor and the hasty, hysteria-ridden measures taken to prevent a new assault. The road-guard detail, like that in *The Pistol*, is a seemingly vital stopgap necessitated by a bureaucratic blunder. As narrator John Slade points out, however, its "necessity" is suspect because the Japanese knew of the American defense plan soon after it was devised, yet it is important that everyone considers the road-guard essential at the time of the story.

Mazzioli, who was probably apprenticed to "the Book says" Paoli, believes that following orders affords security. He both resents and envies John Slade for his ability to think for himself as well as for his greater education—six months at a university. Placing his faith in the wisdom of army organization and army regulations, one of the frailest forms of external salvation ever devised, Mazzioli considers the performance of army duties to be a sacred mission that will shield him from the terror of chaos and the enemy. Thus, it may be an illuminating shock when he discovers that his correct, by-the-book treatment of the businessman Knight, whom he had mistakenly suspected of being a German spy, results in the abandonment of the road-guard by army officials, who are more responsive to pressure from the wealthy than to danger to their country.

In contrast, Knight's ability to do away with the road-guard on an irritated whim merely confirms Slade's sense of the folly of believing in the efficacy and protectiveness of organizations. That his sympathy is for individuals is shown not only in his actions toward other soldiers (he alerts Alcorn so that he will not be found sleeping on duty) but also in his statement to Lieutenant Allison that he could put himself in Knight's place and feel sorry for him, although "he sure didn't need it" (Jones, *The Ice-Cream Headache and Other Stories* 37). Moreover, when Slade remembers a captured Japanese submarine officer, he associates him with a Japanese woman whom he almost married, and his sympathy extends even to the enemy.

Slade's sympathy, however, which reaches out to embrace all suffering individuals, provokes him into a fury at the conditions they must endure. The symbolic equivalent of these conditions is the ever-present wind, which has blown Slade's "mind empty of all past" and "sucked out everything [from it] but Makapuu" (33). As Prewitt might have, Slade likes to sit on the culvert "alone at night, defying the wind," yet he also recognizes that humans are able to stand up to wind only so long before they become "stupid from its eternal pummeling" (40). Hence, his final remark about the disbandment of the road-guard—"that's the way it is"—implies an accommodation with the unaccommodating conditions of life. The significance of his remark is emphasized by his ability to speak it while the wind is blowing hard enough to almost carry his blankets away. Even though Slade does not yet consciously understand, the wind represents the incessant, gale-force pressure of spiritual salvation. Unaccommodating conditions are precisely what humans need to grow, and Slade's final acceptance of the wind implies his acceptance as well of the entire process of spiritual salvation.

The problem of security versus salvation is further illuminated in "The King," even though, unlike Karen Holmes, Richard Mast, and Mazzioli, the members of the college band do not appear to be seeking security. Although the band members appreciate the achievements of risk-taking, hardship-prone jazzmen, they make increasing accommodations to a middle-class way of life that seems to afford protection, as a pistol and army regulations do for soldiers, and thus they surrender developing the talent that suffering might have induced.

Jones's introduction to "The King" describes it "as a good example of the 'Double Plot' story, in which two stories, almost unrelated but spiritually connected, are taking place," and he claimed that "the real story is the story of the college band" (Jones, "The King" 141). He links what is happening to the band and to "King" Jefferson, and a pattern of rise and fall emerges for both. The band starts out as a group when Jefferson is brought back to public attention and breaks up five years later when he returns to the hard life in the rice fields. In addition, the band almost dissolves when the

King dies. In between, the band and Jefferson have accepted the spiritual sell-out of playing dance music instead of the soul-expressive music they value. The compromise disturbs Jefferson so much that upon meeting the five members of the band in New York he warns them against hearing his new group, which plays a watered-down version of jazz that the public likes. Ironically, the group against which he warns the band resembles their own.

The steady decline in the band members' ideals can be traced to compromises with their parents and the public for the sake of staying together and gaining financial security. Considering how many times the members accepted their relatives' help in order to be able to play dance music, which they despise, it is no suprise that they capitulate and enter family businesses after failing to establish the band. In giving up the riskiness of a jazz musician's life for one devoted to business and family, however, the narrator will discover that he has exchanged one form of insecurity for another, as indicated by the sickness of his wife and child. Still, his willingness to compromise and futile attempt to evade insecurity, like that of other band members, indicates the choice of a lesser path, particularly when considering Bob French's claim in *Some Came Running* that an artist is the last evolutionary stage preceding conscious discipleship under a great master.

In contrast, King Jefferson lost trumpet, teeth, and money when respectable people, like the parents of the band members, closed down the notorious Storyville, where he had started out. Jefferson's suffering, however, has provided "power in the trumpet, a strong emotional power, that hit you hard" (146), a power akin to Prewitt's that places him well ahead of anything the band members can do even though it is the only aspect of his playing that has any value. Unfortunately, his wide acquaintance with misery has also enfeebled his ability to play, and less than five years after his comeback he is no longer invited to join professional jam sessions. He becomes a broken old man, although outwardly he is at the height of success. Nevertheless, it is his willingness to place himself in a position to fall that has made him a king, the artist approaching discipleship. The band members, in contrast, have "protected" themselves into mediocrity and a longer time on the path of spiritual evolution.

"The Valentine," part of a series about childhood in the Midwest, of which only five stories were completed, presents one of Jones's clearest images of the place of suffering in the human condition. In his introduction, he argues that "that last scene with that poor little youngun standing out there with his head hid in the coats, totally destroyed, and nobody in the whole damned world knows about it, or gives a good goddamn" is "the state that we all of us are in—give or take a handful" (Jones, "The Valentine"

155). At the same time, though, "the youngun" not only survives that situation but also manages to stand up to the mockery of his peers, proving his
growth.

John Slade's bout of "lovesickness" in "The Valentine" resembles Dave
Hirsh's unrequited loves and stems from the same cause—a self-destructive
combination of ego and vulnerability. His youthfully tender vanity is displayed in his choice of the most popular girl in his class to be his sweetheart,
although he has not yet had the courage to approach her, and in his desire
to give her a gaudy box of candy for Valentine's Day in a manner that would
seem "professional as if he was used to doing it a thousand times" (158).
Two girls in his class are "stuck on him" (167), but he wants only Margaret
Simpson, who is talented and intelligent and has the best-developed chest
in eighth grade.

Although John would like to think of himself as strong and brave, his
fear of rejection leads him to place the chocolates on Margaret's desk and
flee to the cloakroom, actions that leave him no defenses and force him to
admit his cowardice. He knows how foolish he appears when he leans out
of the cloakroom with a silly grin on his face to see her response, and he is
"destroyed" by her laughing remarks to two male companions. Moreover,
he is left with no way to rebuild his belief in his manly qualities or shut out
his awareness that everyone in the classroom finds his behavior ridiculous.
Hence, his decision to walk to his desk in full view of all these scoffing eyes
is perhaps the most courageous of his life, especially since no one there has
the insight to recognize his courage—least of all himself.

Like the preceding midwestern childhood story, "The King," and other
works, "The Ice-Cream Headache" embodies the paradox of outward decline and inward progress. Although the story develops the "failed family
theme" Jones discussed in his introductory remarks and elaborates on his
"attempt to understand the curse of family alienation and where it came to
so many of us during those years" (213), it is clear that three generations of
the Dylan family have been founded in pride and would persist in spiritual
blindness had their material fortunes remained firm and high. Jones was
obviously attempting to use his analysis of these partially fictional characters to make sense of his family's history. The characters bear a strong resemblance to his own family; the grandfather, for example, in personality
and personal history is unmistakably modeled on Jones's grandfather,
George W. Jones.

Edward Dylan, the founder of the family's fortunes, is, like George W.
Jones, more strong-willed and successful than any of his four sons (Jones's
father had three brothers) or his grandson and granddaughter. Moreover,

his term as sheriff—he significantly resembles the western lawman Wyatt Earp, as did George Jones, who also was a sheriff—has fed his already powerful conviction that he knows the one narrow path to God and is therefore qualified to instill morality in others. His methods of imposing his moralistic doctrines on his sons have been as stern as those he applied to drunks and other wrongdoers because he makes little distinction between them, regarding everyone as weak and prone to sin. For Dylan, manhood means asserting strict control over every aspect of life, including sexual impulses. His grandson, Tom, appears justified in suspecting that his grandfather's sexual repression has been the basis for his mean, restrictive treatment of his sons.

Inevitably, such exaggerated control is impossible to maintain, and Dylan is finally forced to doubt his chosen way of life. The fact that all four sons have turned out to be weaklings induces him to wonder about his own virility and wisdom. These doubts, although not yet inducing him to perceive any flaw in his concept of manhood, prompt Dylan to treat his grandchildren more gently than he did his sons. Before his death, he also admits several disastrous misjudgments of society's capacity for change, although he is spared the knowledge of the depression he had similarly failed to anticipate. Dylan has invested in companies that soon will be wiped out (as the value of George Jones's Insull stock deteriorated soon after his death, greatly affecting the financial and social status of his family and giving James Jones an early lesson in insecurity). These misjudgments suggest that rapid changes in scientific knowledge and social structure produce humbling mass insecurity.

Dylan's four sons, having been under the shadow of their father for too long, are ill-prepared to meet the challenges of life on their own. Moreover, they all lack their father's sexual control, and three are killed as a result of entanglements with women. They are the first to have the symbolic ice-cream headache that comes from being greedy for pleasure and trying to eat "too much too fast" (226). The death of the three brothers within five years after their father's death implies their frantic efforts to grab hold of things he had always tried to keep them away from.

The grandson, Tom, is the most obvious victim of an ice-cream headache. Like Hawthorne, Jones provides readers with a plausible physical cause for Tom's illness, a diagnosis of double lumbar pneumonia. Also like Hawthorne, Jones intends readers to entertain a more fanciful idea—that Tom's illness is caused by guilt in advance over his approaching sexual encounter with his sister and her girlfriend Joan. (Paralleling Tom's incestuous desire for Emma, Frank MacShane records that Jones "admitted" that "he had been physically attracted" to his sister Mary Ann, "but, frightened of the possibility of incest, had kept his distance" [*Into Eternity* 127].) Although Tom can recognize the internal and external damage wrought by his grandfather's sexual repression, he has still imbibed the older man's attitude that sex is dirty. He not only passes up the opportunity to go with prostitutes out of fear of the women themselves but also expresses shock that his sister is interested in his pornography collection and likes to masturbate.

Although Tom quickly employs his discoveries about his sister to blackmail Emma into agreeing to a three-way sexual romp with him and her fellow masturbator Joan, he is disturbed by this plan and reflects that if his "grandfather had ever wondered about that 'Mark of Cain' of his in the family—that flaw in the blood passed on in his seed, then he ought to see [Emma and me] now" (228). Moreover, he can only hold a blackmail threat over his sister because she too regards sex as dirty and does not want her parents to know she has such feelings. Yet their belief about sex makes them rebellious and inflames their curiosity; they are prepared to go ahead with their proposed exploration of each other in spite of being certain that they will be ashamed of doing so afterward.

The prospect of being initiated into the longed for and feared mysteries of sex, especially being introduced to them by his sister, is too much for Tom's nervous system, and he succumbs to his illness on the way to the room in his grandfather's mansion where the girls are to meet him. His grandfather's bequest of moralistic Protestantism still holds Tom back and leads him initially to regard his illness as punishment for his projected sin. Fortunately, Tom has a vision of his grandfather pistol-whipping his father for drunkenness and of winking female crotches hidden in his grandfather's right eye and eyebrow that convinces him emotionally as well as intellectually that his father and uncles should never have let the old man make them feel guilty, because "there's nothing in the world that's ever that bad" (235). It is a view of guilt and evil that Emerson and Madame Blavatsky would have appreciated, and it moves Tom far enough along the path of spiritual evolution to free him from ice-cream headaches. Appropriately, his fever subsides, starting him on the path to recovery.

The whirling of a bicycle wheel in his vision may represent the changes brought about by industrialization. If such is the case, Tom's impression that "the bike pedals felt light as feathers" suggests that he has learned how to get along with such changes (138). It also implies that he has come to terms with his guilt and fear of suffering. His desire to replace the rotting, fringed lampshade that he had torn to torment his mother, who kept it as a reminder of their former wealth, demonstrates that he has also come to terms with the past and his feelings about his mother, whom he long resented for her petty-mindedness and complaint-ridden attempts to dominate him. Thus, Tom seeks to build a present and a future based on his vision. Yet he will have to implement this vision cautiously to avoid relapses, because salvation means an end to ice-cream headaches.

The patterns of growth established in these works continue with little variation throughout later works. Spiritually educated characters nearly always replace their pride with selfless compassion, their self-righteousness with sensitivity, their desire for others with an acknowledgment of their isolation, and their longing to change the world with a recognition of the necessary roles of apparent injustice and agony. In addition, they nearly always shed their strongest illusions and frequently go off by themselves. In spite of their sympathy with the plight of others, they realize that they cannot help people because everyone must be permitted to grow through suffering, at least in their present stage of evolution. *Whistle* suggests that those at the level of the leaders, lords, masters, and teachers in the world of bodyless spirits may be pulling all our strings.

Notable modifications in Jones's beliefs occur in *Go to the Widow-Maker* and *The Merry Month of May*, however. In the former, Ron Grant's growth toward compassion and selflessness involves consciously suppressing his worries about his wife's fidelity and falsely informing her that he is convinced of her innocence. Considering Jones's stress on self-honesty in his earlier books, this is a striking change. Moreover, this altered attitude concerning honesty is reiterated in *The Merry Month of May* when Jack Hartley tries to decide whether Hill Gallagher will be helped more by the truth about the affair between Hill's father and Hill's lover or by a lie that will give him time to adjust to an unpleasant situation. Even in these novels, though, Jones is not dismissing the value of honesty but rather questioning its worth as an absolute value.

The other modification worth noting in *Go to the Widow-Maker* is Ron and Lucky Grant's achievement of a single, subjective viewpoint; instead of separating like Warden and Karen Holmes or Dave Hirsh and Gwen French, they go off together at the novel's end after having formed a single unit separated from all other individuals. Except for the special limited case of the two women in "Sunday Allergy," no other couple arrives at a single viewpoint in the rest of Jones's fiction.

The chief modification introduced by *The Merry Month of May* concerns responsibility. Although Jack Hartley also discovers that he cannot be responsible for others, he also learns that humans can help each other in small ways. For example, he is touched by a brief spiritual contact with Ferenc Hofmann-Beck following Louisa Gallagher's suicide attempt, even though Ferenc offers no practical assistance. Jack is similarly impressed by the compassionate activities of the French doctor who tries to save her, even though he suspects the doctor's actions are futile. Thus, the novel suggests that people concerned about their responsibilities to others are functioning on a higher spiritual level than those concerned only about themselves, even though such responsibility is rightly doomed to failure.

A final problem relating to growth concerns the question of gender stereotypes, suggested by Maggio's and Richard Mast's desire to be cowboys, Edward Dylan's resemblance to Wyatt Earp, and Karen Holmes's wish to live traditionally as wife, mother, and homemaker. Mast and Karen are among Jones's characters who come to realize, to varying degrees, that the popular images of manhood and womanhood are hindrances to their growth rather than guidelines for it.

4

Bravery and the Circle of the Sexes

Viet Journal, Jones's personalized coverage of the final period of the American military presence in Vietnam after the peace accords were signed in 1973, describes his encounter with an old beggar woman who had been stripped of all defenses and could no longer save herself—or be saved—from the wretched conditions of her life. Contending that she had not been helped at all by the United States, the French, the South Vietnamese, the North Vietnamese, or the Viet Cong, he observes that "what any of them or all of them might do for future generations would not do her any good at all," and that "she was all of Vietnam to me" (253).

Instead of blaming her situation on a particular country or political ploy, he saw in it a universal masculine failing: the "fifth grader" mentality that goads a man to test himself in dangerous situations and assert superiority through bouts of competition. The childishness of such motivation is manifest in the scene introducing the metaphor: North and South Vietnamese strive to outdo each other in raising their flags, and the American colonel comments that "somebody has said that Vietnam is the biggest fifth grade in the world" (101). The destructiveness of such motivation is shown in Jones's observation on the fighting at Quang Tri: "I could not imagine any soldier wanting to stay in a place like that and fight for it. But both sides did. Stubborn fifth-graders" (102). Moreover, after describing his delight in the "high-making, hilarity-inducing condition" of going dangerously low in a helicopter, Jones admits to being vulnerable to the impulse to do so: "What a weird race we were. There was some of the fifth-grader in all of us" (103-4). It is the same vulnerability analyzed in chapter 3 in connection with his mixed feelings about cowboys.

Jones similarly acknowledges his eagerness to be exposed to the dangers of Dak Pek, fifty miles behind enemy lines and open to attack—an ideal masculine testing ground. Once again confessing how much of the fifth-grader remained in him, Jones notes that there is "an odd conspiratorial physiological alliance between fear and the sense of sex" (219), and that "if all the factors were right, fear could be terribly exciting. So exciting you could get hooked on it like a drug. And want to do it again. Like sex" (218).

Later, Jones adds another focusing device to the fifth-grade metaphor: a simian figure that "visited" him on the night before he went to Dak Pek and at other key moments. Even though he is unwilling to pin down the meaning of the figure, preferring it to have a more resounding complexity and impact, Jones connects the ridiculous, apelike creature with man's incessant pursuit of danger. Moreover, he ties the figure to his fifth-grader impulses when he asks himself, "Could he be a symbol of the race, and our needs for fury and danger and fear and their excitements? Maybe he was a mirror image of myself? Myself before I shaved all over and put on airs and clothes, and pretended to be different? Maybe it was him I was trying to encounter face to face when I went to Dak Pek and Tri Ton" (221).

The figure may also be linked to Jones's attacks of guilt over "the backwardness of humanity. Of the cruelty, the indifference, the Kantian solipsism humanity mostly consisted of. It made a terrible despair" (140-41). Certainly, the simian figure suggests the theory of evolution that Robert Ardrey develops in *African Genesis*, with its emphasis on humanity's development from apes who learned how to use weapons to kill, their murderous impulses being essential to the expansion of their mental capacities. Frank MacShane reports that Ardrey's work "appealed to Jones because of his unsentimental willingness to face facts," which included an agonizingly balanced awareness of the continuing presence and need for "the killing instinct to preserve society" (*Into Eternity* 260). Jones was also aware that failure to modify the killing instinct could lead to nuclear holocaust. He was surely attracted to Ardrey's work because of Ardrey's contention that while "weapons have proliferated and the predatory instinct has become more deadly, . . . 'Our capacity for sacrifice, for sympathy, for trust have evolved just as surely as the flatness of our feet, the muscularity of our buttocks, and the enlargement of our brains' in the long conflict between primates and animals that began in the savannahs of Africa" (*Into Eternity* 261).

Ardrey's detailed image of humanity as inextricably apelike and evolving was well suited to Jones's painstakingly developed perspective, a viewpoint that went back as far as his first story, "The Temper of Steel" (1947). The simian figure, which surely haunted Ardrey when he was writing *African Genesis*, might well have influenced Jones while he was composing his early work. In "The Temper of Steel," Jones links a modern soldier's willingness to save his own life by means of the utmost brutality toward others with the primitive selfishness of killer apes, although, paradoxically, this brutishness may lead to its own surpassing through inducing guilt.

Jones points out in a note at the end of "The Temper of Steel" that his guiding conception was the absence of chivalry in modern warfare. As his protagonist Johnny asserts, the reason the revulsion at the mechanical havoc of twentieth-century warfare expressed in *All Quiet on the Western Front* appears so dated is that the form of grinding, mass-oriented fighting Erich Maria Remarque had found new and appalling was commonplace by the time Johnny entered the army. Beneath Johnny's seeming lack of emotion, however, he is disturbed by the death he inflicts. Even though his hand seems to act on its own, "cunning as animals are cunning" (Jones, "The Temper of Steel" 8), killing becomes a memory he would like to thrust out of his mind and cannot. He disapproves of killing as much as Paul does in Remarque's novel, differing only from Paul in refusing to face his feelings until the memory of the act returns "as a gas-filled corpse rises to the surface of the sea" (6).

The continuity in Jones's attitudes toward he-man masculinity, bravery, and the simian figure slyly hiding within humanity indicates an important element of the unsevered golden thread running throughout his work, inseparably united to which is his attitude toward ultrafemininity and the refusal of responsibility. From the beginning of his career, Jones opposed stereotyping men as strong, silent, cool, aggressive, logical, cunning, tough, and efficient and women as passive, dependent, emotional, vain, virtuous, homemaking, instinctive, and concerned about appearance. As Jones saw it, this polarized set of popular images was rooted in the animal level, tended to form men into callous egotists and women into childish parasites, and dangerously inhibited the spiritual development of both sexes. Moreover, when men strive to abolish all their "womanish" qualities and women seek to destroy their "mannish" traits, they not only wreck their basis for communication with members of the opposite sex but also lose contact with a significant part of themselves. Even more disturbing, seeking to get rid of unwanted personality traits paradoxically results in their reappearance in other forms.

In contrast, Jones's concept of individual salvation and growth emphasizes a movement toward recognition of the mutual spiritual goals of men and women and toward a broader, more sensitive view of the multitude of possible combinations of inherent personality traits. His views were in keeping with the ancient Chinese symbol of the yin-yang described by Johnny Carter in "They Shall Inherit the Laughter," a circle divided between the masculine principle (yang) and the feminine principle (yin). In the yang is a spot of yin and in the yin is a spot of yang. The presence of the spots is intended to show that yin and the yang are neither totally different nor totally separate from each other. Only within the circle containing both can true wholeness or oneness be found. Moreover, the role of sexuality in *Go to the Widow-Maker* in aiding the mutual growth of Ron Grant and Lucky Videndi and enabling them to achieve a common subjective viewpoint suggests that perhaps Jones believed in the power of sexual mystical experience to transcend apparent dualism, as in the Hindu sexual mysticism Benjamin Walker has described: "The supreme bliss that proceeds from ritual sexuality is believed to be the height of religious experience. In this state of non-duality all differences vanish, and everything, high and low, good and bad, ugly and beautiful is held to be the same. It is while in this pose that the couple apprehend the mystery of the whole cosmic process and taste the transcendent bliss of divine experience" (*The Hindu World* 393).

What a leap—from the brutality of dividing war to the bliss of unifying sex. Yet Jones, who made a determined effort to eschew dualism throughout his writing (an effort that is another reflection of his American literary Orientalism), fully acknowledges the fundamental and inescapable parts both war and sex play in spiritual evolution.

Jones's fourth novel, *The Thin Red Line*, devastatingly comments on the "toughness" of men in combat who fail to acknowledge the wholeness of the masculine and the feminine within the circle of yin and yang yet remain subject to it anyway. For example, the names of several major characters— Big Un Cash, Big Queen, Geoffrey Fife, Don Doll, "Carrie" Arbre, "Milly" Beck, and Bugger Stein—demonstrate the pretentiousness and absurdity of the pursuit of he-man masculinity, as well as their doubts about whether they possess even "normal" manhood. By seeking to immerse themselves in maleness, the men commit toughminded acts that reflect their primitive consciousness. Fife asserts his new status of combat-tested veteran, for example, by pulling the beard of a Japanese corpse and fistfighting. In Jones's view, such acts are more representative of the simian figure within than of manliness, and they indicate the arrogance and callous folly of those who perform them. Humanity's evolution beyond apehood moves in the opposite direction, confessing frailty and lack of importance to others.

Although *The Thin Red Line* can be readily understood on its basic levels, where critiques of he-man masculinity and war are powerful and clear, it is built around a philosophy that Jones no longer mentioned directly and that cannot be reconstructed from the information he provided. This means that, as in *The Pistol* before it and all the other works of fiction after it, readers are forced to go outside *The Thin Red Line* to understand it fully. For example, those acquainted with the views on reincarnation Jones's spokespersons spell out in *From Here to Eternity* and *Some Came Running* will detect a reference to them when Fife remarks that if there is an afterlife it is not "like all the churches say" (480). Yet unacquainted readers could not have inferred these beliefs from that statement, which is the only semi-explicit reference to reincarnation in the book. Similarly, although unacquainted readers may note that Stein, Fife, Maynard Storm, and several other characters become humbled by their experiences, lose many of their illusions, and go off by themselves, they would be unlikely to surmise that such actions form part of a process of spiritual evolution.

Yet those acquainted with the rest of Jones's work can probe the highest level of *The Thin Red Line* without great difficulty by applying what they have learned from an attentive study of his first two published novels and seeing where *The Thin Red Line* fits and where new directions have been taken. Jones's earlier writing offers the explanations necessary to work out an interpretation of the novel as a whole. The plotting and characterizations remain largely founded on the set of beliefs described in *From Here to Eternity* and *Some Came Running*, although Jones developed a new approach to group experience and responded to death with greater intensity in *The Thin Red Line*. Once that fact is established and due allowance for it made, the novel can be analyzed on its own terms.

Because Jones had already discussed his philosophy at length on two occasions, why would he describe it again in book after book even when modifying it? Moreover, by abandoning his attempt to present his reincarnationist beliefs directly, Jones attained greater artistic scope in relation to characters and subject; he no longer had to provide an all-knowing spokesperson or devise plots that would depict every facet of his beliefs. By narrowing his themes he could often achieve sharper focus and tighter organization yet still hint at the larger ideas relegated to the background of his work. All in all, he gained more than he lost by deciding to stop discussing his system.

One of Jones's outstanding accomplishments in *The Thin Red Line* is a tightly knit organization based on the closeness and experiential commonality of men in an army combat unit that provides, like any community, multiple possibilities for divergences in spiritual growth and formation of individual karmic bonds. In *WW II: A Chronicle of Soldiering*, a personalized history of the war, Jones notes that the campaign for Guadalcanal described in *The Thin Red Line* was, as "the first American offensive anywhere," fought "when the numbers and materiel engaged were smaller, less trained and less organized," so "there was an air of adventure and sense of individual exploit about it . . . where small units of platoon and company strength still maintained importance" (49). Knowing from his combat experiences at Guadalcanal how much unity existed in the companies, he often treated his fictional (or perhaps semifictional) Charlie Company as a character, even though he never forgot that it was composed of individuals. As Terry Southern has observed, Jones's much maligned use of language was one of his most effective tools in achieving this sense of the collective character of the company:

> There is behind the work a new kind of narrative, it is the "omniscient author" taken toward a logical extreme, where the narration itself, although faceless, without personality, expresses feelings, both of individuals and collectively, in their own terms. . . . Narration which uses four-letter idiom traditionally requires that the narrator emerge as a personality. Jones has ignored this requirement and has given the purely textual part of his work a tone which is in perfect harmony with each incident and character it describes. ("Recent Fiction" 331)

Having established the intertwining of the collective company and the individuals in it through this experimental narrative technique, Jones deliberately alternates between intense occasions when all men in the company react alike (the aerial bombings) and those in which they respond differently (the dangerous run under enemy gunfire, when John Bell concentrates on getting across safely while Charlie Dale is concerned more with showing off his fearlessness and gaining his superiors' attention).

Another of Jones's achievements in *The Thin Red Line* is his ability to maintain reader interest in a set of consciously deglamorized characters. Although he provides as much action as he did in *From Here to Eternity*, the new novel lacks the romantic aura he had placed around characters such as Warden and Prewitt and, paradoxically, describes heroics performed by antiheroes, another reflection of his mixed attitude toward bravery. Bead, for example, has a hysterical victory over the Japanese soldier who attacks him while he defecates, an objectification of Jones's most traumatic personal war experience. The fight excites readers and concerns them for Bead's safety, yet they recognize the ludicrousness of the circumstances and Bead's viciousness in killing his enemy. Even though the incident satisfies a thirst for adventure in fiction, it also compels a complex, unidealized view of the victor.

Jones's decision to give this personal experience to Bead rather than Geoffrey Fife (the character most closely modeled on himself) indicates again his concern with balancing group and individual experience. In a letter to Scribner's editor Burroughs Mitchell on December 2, 1959, he explained that he made the shift from Fife to Bead because "a friend here who read the manuscript made the complimentary comment that Fife is emerging as a fine major character," and he did not "want this" (Hendrick, ed., *To Reach Eternity* 288). Jones permitted no star performers in *The Thin Red Line*, although many characters are fascinating and some speak for Jones on certain ideas.

To a large extent, *The Thin Red Line* seems the fulfillment of Dave Hirsh's concept in *Some Came Running* of a comic combat novel as one "in which *death*, and *mutilation* and *war itself* are comic; instead of horrible" (290, emphasis in the original), and in which men at war are shown to be guided by the same vain, petty, malicious, grasping, narrow-minded motives that dominate their actions in civilian life so the human race will be forced "to take an unvarnished unsugarcoated look at itself for a change" (145). In addition, it uses the same general form that Dave had employed of following "a typical infantry company" of "typical green men" who are "as well trained as any men can be who have never been in combat" from the onset of a campaign to its conclusion (649). *The Thin Red Line* comes close enough to compel comparison with Dave's projected book, although it does not adhere strictly to Dave's outline: It is set on Guadalcanal rather than in Europe, excludes several scenes Dave envisioned, and adds others that challenge or modify his conception.

The heart of Dave's book, and much of *The Thin Red Line*, is the view of death as comic; like the classic pratfall, it deflates the human ego. Dave's theory was that previous writers on modern warfare had emphasized the "horrible horrible horrors of war . . . because their egos could not support this hated indignity of personal death, any kind of death, which they feared they might have to suffer and were so vain they could not stand the thought of" (Jones, *Some Came Running* 145). Furthermore, he had argued, "If you could divorce yourself from imagining it was you, there was nothing funnier in the world than the way a man whos been shot tumbles loosely and falls down. Unless its watching someone slip on a banana peel and break their arm" (145). The Three Stooges-quality of death that Dave describes is the reason "Bell had felt laughter burbling up in his chest" when Kline had fallen with a startled look on his face (*The Thin Red Line* 189-90), and Stein can not "help laughing" at the movement of the "widened eyes" of a surrendering Japanese soldier "slowly crossing themselves in despair as they focused on the advancing muzzle" of Big Queen's rifle, which Queen then fires in the soldier's face (317).

The classical epic-tragic view of warfare asserts that each man's death in combat (or at least each hero's death) is meaningful and noble, thus enshrining the ego of the individual dead man and of humanity. The Jonesian comic view, however, generally depicts men's deaths as pointless, stupid, absurd, and laughable to shatter their illusions about the world and their own importance to it. At the same time, this comic view takes issue with the modern tragic-comic attitude that similarly rejects the epic-tragic conception. Whereas the modern attitude regards an individual's death in combat as truly meaningless and cries out against it (as did Jones in moments of doubt or amid sorrowful, tormenting memories), the Jonesian comic view paradoxically asserts it to be a meaningful part of the spiritual evolution process.

Jones's comic view also valiantly struggles to maintain an attitude of acceptance and compassionate understanding that might even be exemplified by the dead themselves, as shown by the look of "vastly wise and tolerant amusement" on the face of the myopic Greco-Turkish draftee Kral, who had not realized until he was shot that the profession of first scout for which he had volunteered is "a thing of the past and belonged in the Indian Wars, not to the massed divisions, superior firepower, and tighter social control of today" (187). Kral also provides a link between that attitude toward death and Jones's theory of reincarnation through Bell's impression that the more he stares into the eyes of Kral's corpse "the more he felt them to be holes into the center of the universe and that he might fall in through them to go drifting down through starry space amongst galaxies and spiral nebulae and island universes" (187). Although Bell is not ready for the message Kral's eyes reveal and is terror-stricken by his waggish look when Bell tries to tell himself "HERE LIES FOUR-EYES KRAL, DIED FOR SOMETHING" (188), it is a lesson he will eventually learn from experience.

Between the conception of the comic combat novel developed through Dave Hirsh and the writing of a similar work in *The Thin Red Line*, Jones added intense new dimensions of sorrow, outrage, and empathy to his work, possibly from the doubts that always accompanied his reincarnationist beliefs or the agony of reliving the experiences recounted and partially transformed. These dimensions did not destroy or even seriously defy his overall comic conception, which was always inextricably grubby and glorious (in its reincarnationist hope), but they demonstrated the darker aspects of it—the black yin that accompanies the white yang—as Jones would later do in *Whistle*.

Frank MacShane records how Jones "had to relive the fears and terrors he had experienced in the army in order to get them down on paper" and would sometimes "break down and weep while he was writing" (*Into Eternity* 200). He also observes that writing the novel led Jones "to a new awareness of what war does to people," prompting him to assert that "the dead, frozen like flies in plastic, realized—at the moment of death when of course they stopped—that humanity must grow to feeling, to empathy, or become extinct" (200). Significantly, when Jones describes a death scene he had witnessed in which a soldier hit in the throat "cried out, 'Oh, my God!' in an awful, grimly comic, burbling kind of voice that made me think of the signature of the old Shep Fields' Rippling Rhythm band," he ended with the comment, "I felt like crying" (*WW II* 52). Grimness and pain overshadows all traces of comedy and proclaims the need for all humanity to feel the empathy that Jones could never personally evade. But this much needed humaneness is always included in what he meant by compassionate understanding, and his "comedy" is just another device for evoking it.

The death scene in *The Thin Red Line* that refuses to allow readers to distance themselves is Eddie Bead's. When Bead realizes how badly he has been hit, he cries out in amazed agony, and Captain Stein, who had wanted to believe in his ability to care for his men, turns away, "feeling like an old, old, useless man" (251). Fife, who had accepted without difficulty the deaths of Tella and Jacques, finds he is stunned that Bead is dying and uses Bead's first name in talking to him, "something he had never done before" (251). While Bead dies, Fife, at Bead's request, holds his hand and even cradles him; afterward, he crawls "away by himself, weeping in terror, weeping in fear, weeping in sadness, hating himself" (251).

Even in Bead's death scene, though, there is a sorrowfully comic element in the selfishness and pettiness briefly yet tellingly exposed by Fife's hesitation to take Bead's hand out of fear of being labeled a homosexual, even though—or perhaps because—"the act of hesitation was far below the level of conscious thought" (251). Fife hesitates not simply out of concern for what others might think, but because he and Bead have actually committed an act that could be considered homosexual. In a December 2, 1959, letter to Burroughs Mitchell, Jones discussed why he had added a sentence to explain the act Bead and Fife had performed: "I think it very important, because . . . it was unclear to almost everyone whether Fife and Bead were committing pederasty or fellatio. I think this a very important point because if they're having fellatio it places Fife in as equally guilty a position in his own mind as Bead. If, however, it were pederasty Fife could escape guilt by rationalizing to himself that he was committing only a male action" (Hendrick, ed., *To Reach Eternity* 288).

Bead's comment—"I'll do it to you if you'll do it to me" (Jones, *The Thin Red Line* 122)—indicates that whatever they do is mutual, which is why Fife has to struggle with his sense of guilt before physically displaying his concern for Bead. Thus, it is a sign of Fife's spiritual growth that he is able to do so, especially because one of the purposes of a karmic relationship such as this is to help one or both persons move beyond their narrow concerns to a larger perspective—and empathy. In a moment of brutally painful illumination Fife comes to see that he is crying "more because he suddenly realized that he was the only man in the whole company whom Bead could call friend, than because Bead was dying" (251). Ironically—and comically—Fife is wounded only five minutes after he has had this feeling.

Coupled with the grimly and agonizingly comic view of death, a view that can make readers simultaneously weep and laugh at humanity's folly, is the comic view of mutilation and war. Because mutilation and warfare have great potential for lowering men's pride as well as for tormenting them to make them grow, they can be seen as horrifying, helpful, howlers in the same terms as death and also comic in the spectacle they offer of men pursuing trivial, self-centered concerns under extreme conditions. Big Queen, for example, wants to maintain the image of a powerful, cowboy-heroic male when he is forced to pull a corpse from the mucky ooze and take the lead through a jungle where he constantly fears snakes. And Doll considers committing sodomy after accidentally lodging in Arbre's buttocks while the attack is underway. Even the cynically wise Eddie Welsh can be caught up in an absurd enterprise such as trying to stop Tella from screaming because he feels doing so is not "dignified" (241). The most revealing action, however, is Dale collecting the gold teeth of dead Japanese soldiers, a collection that confirms Welsh's observation that war is fought for the sake of property.

In the part of *WW II* entitled "Green and Obscene," Jones remarks that the experienced soldier "was about the foulest-mouthed individual who ever existed on earth. Every other word was fucking this or fucking that. And internally, his soul was about as foul and cynical as his mouth" (70). Greedy, small-minded, and frequently bestial, these men are supposedly the bravest of the brave and in fact do perform extraordinary feats in the most dangerous circumstances, but bravery, too, must be regarded as comic in the midst of war.

In an essay on "Phony War Films," Jones argues that the "really superior combat soldier" is the man who has "become an Animal, a vicious, cruel, shrewdly functioning Animal who saves the outfit time and again"

(*WW II* 67), and certainly that is true of the most courageous, capable soldier in *The Thin Red Line*, the ambitious Charlie Dale. Although he initially fears combat, Dale is sheltered not only by the combat numbness that affects everyone but also by his wall of selfishness. He can walk through a field of fire without worrying because he does not believe anything can hurt him. He is more concerned with making a good impression on the officer-in-charge, getting out of the kitchen, and moving up in rank. In addition, he finds it easy to kill Japanese because he cannot empathize with them. It is not surprising that Dale is outwardly successful; those with the strongest egos have the best chance of thriving materially in either peace or war.

An even better example of the Ardreyan, killer-apelike callousness that constitutes much of the bravery in warfare is demonstrated by the personal vendetta Big Un Cash conducts against the Japanese. Cash sees all Japanese as evil because some Japanese soldiers tortured and killed two American prisoners, and he becomes so enraged by the incident that he kills two prisoners by cracking their heads together. Moreover, he has no sense of personal danger when confronting the Japanese; all he considers is the chance the confrontation gives him to slaughter evil creatures. (In *Go to the Widow-Maker*, Al Bonham, a modern Captain Ahab, experiences the same exhilarating recklessness when destroying sharks.) Not surprisingly, Cash regards himself as an Old West hero, complete with shotgun. His dying request that his wife be told he died "manly" reveals not only his self-image but also how little he has learned. His death wound has come from a "light Nambu" fired by a suicidal, starving Japanese who might have hit someone else; Cash was merely the biggest target and way out in front (434).

Other examples of bravery in battle stem from the soldiers' fears and would not be considered heroic if the motive were known. For example, Bead's response to the enemy soldier in the woods is hysterical, triggered not only by fear but also by embarrassment at being seen while having a bowel movement. It is therefore appropriate that the guilt he feels after killing the soldier resembles that he experienced when his "mother had caught and whipped him for masturbating" (168). Similarly, Don Doll's feat of charging a Japanese emplacement is provoked by his feeling of being unable to endure a stressful situation any longer, and he even cries "Mother! Mother!" as he runs toward the enemy he does not want to encounter (272). Afterward, he, too, feels ashamed of what he has done, but his shame lasts only until others begin to praise him.

It is surely no accident that both Bead and Doll think of their mothers in connection with these incidents. Near the beginning of *WW II*, Jones notes the "sea change" that occurs in American women when they become wives and mothers, causing them to lose interest in sex and be claimed by "all sorts of virtues" that have become part of the popular image of motherhood. He wonders whether young men who joined the army "joyously" soon after Pearl Harbor did so because it gave them a reason to "get away from homes filled with mothers and/or wives" (30). Over and over in his stories, Jones emphasizes the roles such "virtuous" mothers play in instilling masochism in their sons, and he points up the role of masochism underlying bravery in *WW II*, although without specifically linking it to motherhood: "There had to be something somewhere in all of them, in all of us, that loved it. Some dark, aggressive, masochistic side of us, racial perhaps, that makes us want to spray our blood in the air . . . for some damned misbegotten ideal or other" (42).

The one thing that offers all soldiers a chance to be brave and vicious is combat numbness, which operates in the same fashion as the curtain in Dawn Hirsh's mind that separates part of her personality in *Some Came Running* and safeguards against unpleasant realities. While combat numbness lasts, it seals off the sensitive, fearful, vulnerable side of each man's character, allowing the brutal, selfish, survival-at-any-cost side to function. Combat numbness is the thin red line that marks as well as makes the difference between sanity and madness, heroes and learners, and involution and evolution. Jones describes it as being "composed of equal parts of sheer physical fatigue, insupportable fear, and a sort of massive strained disbelief at what was happening" (*WW II* 198) and discusses it as part of the final stage of the "evolution of a soldier," the goal of which is "the soldier's final full acceptance of the fact that his name is already written down in the rolls of the already dead" (54). The chief danger of combat numbness is its effect on men's characters, because it reduces men to the animal level and places or keeps them at the starting point of spiritual growth. Only when combat numbness wears off are men free to experience pain again and resume their development. Yet despite the handicap that combat numbness places on them, many characters in *The Thin Red Line* do grow spiritually as a result of combat experience. Because their growth comes in a variety of ways and takes a variety of forms, each gains a different perspective on war, yet growth always involves a movement away from "masculine" hardness, savagery, and aggressiveness.

The first character who steps beyond the animal level is Capt. James Stein. Because he had wanted to emulate his idealized image of his father, a major in World War I, his recognition of the image's falsity marks a profound change. Although he had been led to regard military command as a noble endeavor, experience makes him see that his beliefs about himself, his father, and war are illusions. In the first experience, when Private Jacques is wounded right in front of him, Stein is disturbed because he is confronted not only with the cruelty of war but also with a contradiction of his self-image of being a benevolent leader. Having deemed himself a protective father to his men, he is compelled to realize what he has brought them to face.

Stein is also shocked when Fife is hit a short distance away from him. The incident makes him aware of the enormous role chance plays in warfare—Jones notes that experienced soldiers learn that "danger only existed at the exact place and moment of danger, and not before and not after" (*WW II* 70)—and the consequent futility of logic and tactics. The lesson is reinforced soon afterward when chance mocks the wisdom of one of his decisions by altering the circumstances on which it is based. Stein may be correct in proposing that a reconnaissance be made on the right, where an attack might preserve many lives that would be lost through a direct attack, if, as he assumes, the Japanese force is reduced there. The unexpected advance of Milly Beck's men, however, leaves Stein without an argument when Colonel Tall, whose decision to descend from the command post Stein also fails to anticipate, arrives to take over. Although the success of his patrol the next day appears to confirm Stein's judgment, he can never be sure whether the Japanese had maintained only a small, weak force on the right when he suggested the patrol or whether they had waited until that night to move a larger force from there, just as he can never be sure whether his decision was motivated by concern for his men or fear for his life.

Jones's answer to the question "Is History Written by the Upper Classes for the Upper Classes?" is, "It would seem that it is" (*WW II* 70). He argues that the upper classes "have a high sense of personal honor and moral integrity the lower classes simply do not have, perhaps because the poor cannot afford them" (70). This inequality leads toward mutual incomprehension between the classes that is reflected in the differing attitudes of officers, usually drawn from the upper classes as Stein is, and the lower ranks. The conflict is shown in the histories of military campaigns, because "the private remembers it from the viewpoint of his lower class ideals, or lack of them, while the historian has written it from the viewpoint of the upper-class commanders and their totally different ideals" (71). The officers' view stresses the role of the strategy and tactics of commanders, but soldiers who fight the battles see them in other terms. Significantly, the example Jones uses to support this contention is "a fight which was won pure and simple because two Pfcs who hated each other were bucking for the same stripes" (71), something all the men in the company know but their commander never learns—and military histories never record. The description fits the conflict between Don Doll and Charlie Dale and their similar role in achieving a victory, something Stein never learns although it has a major impact on his career.

The difference of viewpoint between classes is a karmic collision designed to bring about the loss of illusions and ego reduction of one or both groups. Stein's misjudgments stemming from his upper-class view of strategy (as well as his mistakes concerning his men, the battle, and Colonel Tall) have that effect on him. At the same time, his karma reflects the more general karma, not only between opposing yet interlinked classes but also between warring countries. As Blavatsky contends, "The aggregate of individual Karma becomes that of the nation to which those individuals belong, and further, . . . the sum total of National Karma is that of the World" (*The Key to Theosophy* 202). She also argues that those who are ignorant of karma view its ways as "Providence," "blind Fatalism," or "simple Chance" (*The Secret Doctrine* 147), whereas "those who believe in *Karma* have to believe in *Destiny*, which, from birth to death, every man is weaving thread by thread around himself" (146).

The final experience that clashes with Stein's image-picture of the world concerns his beloved men's slaughter of a small group of exhausted, ineffectual Japanese soldiers, several of whom are unarmed and attempting to surrender. The "victory" this slaughter brings appears bloodthirsty and chaotic to Stein rather than the shining, heroic spectacle his father had led him to expect. As a result of this last revelation, he is well on his way to being freed from his illusions when Tall announces that he is taking away Stein's command. Stein's sudden, weeping awareness that "he could no longer even dislike Tall" carries a half-stated corollary: "And if you couldn't dislike even Tall." It is evident that he has attained an understanding of the way all people, including Tall and himself, remain trapped by illusion until experience reveals their inadequacy (Jones, *The Thin Red Line* 327). His impulse to weep also signifies how far he has moved beyond the traditional image of the stalwart, shatterproof male.

The former officer John Bell also grows, although his development takes a different course from Stein's because his growth stems chiefly from his sexual problems. His special perceptions about combat relate to its sexual overtones, leading him to make observations similar to those Jones makes in *Viet Journal* about the erotic thrill of war. Although Bell's biggest flaw has been his dependence on his wife, Marty, an indication of the powerful karmic bond between them, that dependence is also the source of his sensitivity. A continual fear of losing her torments him and keeps him alert to the knowledge that comes through pain, even when he is under the influence of combat numbness. His sensitized sexual suffering, moreover, is what enables him to perceive how combat numbness turns soldiers into near-automatons guided by a distorted sexual excitement derived from the opportunity to penetrate the enemy through death.

Not surprisingly, Bell feels trapped by the modern state and the highly organized warfare that has taken him away from the genuine sexual excitement of contact with his wife. It is only when Marty writes him a "Dear John" letter that he resigns himself to his isolation and chooses to stay in the army; "he would probably do as little harm there as anywhere else" (Jones, *The Thin Red Line* 492). Even though the letter is the most distressing incident in Bell's life, he responds with sad comprehension of his wife's feelings (although he concedes that his belief that he has always understood her may be an illusion) rather than a wish to hurt her in a way the traditionally masculine Captain Bosche would have approved. The response reflects the considerable extent to which he has worked through his karmic bond with Marty, so that he probably will not have to meet her again in his next incarnation.

A third learner, Welsh, displays less compassion than either Stein or Bell do, but he also shows keener awareness of the absurdity of warfare and his role in it, an awareness that leads him to be nicknamed "Mad" and even approach the madness to which he will succumb in his next incarnation as Winch in *Whistle*. Welsh had started out with an advantage over Stein and Bell because he is able to guess what his combat experience will be like and even feels triumphant because everything turns out "exactly as he had expected and anticipated, thus leaving him with no real shock or trauma: men got killed mostly for statistical reasons, as he had anticipated: men fought well or badly like they would have fought for women or other Property, as he had expected" (375). Although Welsh rages as much as Fife at fighting for "property" that is meaningless to him, he knows he need not have joined the army, because he had predicted when the war would come. Moreover, his awareness of responsibility for his situation grants him a measure of sardonic aloofness that would have proved useful to Fife.

Welsh's major accomplishment, like that of his precursor, Warden, is to recognize that war is a childish game differing from cowboys and Indians only in the greater complexity of the army machinery operating it. He also shares Warden's conviction of being able to maintain integrity within this organized madness by playing countergames, the rules of which he invents and adheres to rigidly. Yet the toll on him to maintain this attitude is greater than it was for Warden because he is under greater pressure. Although Welsh outwardly conforms enough to avoid friction with superiors, he inwardly goes his own way and, when he can, bends the army's rules in directions that please him most at the moment. Instead of distributing grenades like any other noncom, for example, he must toss them to his men like footballs to mock the rah-rah atmosphere of the approaching battle and make his mockery sly enough that the generals watching him will miss it and admire his spirit. Moreover, Welsh has secretly asserted his individuality by such acts as carrying gin in his canteens and imagining himself in a sixteenth-century bathtub when he is in a slit trench.

Without specifically linking it to the character, Jones spells out the dilemma of Warden-Welsh-Winch when he compares "the old-timer first sergeant" to "the Negro mammy slave who ran the master's big plantation house and family with a hand of iron, or the modern housewife who carefully rules her lord and master's life with dexterity from behind the scenes" (*WW II* 122). To gain power and some control over his life within a basic condition of servitude, the first sergeant "must work within the mass of anonymity to find his freedom of expression" and use "duplicity" and "camouflage" (122). Thus, his true self must always be covered up to be asserted, a Catch-22 type of situation equally well known to Ralph Ellison's invisible man. It is not surprising that such an oppressive condition keeps him on the verge of madness, although as Welsh the triple-incarnating character still handles the situation well.

Welsh recognizes that the reason he is in his country's army and at war "from choice, not necessity," in spite of his lack of respect for "home, family, country, flag, freedom, democracy," is that part of him "liked being shot at, liked being frightened, . . . liked shooting at strangers and seeing them fall hurt" (Jones, *The Thin Red Line* 410). The part of him that seeks out such experiences is related to the "penancemaking, selfdestructive thing in his nature which had made him go after Tella" and "would almost certainly make him liable to other such acts in the future" (375). It is also why Welsh jeers at Storm force-feeding atabrine pills to the men to prevent the malaria that might make it possible for them to be shipped out to safety and why Welsh conceals his own malaria and holds on to the disease as a possibly mad assertion of his individuality against military anonymity and to avoid being released from combat.

Paradoxically, although Welsh knows the educating value of pain and cunningly stays in the army as the most available source of it, he advises everyone else to seize any chance to get out and hopes that if he pursues combat numbness "long enough and often enough, it might really become a permanent and mercifully blissful state" (495). The peace that Welsh seeks, however, is not a mind-drugging flight from reality but rather that which comes at the end of the educational process, when he will have learned all that experience can teach him and is ready to move on to a higher spiritual state where pain is no longer necessary. Although he may be wrong in his calculations and may be approaching the thin red line between sanity and madness, he has already learned enough to make accurate predictions about many (although not all) of the experiences facing him and follow the surest path for salvation. Moreover, if Welsh's calculations should be right, then the thin red line is the thinnest of all because even combat numbness could lead to spiritual evolution, which is the only meaningful form of sanity or manhood.

The novel's most equivocal figure is Witt, clearly the descendent of Prewitt (as Welsh is of Warden). Witt has ample opportunity to observe the absurdity of his romantic notions of the role of individual skill and Wild West heroism in battle, but it is doubtful whether he ever examines or casts off his illusions. He is too fond of his image as a Davy Crockett-like savior who single-handedly rescues friends except when officers issue such foolhardy orders that it becomes impossible for anyone to prevent disaster. Unfortunately, his officers seem prone to such orders, and Witt seldom has a chance to save anyone. The Ding-Dong Trail roadblock massacre should have opened his eyes because he was unable to help others and could barely save himself. Yet Witt finds it convenient to protest against the officer who ordered the roadblock in the same way he has protested against so many officers in the past. He must protest against circumstances, superiors, and the nature of the universe to avoid recognizing his own inadequacies.

Nevertheless, Witt's freedom of movement and ability to assert his individuality provide a balance to John Bell's vision of himself and the others as automatons, and the juxtaposition of Witt's and Bell's opposing pictures of reality implies a subjective element in each. Although Bell's picture fits in better than Witt's with the description of how fellow soldiers behave under the influence of combat numbness, it fails to take into consideration the varying responses of the men in his company concerning what happens to them on the battlefield and what they do while experiencing combat numbness. Moreover, it ignores the contrasting ways in which their characters develop after battle. Thus, even though Bell's viewpoint reveals a major truth about combat, his is not the only truth. Appropriately, *The Thin Red Line* ends with the statement that "one day one of their number would write a book about all this, but none of them would believe it because none of them would remember it that way" (495).

There are moments in *The Thin Red Line* when an experience is strong enough to affect everyone in the same way and it becomes possible to talk about a group vision. Yet most of the time each character is bound inside an individual subjective world that must inevitably conflict with those of the other soldiers. As always, the purpose of such karmic conflicts is to disturb the illusions of one or both of the colliding consciousnesses. George Band's illusions of the respect inspired by his leadership and the joyous camaraderie of men in battle, for example, are shaken by Private Mazzi, who is more concerned about his friend Till's observation of Mazzi's subjective terror during the attack on Boola-Boola Village than about the faults Mazzi is denouncing in Band. Similarly, both Doll and Arbre are upset by the discovery that each considers the other a homosexual, although each regards his own readiness to perform certain homoerotic acts as normal. Other examples of such confrontations are Fife's assertion of educational superiority at a time when Witt is wrapped in self-pity over a self-exile from Charlie Company; Doll's attempt to assume "paternal responsibility" for Fife by offering him a position in his squad only to feel conned when Fife gratefully accepts the offer; and Bosche's reluctance to live up to his announced willingness to back his men when Beck, speaking for all of them, asks him to protest the division commander's order to remove their beards.

As was the case in *Some Came Running*, all of these clashes between subjective worlds create karmic bonds that will probably have to be worked out in future lives. Yet they all further the movement across the thin red line from involution to evolution and prove that even modern warfare cannot damage human character enough to halt this progression. The presence of a man eating an apple at the end of the novel therefore suggests not only the loss of innocence Paulette Michel-Michot has emphasized but also the fortunate fall in which man's separation from God is merely the starting point for a gradual development and reabsorption into God. Nevertheless, the men who will cross that thin red line are not the proud, brave, supermasculine animals who fight wars but the sensitive humans who emerge from the suffering of combat.

Although Jones recalled that his early story "Greater Love," published in the same year as *From Here to Eternity*, was his "first real attempt at writing seriously about combat" (*The Ice-Cream Headache and Other Stories* xiii), his viewpoint in the story was similar the one he developed in *The Thin Red Line* and carried over into *Viet Journal:* Combat deaths are howlingly "comic," and the simian bravery of emotional fifth-graders (Prewitt envisioned schoolboys compelled to attend to their daily lessons whether they want to or not) reeks of Ardreyan irony.

In "Greater Love," Quentin Thatcher, like his fellow clerk Geoffrey Fife, starts out identifying manhood with the usual combination of courage and callousness only to wind up mocking the supposed nobility in that mixture. On one level, the story's title—"Greater Love"—is ironic because the stronger form of love that Thatcher manifests is not for his brother Shelby but for himself and the act of killing necessary to ensure his survival. Despite Thatcher's assertions that he longs to go into battle with Shelby to protect him, in actual combat he walks unobservingly past his brother's body. Moments before entering combat, he had witnessed two soldiers who reminded him of marionettes; marching up the hill as they did, he resembles one, too.

Flaunting his masculine pride at having killed a Japanese, Thatcher places the dead soldier's bridgework between his helmet and liner and strikes a pose as the "immortal infantryman" (Jones, "Greater Love" 139). He also reveals his inhumanity in this moment by an absence of emotion at a photograph of the dead man's wife and baby. His only concerns are to induce the first sergeant to admit that clerks—Thatcher is a clerk—can make rugged, macho soldiers and to berate his brother, whose death he has yet to comprehend, for not displaying aggressiveness like his.

The concept of death in "Greater Love" is the same as in the lyrics of "Don't Monkey around with Death," the painfully comic song John Bell composes in *The Thin Red Line:* "Dont futz around with the Reaper, He will only make you smell" (74). The stench of the buried men whom Thatcher and his fellow soldiers dig up reminds them that their fate will also be comic rather than tragic. Although Al Zwerman seeks to give belated dignity to his brother's death by keeping comrades' hands, shovels, and eyes off his corpse, his attempt to protect his brother Vic's modesty proves to be a hollow victory because death ensures men's humbling.

As Jones observed in his introduction to the story, it is easy to spot the resemblance between the first sergeant and Warden and Welsh. Like Warden with Prewitt and Welsh with Fife, the first sergeant, realizing that Thatcher's idealism and protectiveness toward his brother may get him killed, is trying to teach him a lesson about living with injustice and admitting his own inconsequence to the running of the company, the universe, and his brother. This is clearly another master-disciple relationship, the object of which is to enable Thatcher to gain the knowledge and attitude he needs to cope with rapidly approaching combat experiences.

One reason the first sergeant changes his mind about letting Thatcher go on the graveyard detail with his brother is that he recognizes that it will compel Quentin to see the bestial products of combat. The simian figure will be slyly posing and preening behind the lack of nobility or individuality of the corpses. Although he has no way of knowing that Vic Zwermann's body will be there, the first sergeant wants Thatcher to become accustomed to such sights so he will not be dismayed and horrified when he encounters them in battle.

Later, the first sergeant approves of Quentin's faking stance in front of the dead Japanese soldier, an indication that Thatcher is beginning to share the sergeant's vision of combat as a game and has placed himself at an emotional distance from the slaying to continue functioning. Thatcher's reference to his fallen brother tells the sergeant that he has witnessed the worst of disasters and has kept going, which is why the sergeant tells him that he is doing fine. Thus, a further implication of the story's title is that greater love is shown in the first sergeant's effort to teach Thatcher how to take care of himself than in Thatcher's attempt to protect his brother. Yet the training the sergeant gives Thatcher is on a low level and based on the premise that a man must act selfishly and callously to live through combat. The first sergeant's advice nevertheless seems effective and reasonable, and life itself will take care of sensitizing Thatcher through the grief he will soon feel over the death of his brother and the misery he will experience each time his combat numbness wears away.

❖

Jones's fifth published novel, *Go to the Widow-Maker*, throws new light on the author's various earlier comments about bravery and manhood by placing them in the context of Lucky Videndi's theory of the circle of the sexes, a concept that has much in common with both the symbolic circle of yin and yang and the warning to initiates in *Light on the Path* to refrain from shunning the soiled garment flung on their shoulders. The idea of the circle of the sexes holds that when men seek to become super-masculine and eliminate everything womanly in themselves they take on more and more feminine traits. The same consequences hold true for women who try to be ultrafeminine and for men and women who deny their sexual identities. In *Some Came Running*, for example, Gwen French's efforts to avoid the feminine characteristics she despises cause her to acquire more than she had earlier.

Go to the Widow-Maker also stresses key resemblances between women and men. Even though Ron Grant strives hard to attain he-man aggressiveness, he has an equally strong desire to become a slave to a woman. Similarly, although Lucky Videndi emulates the passivity of an ultrafeminine woman, she has an urge to assert her independence and dominate the men who care for her. Both she and Grant must overcome penchants for risk-taking and excessive dependency before they can hope to build a lasting marriage; their union is only made possible by similarities in their characters and ideas.

Like most stories of requited love, *Go to the Widow-Maker* becomes sentimental at times, particularly because, as all biographies of Jones demonstrate, this roman à clef sticks close to the details of his meeting and marriage to Gloria Mosolino and the subsequent breakup of his fourteen-year relationship with Lowney Handy, during which "Lowney lunged at [Gloria] with a bowie knife" (MacShane, *Into Eternity* 156). Fortunately, the sentimentality appears primarily in the early part of the novel, where an exaggerated glow suffuses those scenes in which Grant (Jones) first meets Lucky (Gloria), notes that her friends adore her, and introduces her to his awestricken friends. She seems a little too charming, a little too perfect, and the early stage of their love seems overly glamorous and idealized. The atmosphere of these scenes is reminiscent of the Hollywood depiction of love in high society during the 1940s, and Grant's references to his desire for a Clark Gable-Carole Lombard relationship are somewhat forced.

Sentimentality disappears, however, once Grant and Lucky begin to fight. The conflicts between them are credible and compelling, and both emerge as complex, fascinating characters. Jones's overall concern with growth takes a more secular turn here, enabling him to accomplish something that only a few novelists have done well: detail the gradual development of a mature, durable love that by all accounts he found in his own marriage. He makes a probing, painfully revealing, psychological study of the lovers' slow but discernible movement toward acceptance of the responsibilities stemming from their love. As Jones points out through his narrative, mature love can only be attained after both partners detect and overcome a number of childish components in their personalities. The union of Grant and Lucky is believable in the end because of the harrowing steps each has taken in gaining self-awareness and adapting to the other.

As in *The Thin Red Line*, Jones displays considerable skill in structuring, and his subplots blend well with the main romantic plot derived from his own life. Readers are never permitted to lose sight of the developing relationship between Grant and Lucky; even when both of them are "off-stage," characters continue to discuss them and provide information about the problems they face. Moreover, Jones constantly correlates Grant's encounters with women and his experiences underwater, emphasizing that whenever he has trouble with either Lucky or Carol Abernathy (Lowney Handy) he tries to reestablish his manhood by confronting dangerous situations while skin diving. Bonham, who compensates for the deterioration of his marriage by hunting sharks, follows the same pattern. In addition, Jones links romantic episodes to the skin-diving ones by focusing on the same characters in each.

Jones's increased economy in plotting is also shown in his ability to interweave parallel and contrasting situations (as well as autobiography and fiction) into the same actions so they influence each other. The best example concerns the way he meshes the subplot involving Al Bonham and Cathie Finer with the story of Grant and Lucky. Cathie and Bonham's recklessness not only contrasts with Ron's and Lucky's growth toward maturity but also reinforces the Grants' decision to shoulder their obligations toward each other and live in a more responsible manner. When Bonham calls Grant for help after the police find him with Cathie Finer, he has the opportunity to witness the disastrous results of Bonham and Cathie's risk-taking and can report them to Lucky. In addition, Bonham's downfall leads to the failure of the schooner company in which Grant had invested and teaches Grant another lesson about the need for avoiding senseless risks.

Jones's supposedly inelegant language may have contributed as much as his plotting to the effectiveness of *Go to the Widow-Maker*, because it seems well-adapted to the psychological probing of the rough-hewn, masculine attitudes he was exploring (Thompson, "The Professionals"). As in *The Thin Red Line*, Jones worked the language of his characters into the narrative, noting in a letter to William Styron on November 24, 1966, that he had let "various characters describe their own various actions to themselves in the second place, thus giving them a reflective viewpoint of their own actions which if described by me or them in the present would have been impossible" and attributing this method to Ford Madox Ford in *Parade's End* (Hendrick, ed., *Into Eternity* 313-14). Observing that most of Jones's characters in the novel "belong to a new and nameless class" consisting of "proletarians who have become rich since the war" without changing "their tastes nor their manners nor their speech," Thompson describes how he shrewdly manages to connect the language such men use to each other with their underlying attitudes of "masculine aggression and sexuality and solidarity, largely through its obsessive obscenity" ("The Professionals" 16). Beyond that achievement, Thompson sees an even greater, more general, triumph in Jones's handling of such language:

> [Jones's] use of the proletarian dialect of obscenity allows him an entirely new accuracy of fact and of valuation in speaking of sexual experience. . . . It is a profound honesty, a willingness to connect physical experience with

feeling that neither pornographers nor those who speak only of the feelings and obscure the physical can hope to manage. As he manages this about sex, so he does about aggression. Jones uses the language of masculine aggression, knows how to assess its undertones of sexuality, and in the action he presents, he shows the consequences of these feelings. Those who imagine he is simply praising the male world do not understand him at all. (17)

In that respect, Jones's apparent flouting of established modes of expressing sensibility in literature has led to a gain in intricacy and delicacy in the examination of important areas of contemporary experience.

The central problem in *Go to the Widow-Maker* is Ron Grant's obsessive concern with his masculinity. He is driven by a need to do something spectacular to establish his manhood yet finds no act sufficiently daring enough to accomplish that; he always discovers some flaw that leads him to dismiss every feat as pointless and unmanly. Only at the end of the novel does he realize that he can never succeed in the quest to establish his masculinity by external means and that he has badly mistaken the nature of manhood. Engaging in such a quest leads to denial of valuable "feminine" components in his personality, and continual pursuit of this impossible goal would lower him to the animal level. As a result of these revelations, Grant frees himself from his hero-worship of men such as Bonham and Jim Grointon and returns to his more appropriate task of writing sensitive, uncompromisingly realistic plays.

To a large extent, Grant's fifth-grader impulses spring from his need to compensate for his constant humiliation by Carol Abernathy, whose chief hold is the guilt she has instilled in him for having once offered her to a friend. In addition, he has taken the role of being her "foster son" half-seriously, a stance they had acted out in front of a *Life* magazine reporter (A. B. C. Whipple) to preserve Carol's and her husband's reputations. Seeing her as a foster mother has complicated his feelings toward her; moreover, he has allowed Carol to become the moral arbiter of his writing and endured many tongue-lashings for misdirecting his energy toward sex and other pursuits instead of concentrating on his work. Although Jones gives Carol this attitude of Lowney Handy—one from which he had suffered—he converts Handy's beloved masters of the East into Carol's idea of the gnostic masters of wisdom and provides few hints in Carol of the ideas about theosophy and transcendentalism he had shared with Handy, perhaps because he still adhered, amid ever-present doubts, to most of them.

Grant's feelings about women have long been complicated by latent masochism and the realization that *"what he really wanted was to enslave himself to some woman and become her creature, her groveling possession, contemptible, and contemptuously treated by her"* (Jones, *Go to the Widow-Maker* 225, emphasis in the original). That feeling has provided much of the basis for his relationship with Carol, who shows little reluctance to shower Grant with belittling remarks and physical abuse, yet he has always been able to reflect that his awareness of this desire is "why all these years he had had to be so careful in picking himself a wife. He must not pick a bad master. . . . But, of course, he would have to be the boss in the family, too" (225).

Because Grant views himself as deserving to be outcast, he constantly expects to be rejected and yet resents any action interpreted as rejection. Thus, his natural response to Lucky's refusal to go to bed with him on their first date, like Dave Hirsh's to Gwen's rejection of his advances, is to question what is wrong with himself and be angry with her. His chief worry has been that he is a coward, and he has come to idolize hard, irresponsible men, whom he mistakenly regards as more courageous than himself. He considers Jim Grointon, for example, to be a superior being because of the things he "could do in or on or above the sea, diving, sailing, flying, even the camping, all the romantic, and *real*, things that the bourgeois, small town, and now pseudo-intellectual, types like himself . . . wrote about" (490).

Grant's insecurity about his manhood, and his semiconscious belief that he deserves to be treated with contempt, can be traced to "his terrible and lifelong inferiority complex" (79), a consequence of which is the "'rejection syndrome' built into his psyche that could be triggered by the slightest and often most inoffensive thing" (459). Further undermining his self-confidence are fears that by "unmanning" Hunt Abernathy (modeled on Harry Handy), and contributing to Hunt's alcoholism through his affair with Carol, he has also unmanned himself. Moreover, the fact that Carol has become Grant's "foster mother" and Hunt has assumed the role of his "foster father" increases Grant's shame over his relationship with them.

Once Grant accused a fellow writer, Doug Ismaileh, of trying to use him as a father figure to be destroyed (reflecting an attitude Jones detected in Tom Chamales and one that many other American male writers have held), yet Grant, too, searches for a substitute father, viewing not only Hunt as such but also Al Bonham and, to a limited extent, Jim Grointon. When Grant goes skin diving with Bonham, he feels "very much the son to Bonham's massive paternalism," a reaction to Al's competence in the water and huge size (14). Later, Grant notices that Grointon "usurped a sort of parental superiority" (488), but he is displeased because he is aware that Grointon, trying to appeal to Lucky, is performing for her benefit and striving to place Grant in the role of child. As much as Grant admires Grointon, he is not prepared to surrender his wife to him, and he develops a semi-Oedipal jealousy toward Jim Grointon.

Another reason Grant is drawn to men such as Bonham and Grointon as heroes, friends, and fathers is that he regards them as the last individualists in an overly organized world. Because he considers the organization of modern societies a universally emasculating although necessary force, Grant longs for a way of life in which a man can still experience freedom. A skin-diver's life, he argues to a novelist friend, "is the last frontier left to an individual to do individual work" (75). He is sure that individualism, adventurousness, and toughness form a better trinity than organization, security, and sensitivity, although he will later question that judgment.

In his poem "Harp Song of the Dane Women," the epigraph for *Go to the Widow-Maker*, Rudyard Kipling contrasts women's world of "the hearthfire and the home-acre" with men's world of the sea as "the old grey Widow-maker" or the pursuit of security and the pursuit of danger, and that contrast represents the conflict within Grant. The women in the poem question why men should forsake them for a life that offers self-destruction as its goal, and Lucky Grant might well ask the same. A connection is always made between Grant's difficulties with women and his desire to assert his manhood in the sea. Just as his impetus to learn skin diving comes from his rebellion against Carol's castrating domination, his later quest for ever more dangerous experiences underwater stems from an increasing alienation from Lucky. Once Grant becomes a "self-convinced" cuckold, as he tells her, he finds that he is "much braver underwater" (581), although his foolhardy risks really indicate that he has stopped caring whether he lives or dies.

Ultimately, Grant learns that his course toward manhood culminates not in the partially sensitive, partially admirable Bonham but in the foul-mouthed, petty-minded, larcenous simian figure Mo Orloffski. Orloffski, a total individualist, has no respect for law or society and no concern about the feelings or property of others. Once Grant realizes that he is beginning to resemble this supreme specimen of animal man, he recognizes that he must change direction. At the end of the book, he reflects that he and Lucky need to stick together because "alone, they didn't either one of them have even that much of a chance. . . . In these Orloffski and Bonham woods" (617), a signal of new understanding of the callousness and destructiveness in the anarchic lives of men he had regarded as mentors.

In a speech to Lucky after returning from an impossible-to-win fight with Orloffski in which he has been pointlessly and stupidly beaten, Grant reveals the extent to which he has come to terms with his insecurities about masculinity. The image of a boy who becomes obsessed by the great difference in size between his father's penis and his own and who internalizes that image applies to Grant's own case. For example, his idea that the "boy" can never grow up because his memory of that disproportion remains a subjective reality, or image-picture, to him even though his physical size will change depicts Grant's inferiority complex and the discrepancy between the way he views himself and the way others see him. Time after time, he believes he has acted like a coward when others applaud him as cool and courageous. What he needs to learn most, and what Orloffski miraculously beats into him, is self-acceptance.

Others who have also mistakenly seen themselves as boys when they are men, Grant believes, are hindered from acting maturely. Boys do not know how to handle sex or act tenderly and responsively with a woman; neither do they comprehend how to interpret and diminish international and local conflicts or deal with social and moral issues. Hence, men who see themselves as boys "take refuge in bravery. . . . Only by being brave can they be what they think—hope—is manly, a man. . . . So they make up games. The harder the game, the braver the man. Politics, war, football, polo, explorers. . . . All Daddy's great huge cock they remember but can never match" (Jones, *Go to the Widow-Maker* 608).

Grant's assertion to Lucky that "I'd like to think, I think I maybe am, growing up to my father's cock" (608) implies that he is abandoning his belief in bravery as the chief criterion of manhood and will mature in other respects as well. He has just put aside his masculine pride and assured Lucky that he has become convinced that she did not have sex with Grointon, even though he still harbors suspicions. Her possible infidelity severely tests his manhood because he regards cuckolds as the unmanliest of men; overcoming his outrage and humiliation requires self-control as well as self-acceptance. More important, accepting Lucky on these terms requires him to consider another person's concerns equal to his own.

The willingness to face Lucky as an equal is vital to maintaining the single viewpoint she and Grant had attained in the first days after their marriage, when "some occult alchemy of close warm wet sexuality" had enabled them to relate to each other as if they "had actually become one personality, the two separate eyes in one head as it were" (375). This sense of fusion seems to imply an important evolutionary advance toward the final fusion with Brahma or the Over-Soul, and the emphasis on vision suggests Emerson's image in his essay on "Nature" of the "transparent eyeball" through which "the currents of the Universal Being circulate" (*Selected Essays* 18).

The role of sexuality in helping them achieve a single viewpoint also hints at a mystical view of sex similar to that of the Tantric stream of Hinduism and Buddhism Benjamin Walker has described, which posits that "there is an intimate connection between cosmic creation and the primal urge of men and women; and differences are resolved and harmony achieved between the macrocosm and the microcosm through sexual union" (*The Hindu World* 392). Walker also notes that for those who believe in Tantrism, "the sex act is . . . regarded as the channel for the highest spiritual experience and a means of salvation" (392). The fusion vanishes after their argument about Grant's affair with Carol but reemerges at the end of the book when Grant reflects that "maybe, if he hung on, if *they* hung on, they might someday again achieve that sort of strange wonderful Single Viewpoint they had once had" and then believes he can see in Lucky's "eyes that she had been thinking the same thing" (617-18). The possibility that Grant and Lucky may be able to attain a durable, and even permanent, merging of their separate subjective views thus indicates not only the strength and meaning of their love but also the opportunity given both to move to a new spiritual level.

In many respects, Lucky acts as Grant's master, although in other respects he acts as hers. From the beginning of their relationship she recognizes the importance of his writing and encourages him to concentrate on it rather than on skin diving and similar pursuits, rightly valuing the emotional perceptiveness in his plays and his passionate yet gentle lovemaking over his brutalizing quest of danger. It is not only her consciously directed encouragement that helps to sensitize Grant but also her indirect effect through the suffering she arouses in him.

Lucky's beneficial impact even extends to the lovemaking she had found so pleasing in the early stages of their relationship. The first time Grant meets Lucky, he is bent on satisfying his animal desire as soon as possible, yet after their marriage he observes that their sexual closeness culminates in a shared viewpoint, thereby learning that sex on this level is akin to spiritual union. Later, when they become estranged, Grant makes the equivalent realization that the "fucking privileges" she is willing to extend are unsatisfying because what he wants to do is make love.

Grant's final willingness to accept Lucky even if she did have sex with Jim Grointon demonstrates not only his increased movement toward the unselfishness he had begun to display in their sexual relationship—unselfish sex that moves them toward the larger self of the single viewpoint and, ultimately, toward the Over-Soul—but also his greater flexibility in outlook. Much of the difficulty he experiences in accepting his masculinity can be traced to his rigid, stereotyped notion of a man as self-contained and unthinkingly brave. Once Grant gets beyond that, he is free not only to assess his virtues more accurately but also to adopt a more personal set of values. His acceptance of Lucky's possible unfaithfulness, however, also compels him to modify a personal value derived from experience. Because he had believed that infidelity by either partner kills something vital that can never be regained in a relationship, he must admit that he is acting counter to his convictions in deciding to continue with her.

Yet Grant has remained true to Lucky (except for sleeping with Carol on two occasions to avoid humiliating her), and he has reason to hope that Lucky will be faithful to him. He remembers the argument of their psychiatrist friend Ben Spicehandler that even if Lucky betrayed him with Grointon "maybe she's sorry. Maybe she's learned something. Something about where the real importance lies" (Jones, *Go to the Widow-Maker* 593). Functioning in his role of master based on knowledge gained from his irresponsible actions during the early stages of his marriage with Irma, Ben asks Grant whether he expects "everything in life" to come to him "without paying for it" and thinks himself "too big and too important" to be willing to teach a little of all he claims "to know about life" (592-93). Just as Ben has been taught a lot by his temporary abandonment of Irma, he expects that Lucky will also gain greater insight from whatever mistakes she has made, and, he implies, the same principle also holds true for Grant.

Grant bitterly remembers his overlarge sense of obligation to Carol and too quickly dismisses Ben's point that the troubles with Lucky may stem from a fear of responsibility similar to Ben's toward Irma. Moreover, Grant's sense of responsibility has always set him apart from the "accident-prone" Bonham, the untrustworthy Grointon, the crude Orloffski, and the pugnacious Finer. He had nevertheless been reluctant to abandon the known problems of dealing with Carol for the unknown problems of living with Lucky and later, when Lucky turned hostile, took refuge in a pursuit of danger instead of facing his problems and making decisions about them. Only at the end of the novel does he seem truly willing to assume the responsibility of living with a woman and placing her desires, emotions, and welfare alongside his own.

Apart from his involvement with Lucky, Grant's only experience for which it seems worth taking risks is his mystical excitement in a cave during his first dive, the type of communion with nature as the embodiment of universal being that Emerson applauded, although he would probably not have felt comfortable with Jones's sexual approach. On the way down, Grant feels that "everything, all problems, all plans, all worries, 'mistress,' her husband, new girl, the new play, sometimes even consciousness of Self itself, seemed to have been swept from his mind by the intensity of the tasting of this new experience, and new world" (12). His escape from the confinement of self, a key element of the experience, prepares him for the "strange spiritual excitement" he develops in the cave (16) and for his feeling that the "seventy-eyed monster, all head and almost no body, resting on the sand floor" might be "the Great Being Himself" (17). Moreover, Grant feels "himself beginning to get an erection in the dim stillness" as he always does "when he found himself alone in an empty church. . . . Was it the privacy?" he wonders, "Or was it maybe the nearness of God? the nearness of Unknowable?" (17). He vows to return and "masturbate, come like a fury, and watch his milky semen swirl and mingle with the green water which itself swirled about his body with every tiniest movement" (17).

The passage suggests the role of semen as a link between the physical and the spiritual, something also implied in *From Here to Eternity* during Prewitt's astral projection by the "jism cord" connecting the "one of him" in his body with the "other of him" that "had gone off the world like a spaceship" (579). When Grant does return to the cave, however, he finds he does not want to masturbate after all. Perhaps the desire for auto-stimulation would have been the kind of wish-fulfilling substitute for sexual union with the deity that it usually is for such union with another human. Instead, Grant swims "back and forth across the cavern, delighting in the movement of the water against his naked crotch" and then discovering immediately after he leaves the cave that he has "quietly" and "mysteriously" lost his erection (Jones, *Go to the Widow-Maker* 205).

Although the experience in the cave shows Grant the awe-inspiring yet friendly and beneficial aspect of the sea (the white yang), he also observes the more sinister side of the sea (the black yin) when he dives to retrieve the car containing the dead Jamaican businessman and Anna Bottomley. Although the couple has brought about their own destruction through reckless sexual play while driving, the sea is the instrument that kills them. Yet when accompanying Bonham to recover the bodies, Grant is paradoxically confronted by an image of birth; the density of the sea reminds him of amniotic fluid, and the anchor chain stretches from the ship to the car like an umbilical cord. This hint of the indivisibility of birth and death is compounded by Grant's impression that the businessman's body, as it is lifted, looks "for all the world like some dead soul rising to some skim milk heaven" (294), especially because the image of "skim-milk" in this context also suggests semen. The sea embraces everything in the same way the process of evolution does; self-destruction blends into the movement toward oneness with God.

Because Lucky is unable to share these underwater experiences, she sees only the cruelty of the attacks Grant and the other men make on the fish and the danger of the situations he faces. Having recently lost her South American lover, Raoul, who died taking part in his country's revolution, what Lucky wants is a man who can act as a father and protect her from every hazard and hardship. She thus becomes victim of a variation of Grant's obsession with a childhood memory of his father as a man of immense stature and power. Lucky also regards herself as a child, although unlike Grant she feels no compulsion to try to measure up to an adult world. Her father looms large in her mind, however, and it is hard for her to consider any man, including Grant, as being on the same level with him. She long continues to feel that if her father had remained alive throughout her girlhood she might not have become as promiscuous. At any rate, she would have had someone on whom to lean and who could relieve her of the burden of self-responsibility. Accordingly, she seeks a man who will be responsible for her life and can be blamed for everything she finds wrong with herself, guide her firmly, and yet cater to her whims.

Lucky's attempts to find a man who will take control of her life indicate that she is succumbing to an ultrafeminine woman's wish for dependence, fearing, like Karen Holmes in *From Here to Eternity* and Dawn Hirsh in *Some Came Running*, that she can not gain security through her own efforts and yearning to have a man provide it for her. Yet no matter how much Lucky longs for a man to dominate her, she also wants to make her own decisions and live as she pleases, a mingling of wishes that mirrors Grant's longing to be simultaneously master and slave to a woman.

Because full satisfaction of her opposing desires is an impossible task, Lucky must reach a compromise. Doing so will be far from easy, however, because she leans heavily toward ultrafeminine passivity. She needs, for example, to have her roommate perform simple tasks such as arranging for tickets or a ride to the airport. It is in no way surprising that she is passive in sex as well. Lucky's penchant for cunnilingus increases her exertion of power over men in sex while lessening her active involvement, thus forming a temporary union of her drives for dominance and submission and of Grant's similar drives. Her passivity is both fundamental and a source of delight to her, and it is a sign of growth when she takes a more active part in sex with Grant after the night of her temptation by Grointon.

When Lucky invites Grant to make love to her after he returns from fighting Orloffski, she further demonstrates her new aggressiveness and concern. When Grant points out that he can not do it her way because of his broken nose, she quickly replies that "fucking's fine" (609), indicating that she is less interested in her own pleasure than in expressing her affection for him. Like Grant, she had allowed herself to drift into the wedding, and she similarly must shoulder her share of responsibility for the marriage to make it continue.

Even before she met Grant, Lucky's propensity toward passivity and her admiration for forceful, athletic males had been tempered by realization that super-virile men often have something awry in their characters. Her college affair with a captain of the football team had taught her that such men generally "preferred the company of men to being with a woman" (262), and the combination of that experience with her study of the "circle of *politique*" in political science leads her to develop a theory of the circle of the sexes. Just as the circle of *politique* posits that "you could only go so far Right without becoming Left" and vice versa, Lucky's circle of the sexes argues that "when you became more Masculine than normal . . . you automatically came closer and closer to the Feminine" (263). Applying the theory to the loutish brute Orloffski, Lucky picks out the feminine traits in his personality: "his physical vanity, his preoccupation with his own beauty (?!), his posing," and "his preening" (263). Moreover, the analyses of Orloffski and the circle of the sexes not only fit in well with her conclusion that super-masculine males "*were* all fags together, in a totally non-fag non-sexual way" (263) but also place her at a psychological distance from such men. Although the analyses should warn Lucky also against the dangers of becoming more feminine than feminine, applying that part of the theory takes her much longer.

Her judgment of men is clouded by a feeling, spurred by bitter recollections, that there was "not one of them but who had lied to her about something" (262). That history of deception is the reason she becomes so disturbed upon learning that Grant has lied to her about his involvement with Carol. She worries even more that his ability to lie so successfully in the past means that he could deceive her again in the future. Hence, she is confronted with the problem of how to live with her distrust in the same way and to the same extent that Grant must cope with his suspicions about her.

Lucky also distrusts herself. Still influenced by strict Catholic morality, Lucky thinks she may be sinful or even evil. Yet she has established such a sophisticated veneer that it takes Grant a long time to discover that she suspects herself of being a whore although she "turned it around and made it look as though Grant (or someone) thought of her that way—and then hated him (them) for it" (460). Grant recognizes that Lucky displaces her attitudes onto others like he does, and he observes that this process "was probably all as automatic and uncontrollable as Grant's own 'rejection syndrome'" (460).

Just as Grant must achieve self-acceptance to free himself to love her, Lucky must conquer self-hatred to express her love for him.

Lucky's shame over her lack of sexual virtue before marriage demonstrates another flaw in the concept of ultrafemininity, because even though she has made no effort to live in accordance with the image of a "good girl," the concept has conditioned her to despise herself. Despite her shame over her past and her longing to escape the empty pattern of life she had established in New York, Lucky wants to retain the freedom and irresponsibility she enjoyed before joining her life to Grant's. Because Grant has made it clear that he regards marriage as a monogamous institution, however, she is compelled either to accept that limitation on her sexual life or abandon the marriage, a demand made increasingly difficult by growing estrangement between Grant and her.

Even before their marriage, Lucky had resented the inhibitions she imposed on herself as a result of her attachment to Grant and felt a need to get even with him for having taken away her independence. Therefore, when she realizes that Grant is vulnerable, she decides to make him "pay for everything," particularly "for having made her fall in love with him" (248). Grant's deception about Carol provides additional motive, and Lucky's ideal form of making him pay would be to commit adultery with Grointon. Yet doing so might mean exacerbating her whore complex as well as destroying the marriage. Moreover, her desire to strike back at Grant for undermining her independence has always been accompanied by fear of punishment for her past life by being deprived of Grant. Even if she did have sex with Grointon, she discovers that the renewed excitement was not worth the risk of destroying her future with Grant.

The temptation Grointon holds out is the possibility of fulfilling two fantasies. First, Lucky associates him with "a cocky, dirty, arrogant young fellow" whom she had imagined taking on "as a one-or-two-night-stand stud and then gently but firmly" dismissing to see how he would react (361). Going to bed with Grointon would also satisfy her "played-out-in-the-full-imaginative sexual fantasy of her screwing another man in front of Ron" (255), yet, as Grant warns her, "fantasy isn't reality," and, ultimately, she must choose between the two (353).

The primary obstacle to Lucky's choice of reality is her belief that she is not real, which is comparable to Grant's impression that he is still a little boy. Accordingly, she, like Grant, places little value on her decisions, feeling that "whatever she said or did didn't really count" (254). Her sense of unreality is tied to an ultrafeminine desire to be charming, which necessarily involves a lot of role-playing. Yet women—or men—who play too many roles may lose contact with their inner selves, begin to wonder who they are, and separate themselves from individual observations about life and personal values.

Although having sex with Grointon might seem unreal to Lucky, it could have devastatingly real consequences for both Grant and herself, because she comes close to trading a potentially rewarding reality for the brief satisfaction of a daydream. Still, either by reasoning it out in time to resist or by succumbing to Grointon and rediscovering the emptiness of such seductions, Lucky learns the importance of making meaningful choices and substituting responsibility for risk, a discovery that parallels Grant's realization that manhood demands maturity of judgment rather than childish confrontations with danger. As a result of this lesson, Lucky accepts her own reality and assumes the burden of accountability; yet because she makes her commitment first, her new convictions are severely tested by Grant's suspiciousness and anger. Only at the end of the novel, when both have become equally committed to their reciprocal obligations, does their marriage truly stand a chance of survival.

Jones's penchant for creating and examining parallel situations and personality traits paid large dividends in his treatment of Grant and Lucky. He more than amply reinforces his theme of the circle of the sexes by a careful, convincing analysis of the Grants' major similarities amid obvious differences. By demonstrating in elaborate and telling detail how they both come to accept the mixture of masculine and feminine traits in their characters, even though Grant retains his full share of aggressiveness and Lucky continues to lean heavily toward passivity, Jones presents a credible picture of their progression toward placing maturity and responsibility above risk-taking and excessive freedom. Above all, Jones reveals how Grant and Lucky, like the more perceptive members of Charlie Company, lean toward neither sadism nor masochism and learn that humane masculinity and humane femininity are not intimidated by popular preconceptions about what a man or woman should be. These carefully crafted revelations help produce one of the few depictions in literature of what it takes to make a sane, mature, and durable sexual relationship.

The remaining story-beads from *The Ice-Cream Headache and Other Stories,* "Secondhand Man," "Just Like the Girl, and "The Tennis Game," are somewhat looser and more widely separated than Jones's other novel- and story-beads, but they still have an unsevered golden thread of reincarnationist beliefs running through them, and their themes parallel those in

Go to the Widow-Maker. "Secondhand Man," for example, describes a marriage plagued by problems linked to the confining and distorting animal-level stereotypes of what men and women should be, whereas "Just Like the Girl" and "The Tennis Game" deal with the parental origins for the masochism that both damaged and sensitized Ron Grant as well as many of the soldiers in *The Thin Red Line.* Like the rest of Jones's work, moreover, the stories are reminders that psychological problems, whatever their origins, are equally spiritual problems and relate to growth and individual salvation.

"Secondhand Man" (1948) offers an earlier version of some of the problems Grant and Lucky face, because Larry and Mona Patterson both try to live according to popular notions of manhood and womanhood. Larry, however, fails to cast aside these conceptions, thereby losing his chance to develop a more meaningful way of life. Mona, however, manages to overcome her ultrafeminine passivity and belief in the virtue of weakness. By shedding her illusions concerning masculinity and femininity, Mona gains the strength her husband forfeits, yet she discovers too late that a lasting relationship such as Grant's and Lucky's must be built on mutual growth as well as mutual disentanglement from glamours.

One meaning of the story's title comes when a doctor tells Larry that a man of forty has become "Second Hand to our Jobs, to our country's military strategy, to the money we hope to make and then cant spend" (60). In another sense, however, Larry probably became a secondhand man long before forty, because he has always been influenced by the opinions of others about what he should aim for and how he should act. Upon going into town after being contentedly isolated with his wife for seven weeks, for example, Larry immediately worries that people may look down on him for living as he does. In fact, everything he does and feels in town is nudged into his mind by others, and there is little doubt that this has been the pattern of his life. His lament is that "God is Will" (Jones, "Secondhand Man" 78), and the fact that he has no will betrays the self-pity that chains him to his secondhand life with its secondhand values and emotions. Even his flickering effort to resume his life in the woods after returning from town fails because he tries to imagine himself as an Indian with an Indian's closeness to nature rather seeking to regain the more personal attachment he had formed during the preceding weeks. Moreover, the independence he had previously appeared to achieve in the woods appears to be secondhand, too, because it can only be maintained by the absence of other people.

Mona Patterson had argued that weakness might be a virtue, because "to be strong you have to be—dogmatic" (61) and weakness forces men to depend upon each other more; yet Mona is only half-right in her appraisal of its value. She makes sense when pointing to the arrogance in Wyatt Earp's type of independence, which rides roughshod over others, and when she implies that the greater emotional vulnerability of humanity is a spiritual improvement over the social and material self-reliance of nineteenth-century American pioneers. She has misjudged the end of this increased vulnerability, however, and is bound, like Larry, to the lesser conception of the God of Love instead of moving on to Jack Malloy's God of Acceptance. Her illusion is that the weakness she and Larry have confessed to each other can lead them to a combined vision of life that will hold them together and enable them to attain a mutual strength greater than each could have gained individually. Thus, her husband's small acts of taking a beer and talking with the blond waitress seem like a large betrayal to Mona, because they imply not only that his dependence on her is far from complete but also that his vision of life has remained different from hers. Her refusal to discuss the problem with him suggests a retreat to her earlier pattern of fleeing from difficulties through silence. Still, Mona's quiet acceptance of his later drunken condition indicates that she may have reached an understanding of her essential aloneness, which can never be overcome in the way she had hoped to bridge it with Larry. After all, she is described as looking "strong," and she is preparing to establish independence by owning a design shop when they return to Baltimore. Although there is not enough evidence to be certain Mona has not become hard like Earp (or the Earp-like Edward Dylan in "The Ice-Cream Headache"), it is likely that her strength has come through surrendering an illusion. If that is true, she is well on the way to becoming a "firsthand woman."

In contrast to Mona Patterson's theories about the value of weakness in men and women, although in keeping with her probable understanding through experience at the story's end, two other stories in *The Ice-Cream Headache*—"Just Like the Girl" and "The Tennis Game"—demonstrate the dangers of excessive dependency resulting from such weakness. Both stories trace the development of masochism in a young boy who will be scarred for life by his current experiences. The emphasis on the perils of masochism counterbalance Jones's many warnings on the dangers of masculine aggressiveness, although he has also shown how the two may be linked and form an even greater potential for destructiveness of self and others.

The events in "Just Like the Girl" are viewed through the eyes of a young boy named John, whose parents closely resemble those of Dave Hirsh in *Some Came Running* (and Jones himself). Both fathers are irresponsible, heavy-drinking woman-chasers, and both mothers are ignorant, hypocritically malicious, religious fanatics. The fathers publicly place their own desires above the needs of their families; the mothers try just as hard to force others to meet their needs but disguise such efforts under the sacred cloaks of duty and motherly and wifely self-sacrifice. The major difference between John's and Dave's parents is that John's father holds to an idealized image of his wife and sees his son as an extension of himself, whereas Old Man Herschmidt openly despises his wife and children. The difference is significant, however, because it renders John's father more vulnerable than Vic Herschmidt.

Judging from the title alone, John's mother will likely mold him into one of those males who seek dominant wives, and there is some evidence of this not only in John's submission to his mother but also in his fantasy about Phyllis Jenkins (he pictures her having sex with him only after he has protected her against more aggressive males). In addition, John's mother has implied that the only way he can prove his love is by doing what she asks, and the association between love and service is one he can carry over into a relationship with a wife. Significantly, John's last sexual daydream in the story is covered by his mother's face.

John's fantasy about Phyllis is based on his reading of James Fenimore Cooper and implies the continuity through two centuries of American male chivalric worship of women's purity, which, coupled as it usually is with a desire for their bodies, leads inevitably to sexual guilt. In a sense, John is the perfect victim for his mother (and eventually for other women) because he has so combined his love for her, his sense of honor, and his restricted sex drive that he will experience failure in any of these areas as failure in all of them. That is why the attempt to alter his sexual-heroic fantasy to let him accept his father's money, which he considers a bribe for his affection, is doomed from the beginning. John cannot be disloyal to his "defenseless" mother without endangering his pattern of sexual excitement and his self-image of being a man of honor. The same motivation also lies behind his longing to engage in the war that his father fears will begin within ten years. His father is right when he says that John has guts, but John's courage is more the product of his mother's impact than his father's and is therefore subject to her control. When his father's hope to influence him is defeated, John's future defeats at the hands of his mother and any other woman with whom he becomes involved are foreshadowed. Although his mother had said, "Someday the women will be free" (Jones, "Just Like the Girl" 17), and his father had said, "Someday the men will be free" (22), they and John will not obtain that liberty as long as they remain emotionally dependent on the opposite sex, whether as spouse, parent, or child. Such dependency is karmically binding, and to evolve spiritually they must move beyond all dependency, either to the isolation of compassionate understanding or the shared single viewpoint, although both patterns preface further movement toward eventual reunion with God.

In "The Tennis Game," John Slade (who also appears in "The Valentine," "The Way It Is," *From Here to Eternity*, and is likely John in "Just Like the Girl") similarly responds masochistically to his mother's attempt to control his life. Although he struggles against her through secret activities, especially the mental games he values because they are things "his mother wouldn't know about, or his father, or any of the other grownups" (Jones, "The Tennis Game" 108), John expects to be defeated by her in every major outward contest and has learned to identify himself with literary heroes who display nobility amid failure. His mother has imbued him with "a consuming luxurious hatred" for himself, her, his father, and everyone else (199), yet he feels that the one way he can successfully strike back at her is by hurting himself. This sense of "getting even with her" (200) is why he can take pleasure in "grinding the gun barrel in his pants hurtfully" (199).

Still, the dominion John has allowed his mother extends to his sexual fantasies, such as the jungle explorers game in which he feels excitement in being captured and tortured by naked Amazons, and has become so pervasive that he does not hesitate to admit that he and Alice Pringle have been urinating together when his mother calls out to ask what they are doing. Although he has observed the way his mother has exaggerated their poverty so that she will have "something to hold over his father when he got drunk" (200), he has not yet examined her similar purpose in instilling guilt in himself. Later, he wonders why he told the truth about Alice and himself when his mother had no other way of knowing what they were doing, yet it is evident from everything else he does that he accepts his mother's view of his action as "a filthy, dirty thing" (207) and finds her whipping perversely satisfying.

At the same time, John feels his punishment as so bitter a defeat that his memory of the incident almost destroys the pleasure he takes in a tennis game he has miraculously been allowed to play although he had anticipated that his mother would make him work all day. Not surprisingly, the memory of the punishment casts a pall over the game and helps shape his decision to concentrate on the role of a defeated German baron. John's revealing response to "the baron's" loss of the game and everything the baron valued in life is a desire "to play with himself" (210).

All the games John likes to play are sometimes cruel, and most of the cruelty is directed at himself, either directly as in the jungle explorers game or indirectly as in his role of the baron. This element of his personality is depicted most fully in relation to his lead-soldier battle. The setup of the game, in which John shoots at lead soldiers and damages cherished pieces, also indicates his masochism, and his conviction that they must be shot in the name of realism is based on a feeling of reality as consisting of injury and misery.

Because he has divided his two toy armies into "good guys" and "bad guys," he believes he should want the good guys to win, yet his more natural impulse, which he is beginning to favor, is to let the bad guys slaughter the good guys as the Arabs did the French Foreign Legionnaires in *Beau Geste*. The one time he did let the good guys rout the bad guys, "he felt half sick and strangely astonished" (204); for John, the good guys must always lose. It is the only way he can view himself as one of them. That viewpoint involves him in a vicious circle, however, because he is forced to persist in defeat to retain a now-preferred self-image. He no longer requires his mother's release, but rather he needs an evolution-impeding image-picture of being a martyr to her will and the bitter enjoyment of the agony he has permitted her to arouse in him.

Jones's sixth and seventh published novels, *The Merry Month of May* and *A Touch of Danger*, also stress the need for men and women to refrain from guiding their lives by popular notions about manhood and womanhood and find a way of expressing sexual identity that leads toward neither sadism nor masochism. In *The Merry Month of May*, narrator Jack Hartley has attained a fairly high level of maturity and sensitivity through his awareness of his failure to accomplish his major goals, and he has wisely accepted a tough-minded yet sensitive woman as his master in several important survival techniques. Moreover, Jack's compassion and understanding contrast favorably with the aggressive selfishness of Harry Gallagher and other traditional male figures. Despite a few remaining illusions, which he is beginning to lose, Jack displays the best approach to attaining humane manhood.

Although Frank "Lobo" Davies, the narrator of *A Touch of Danger*, begins at a lower level than Jack, he also evolves spiritually. Like Jack, Lobo's ego has been reduced through failure in work and marriage. Even though he has always been overly aggressive and combative, he has learned to limit the injuries he inflicts on others and accept his inability to secure anything approaching absolute justice. In addition, he has advanced enough spiritually to serve as master to the much younger Marie, whom he tries to teach to care for herself and move toward his level of insight. He finds Marie an apt pupil because she also has acquired humility through consciousness of her mistakes and begun to come to terms with her isolation in the world. He is further impressed by her combination of courage and ability in the "masculine" activity of skin diving. Lobo and Marie provide another example of the similarity between men and women, particularly when they are able to progress spiritually.

Because both Jack Hartley and Lobo Davies place heavy emphasis on acting with a concern for others and an awareness of consequences, they carry forward Ron Grant's final call for the replacement of selfishness and risk-taking as the basic criteria for judging men and women. The question doing so raises about the wisdom or folly of acting in a "responsible" manner will be explored more fully in the next chapter.

5

Individual, Social, and Karmic Responsibility

In *Some Came Running*, the biggest bead on Jones's American Orientalist unsevered thread, Dave Hirsh asks himself whether any human could live a "whole lifetime and cause no one any pain." He answers, as he believes Bob French would have, that "we were all *supposed* to cause each other pain" (1233). But should we provoke that pain or let it arise at will from social interactions, springing as frequently from attempts at kindness as from conscious cruelties? Although Dave does not answer that question directly, he evolves to a spiritual stage of compassionate understanding in which he has no intention of hurting anyone, although his approaching death and the karma he leaves behind will soon produce immense, growth-inducing pain in Bob and Gwen French.

Dave also wonders whether we are "responsible for the pain we cause in others" or only "for the pain that *that others cause in us?*" (1231, emphasis in the original), leaning toward the latter solution. These are essential questions. As Dave discovers, virtually all strong social relationships involve karmic binding and agonizing collisions between each person's illusory image-pictures of the world. Where does responsibility begin—and who does it benefit?

Although few would deny that responsible people—those who care about others, readily help in whatever way they can, and do not keep people waiting before repaying *their* debts (although they might have to wait awhile for what they are owed)—are superior to irresponsible ones, yet they probably have not attained the highest level. Responsible men and women have learned that the greatest danger of irresponsible behavior lies in its close association with animal selfishness, resulting in simian figures such as Charlie Dale in *The Thin Red Line* and Mo Orloffski in *Go to the Widow-Maker*. They have not yet discerned, however, that their efforts to help others may also be prompted by vanity. Such vanity is likely a function of the mental level and originates in the assumption that you can arrange other people's lives for them better than they can do so for themselves. Hence, before moving to the spiritual level a responsible person must find out how to display compassion without seeking to alter its object. That is by no means an easy task, because standing aloof and trying not to interfere does not work. Bob French, for example, discovers to his sorrow in *Some Came Running* that you cannot wash your hands of the responsibility for another's decisions when that burden is thrust upon you. He is forced by his realization that he had erred to confess to his daughter, Gwen, "I, with my notion of trying to avoid new karma: I, . . . in trying to follow 'God's Will' and not interfere, or let my own feelings interfere—*I* refused to be a *part* of God's Will" (1253).

Nevertheless, as Bob points out to Dave Hirsh, "Each man must find his salvation in himself alone" (1231). Taking Bob's view, the only true responsibility is individual not social. Men and women must shoulder full karmic accountability for the way they have conducted their lives and try not to lay that burden on anyone else, not even on domineering mothers like those in "Just Like the Girl" and "The Tennis Game" or army generals like Sam Slater who seek to control everyone below them through fear of authority. At the same time, they need to regard even their worst mistakes as essential parts of their spiritual education. Once evolved to this level, they will be freed from the passion to change the world. Responsible people, however, should keep in mind that anyone who has mastered some area of experience can offer limited assistance to a disciple who has learned enough to comprehend and act on such guidance. Ben Spicehandler, for example, assists Ron Grant in *Go to the Widow-Maker* to understand a bit more about love and responsibility, and Rene Halder teaches him about looking out for practical pitfalls in the worldly snare of finances.

Like a responsible person's desire to help others, both the radical dream of transforming society and the conservative need to keep it unchanged (the most important colliding consciousnesses in *The Merry Month of May*) spring from pride, because both radicals and conservatives believe that they alone know the best way for everyone else to live. Yet as Jones's partly factual reporting implies, radicals and conservatives, including even a wily, stiff-necked politician such as Charles de Gaulle, cannot escape being educated through the conflict. When each group tries to force its subjective vision on the other, it makes the ego-reducing discovery of not being as competent, collectively and individually, as it had thought. The vision so highly prized is an illusion. The relationship between radicals and conservatives is less a social than a karmic one, probably to be worked out through many lives until being freed from the illusions binding them together.

Then, radicals as well as conservatives will gain their first real chance of moving beyond the suffering caused by the desires and socially immersed values of their egos and eventually become masters of their progress toward reunion with God.

❖

Jones's sixth published novel, *The Merry Month of May*, a fictional exploration of the 1968 Paris student rebellion, is his most ambitious attempt to probe the social implications of his spiritual philosophy. Noting how the rebellion began in an impulse of social concern and ended in an expression of self-destructive irresponsibility, Jones compares it to the karmic father-son battle between his characters Harry and Hill Gallagher and implies that both social and the family conflicts originate in the pride and illusions of each participant. He also employs a lengthy series of actual events as background and indicates some ways in which the behavior of contemporary historical figures such as Charles de Gaulle and Dany Cohn-Bendit fits the pattern of the spiritual evolution process. His philosophy can be applied to actions in the real world and not merely to behavior in his carefully controlled fictional universe.

In some ways, *The Merry Month of May* is an unexpected and striking addition to Jones's canon, dealing with social conflict in terms of overt social comedy and subtle, unobtrusive symbolism. Jones maintains an ironic tone throughout, casting all the characters, including the narrator, in a comic light and preventing readers from becoming emotionally involved in the novel's many political and personal clashes. This lack of involvement was meant to free readers to contemplate the book's various social, spiritual, and symbolic meanings in the same way that Bertolt Brecht, for example, sought to create detachment so audiences could focus on his ideas. Yet it is a mixed achievement. Although the distancing between readers and characters works well in various scenes involving Jack Hartley, such as his half-ludicrous, half-serious temptations by Samantha Everton and Louisa Gallagher, and in the account of the students' revolutionary activities and the government's counter-stratagems, it is never entirely right in relation to the three Gallaghers, the central figures in the book. Potentially one of Jones's finest works, *The Merry Month of May* needs either to put readers closer emotionally to the Gallaghers by making them vital, sympathetic figures of tragedy or remove readers further from them by turning the family into sharply defined caricatures. Instead, Jones adopts a middle ground that is uncertain and not quite satisfactory although still intriguing.

The problem may have been that Jones sought to develop the three Gallaghers into an unwieldy cross between individual characters and representative types, giving them neither the complex, particularized attention he lavished on Ron and Lucky Grant nor the basic, resonant qualities he found in Welsh and Witt. Instead, they are vehicles for his social commentary and symbols, much as the "characters" in *The Pistol* although without as much justification or generic achievement, as James Giles discerns in the shorter novel. Jones, after all, is primarily concerned with showing the social effects of the temporary nationwide abandonment of responsibility provoked by the Paris student rebellion, and the Gallaghers are a small-scale reflection of that national event and the powerful social forces that shaped it. Yet he manipulates the family's downfall a little too openly to make it either fully convincing or seriously disturbing.

The chief difficulty with Jones's depiction of the Gallaghers is that he never sufficiently fleshes out the positive traits they all supposedly possessed before their downfall. Readers are told in a single paragraph about the sacrifices that old-time radical Harry has made for his social concerns but find that hard to believe because such concern fits in so little with his present character. Jones pays so much attention to Harry's latent selfishness and swift descent into irresponsibility and viciousness that Harry seems to be a bastard from beginning to end and almost outside the bonds of karma, although one of Jones's important points is the effect of karmic relationships on Harry. Similarly, Jones describes Hill Gallagher's desire to expose the hypocrisy behind his father's claim to radicalism and hurt Harry more clearly than his wish to improve the plight of the downtrodden, and Louisa Gallagher's frequent disregard for reality more than any genuineness and value in her idealism.

Yet without believing in a positive side to the Gallaghers' expressed sense of social responsibility, readers cannot regard their flight into irresponsibility as poignantly destructive or feel that they have lost anything cherishable by it. Even worse, if readers cannot believe that the Gallaghers will discover having lost something precious through their folly, then the basis for their future spiritual evolution is imperceptible. Readers can never fully share Jack Hartley's sadness over the family's fate because they have never been allowed to share his illusion that the Gallaghers are a "happy American family" that has everything, including a sense of social concern.

Such flaws, however, should not obscure Jones's many fine achievements in *The Merry Month of May*, including his notable creation of Jack Hartley, Samantha-Marie Everton, and minor characters such as Dave

Weintraub, Anne-Marie, Ferenc Hofmann-Beck, and Martine, who all display the kind of vitality and ability to fascinate that is missing in the Gallaghers. In addition, Jones portrays the activities and ramifications of the student rebellion in intricate and intriguing detail. His use of symbols, such as the river, the barricades, the laying of the paving stones, and the historical background of several famous buildings in Paris, is natural and skillfully crafted. George Garrett has noted that although it is "shorter by half than any of Jones's other major novels and (necessarily) told in a more polished style, *The Merry Month of May* is also the novel in which Jones makes the most extensive and functional use of *place*," so that "Paris, surviving all tragedies, public and domestic, is brilliantly, lovingly evoked, becoming, in essence, a central character in the story" (*James Jones* 148). Thus, the novel could have been extraordinarily powerful and profound had Jones's depiction of the Gallaghers been more satisfactory. The book is still compelling and modestly illuminating, splendid in conception yet only one-half or two-thirds successful in execution.

Throughout *The Merry Month of May*, Jones's narrator, Jack Hartley, stresses the importance of acting in a responsible manner, and, as the novel progresses he begins denouncing the irresponsible behavior of the French government, the student rebels, the Gallagher family (except for McKenna), Samantha-Marie Everton, Sirhan Sirhan, and himself. Moreover, Jones implies a connection between the havoc wrought by the collective decision of the students, citizens, and government of France to take a holiday from responsibility and the disruption of the Gallagher family caused by their decision and Samantha's to place their desires above their commitments. As always in Jones's fiction, such irresponsibility has value because it leads individuals to experience the woe that induces insight. Although Jack Hartley argues that the aim of civilized education is to teach self-control and that "the whole point of civilization is to help each other make life less cruel" (272), he, too, discovers that the primary way anyone learns anything is through the agony of having erred. His enlightenment comes from recognition that he is "a failed poet, a failed novelist," and "a drop-out of a husband" (11).

Jack Hartley's role as an honorable man in a society—indeed, in a world—where honor seemingly has no place or value may not be readily apparent, especially because he seems absurd about such matters as his concern over the sanctity of his morning toilet ritual and his devotion to his favorite *pissoir*. Jack, however, gradually gains readers' respect by the contrast between his behavior and that of almost everyone else. He always strives to do the right thing, although forces conspire to defeat his intentions. He also continues to cherish illusions that lead him to inflict as well as receive sorrow. His most persistent illusions are that decent actions can influence events in a directly beneficial way and that humane intervention can bring careless or bitter people to their senses.

Jack's first intervention is based not only on the illusion that he knows what is good for other people and can induce them to do it but also on his misconception that the Gallaghers are a "perfect happy-American family" (13). He wants to believe in the strength of the ties among the Gallaghers because of his distress over the failure of his own marriage. Jack must later admit, however, that perhaps it was foolish to talk Louisa into confronting Harry about other women, even though he does not regret the birth of his goddaughter McKenna, the result of this confrontation. Although Jack takes the role of godfather almost literally, his failure to bring about a second reconciliation—he encourages Harry to confront Louisa about her apparent sexual involvement with Samantha—suggests that he was not as responsible for the first reconciliation (or for McKenna's birth) as he had imagined.

Jack's decision to tell Hill that he thinks that Samantha has gone to Cannes with Harry, Hill's father, is equally unsuccessful. Even though he tries to consider what would be best for the boy on a long-range basis, Hill is not prepared to face the truth. Jack's subsequent effort to keep Hill from retreating into a life of passive mysticism is equally a failure. When Jack tries to tell the young Gallagher about his own vague comprehension of the purifying function of suffering, an idea gleaned from the way his hand was healed through union with the blood of a deer he shot, all Hill understands is the statement that the incident made Jack decide to stop killing. Because Hill only listens to comments that reinforce his own beliefs, Jack never has a chance to convince him to reconsider his newfound approach to life.

Naturally, Jack's efforts to induce Harry to place family obligations above fantasy and get Samantha to abandon all contact with the Gallaghers fare no better than his pleas to Hill. And his session with Samantha is even less fruitful and more embarrassing because she subjects him to a temptation that both shocks and allures him. Jack's resistance to her wiles, however, shows how Harry could also have resisted—had he chosen to.

The enormous difficulty of making the right choice becomes clear when Louisa Gallagher asks Jack to make love to her and reassure her of her womanhood after Harry has accused her of being a lesbian; she also intends to get even with Harry because of his affair with Samantha. This time Jack refuses to interfere in the family quarrel and takes the honorable course of refusing to sleep with a friend's wife, yet afterward he wonders whether it would have been better for everyone if he had done as she wished. Still, there is no guarantee that such an affair might have made any difference. It is likely that even if Jack had taken her sexually—either on his Second Empire couch or the floor—Louisa would have been comforted only temporarily. She might even have come to regard Jack as another betrayer taking advantage of her.

Finally, Jack endeavors to help the suicidal Louisa, who is in the hospital, by loosening a restraining strap to ease her physical discomfort. His act almost enables her to free herself from the apparatus that is keeping her body alive, and this failure seems symbolic of all his efforts to act responsibly. Moreover, Jack's struggle to talk Louisa into saving herself seems equally symbolic—and equally futile.

Jack's biggest flaw is overprotectiveness, which he primarily directs toward Louisa and McKenna but at times extends to Hill, Harry, and even the student body of the Sorbonne. The danger in such overprotectiveness, as Hill points out in relation to McKenna, is that it "spoils" the person who is protected and leaves her—or him—insufficiently prepared to cope with life's difficulties.

Yet in spite of all Jack's failures and flaws, he is sympathetic and retains readers' respect because of his humility and concern for others. When he tells Weintraub that he knew in advance that de Gaulle is about to release gasoline for the Pentecost weekend, thus undercutting the student rebellion, Jack admits that his ego had prompted him to volunteer the information and reflects to himself afterward, "I didn't much like myself. Damned ego" (262). Moreover, although initially much of his motivation for helping the Gallaghers springs from his desire to preserve his illusion that happy, close-knit family life is possible and desirable, Jack persists in offering assistance to them long after they have lost all pretense of remaining a family unit.

Coming to recognize the small effect anyone has on anyone else's life, Jack wisely concludes that he cannot alter the Gallaghers' mistakes or their misery and has no choice other than to accept things as they are. Yet he also feels that this need does not mean he should abandon his sense of responsibility or isolate himself. During a time of crisis involving Louisa and McKenna, Jack turns to Ferenc Hofmann-Beck because he needs a confidant. Even though Ferenc can make no useful suggestion for improving matters, Jack feels "somehow relieved" and "suddenly, for no apparent reason, [he] liked [Ferenc] very much" (253). From this experience, Jack learns that although such contacts change nothing, it is still valuable and comforting to touch and be touched by someone's spirit—if only briefly.

The index of Jack's development toward acceptance and compassion-ate understanding is his response to the river, which represents life itself and, more specifically, the path of evolution. On the day the police take over the Sorbonne, Jack looks out of his window and reflects, "It was al-ways there, that sadness of the river, of the flowing of the river" (28). Later, reflecting on the unhappiness of a bachelor's life, Jack thinks to himself, "that was no kind of mood to have living alongside the dark, flow-ing river" (161). Most of the other references associate the river with dark-ness, movement, and sorrow.

In spite of these qualities, or rather because he eventually recognizes their meaning and value, Jack starts to turn to the river for comfort. When Harry tells Jack about his decision to leave Louisa for Samantha, for exam-ple, Jack looks "away, out the window at the river" as he listens, because he thinks "that might help" (312). And as the disasters involving the Gal-laghers and those closely associated with them mount, he stares increas-ingly at the river (316, 317, 328, 332, 353, 354, 355). What he begins to see when he does so is that all these incidents are part of the flow of history and the spiritual evolution process.

His final encounter with the river occurs after the student rebellion has run its course and the Gallagher family has divided into separate, suffering tributaries. Jack is attracted by the music of two students playing for money on a public thoroughfare. The traditional music suggests links with the past and the flow of history, and the place they have chosen to perform is an older, character-filled bridge scheduled to be replaced by a modern, four-lane one, just as the humanistic, freedom-asserting bridge that students had at-tempted to build with workers and their fellow citizens had been torn down in favor of the government's smoother, anti-individual one. As Jack listens, the "thin, brave, piping music" spreads "upriver in the breeze," thus re-flecting the spirit-strengthening continuance of each individual in the evo-lutionary process and the brave beginning each soul makes in each new incarnation (360). It heartens Jack (whose last name, Hartley, suggests both "heart" and "hart," as in the deer he shot and was healed by) to see the stu-dents determined to persist in facing life in spite of the inevitable further pain that awaits them, and he becomes aware of the "lengthening sunlight" as he walks home (361).

In contrast to Jack, Harry Gallagher so pursues the path of irresponsi-bility that he has developed "a very cruel mouth . . . like the mouth of an Arab pasha" (276). The mouth has been fitted to Samantha's "street Arab grin" (132, 140), linking Harry and her to the "silly little Arab immigrant boy" Sirhan Sirhan" (300). By the time he joins her in Israel, a fertile ground for "Arabs" destroying themselves and others, Harry has betrayed everyone and everything that had any meaning for him. (This implied view of Arabs unfortunately reflects and helps perpetuate a widespread American prejudice against them, a rare failing in Jones although it likely stems largely from his response to Sirhan's crime.)

First, Harry, resenting Hill's revolutionary activities because they have edged the older radical out of the limelight, becomes as much of an enemy to his son as de Gaulle has been to the students. Although Harry felt he had established himself as a fighting radical on the basis of past risks and sacrifices, Hill looks upon his father's present life as an ease-filled, money-protected sham, provoking Harry to prove himself a better man than his son. Even though he has long been tempted by Samantha, Harry does not go after her until, seeing her with Hill, he deduces that they have been sleeping together; "taking control" of her would allow him to assert his sexual superiority. He is similarly pleased to be invited by Hill's cinema committee to write and direct a propaganda film of the revolution; doing so affords him another chance to crow over Hill. Following Hill's angry resignation, Harry carries on the project just long enough to show how much greater his experience and skill are than that of the students. His subsequent abandonment of the project is a multiple betrayal, because he not only violates the trust the students place in him but also his own radical ideals and his son's revolutionary cause.

Even though Harry's selfishness and indifference toward others have always been latent parts of his character, the key to his renunciation of his commitments and concern for others is his involvement with Samantha. As their affair progresses, Harry comes to disavow duty, love, sympathy, and tenderness like she does. Not surprisingly, considering Jones's emphasis on this theme throughout his work, the source of Harry's absorption with Samantha is his "fantasy" and the masochistic impulses behind it. As Harry defines it, male masochism occurs when a man places a woman's sexual gratification above his own and stimulates her to orgasm, obliterating any awareness of him as having instigated the pleasure. Thus, sex, as Harry desires it, becomes a mixture of delight in physical activities and pain in the thought that a woman, at the point of her greatest excitement, has lost interest in him as an individual. Moreover, the masochism underlying Harry's preoccupation with cunnilingus, which motivates his sexual proclivities, becomes intensified when two women are involved, particularly if they are more interested in each other than in him. Perhaps the main reason he is attracted to Samantha and the type of two-woman fun she is ever-ready to provide is that she offers him pain sugar-coated with pleasure and thus summons him to abandon comfort and complacency for the sake of an evolutionary form of education. As Annie Besant's remarks on "The Use of Evil" suggest, what he will learn when the sugar-coating wears off is that "the gratification of all desire which is not going upwards is a womb of pain" (*The Spiritual Life* 144). He will then move beyond such desire toward the peace that surpasses understanding.

Samantha also calls Hill to enter a karmic relationship that will advance his spiritual education, but the source of her appeal to Hill is different from the lure that caught Harry. Apart from the probability that Samantha is Hill's first highly skilled sexual partner, Jack implies, while questioning the boy about his reasons for falling in love with her, that Hill may share the same goal that Dave Hirsh had with Ginnie Moorehead in *Some Came Running:* helping a socially disadvantaged girl overcome the influence of her terrible environment. "Is it because she's a black girl?" Jack asks. "And you feel that's part of your Revolution?" (Jones, *Merry Month of May* 198).

Although Samantha's mother is a wealthy Haitian singer who has sent her daughter to the most exclusive schools, Hill's vision of her is filtered through his doctrinaire liberal attitudes. Just as Dave failed for so long to see the cunning side of Ginnie, Hill remains blind to Samantha's cunning, inevitably becoming, like Dave, the dupe of a "helpless" woman he loves. Then, as Wally Dennis did over being dropped by Dave Hirsh's niece Dawn, he goes into a tailspin because Samantha leaves him first; he does not want anyone else to do the things he had enjoyed doing with her. He has become possessive in spite of his philosophy of sexual noninvolvement.

Resenting the way his parents tried to stay together in spite of extreme dissatisfaction with each other, Hill has denounced the monogamistic approach to love for being unrealistic, hypocritical, and emotionally harmful. In its place, he would have liked for himself and McKenna to enter into sexual relationships without feeling concern for their partners and be able to walk away undamaged any time their affairs were no longer fun. Nevertheless, his involvement with Samantha teaches Hill that the evolutionary process continues as before, despite any ideas people develop to bypass or defeat it. Moreover, it is ironically appropriate that the worst misery he must endure comes from a woman who practices his philosophy and exposes his illusions about it.

Hill's transformation through Samantha is nearly total; before meeting her he was an activist who believed that his views on anarchism were worthless unless he and his friends tried to put them into practice. After he meets Samantha, he seeks a life of utter passivity through drugs and semi-isolated meditation. Moreover, although he previously struggled to assert his convictions, he has come to defer to the *I Ching* and let that overly general, confusing book guide his thoughts. He once claimed to be working in the interest of others, yet his retreat in the Spanish caves is devoted to self-contemplation and individual salvation, although the means he has chosen are those least likely to assist him to his goal. Jones's attack on this type of passive mysticism may reflect his earlier suspicions about the spiritual path taken by W. Somerset Maugham's supposed yoga master in *The Razor's Edge*, but they could be linked as easily to his views on the hippie life-style. Just as Hill's earlier effort to protect himself through a casual approach to sex had failed, it is likely that his attempt to shield himself against sorrow through drugs and mysticism will also break down, compelling him to start back up the true path to individual salvation.

Like her husband and son, Louisa Gallagher also strives to evade suffering and undergoes a startling transformation of character, with Samantha again as the karmic catalyst. The allure Samantha holds for Louisa is similar to that she held for Hill. Louisa also believes that Samantha had a deprived childhood and wants to rescue her from the results of it, although she thinks that Samantha's deprivation lay not so much in being black as in having a lesbian for a mother. Louisa's desire to play mother and savior ironically brings out her own latent lesbianism and leads her to have enough physical contact with Samantha to be disturbed by her husband's accusation that she has become what she despised. Her subsequent, ill-fated attempt to seduce Jack as a way of denying her arousal by Samantha is equally ironic, because Louisa had hitherto been puritanically obsessed with pulling her skirt down to avoid exciting any man other than her husband. Her further endeavor to flee from self-awareness by stuffing herself with a suicidal dose of pills results in hospitalization. As she lies in an oxygen tent, Jack inadvertently parodies the love he had refused her by lying on top of her nude body after foolishly loosening a strap that restrains her. She had placed her faith in reason and now exists as a vegetable, yet perhaps someday she will become aware of herself again and be able to confront the enormity of her errors.

Why has Samantha, who understood the three Gallaghers far better than they ever understood her, played so wantonly with their lives and invited them all to cast aside the way of life they worked so hard to fashion? What made her impishly decide to provoke them into dissolving their ties with each other and betraying their social concerns? These questions become doubly important because of the parallel between the effect of Samantha's hedonistic irresponsibility on the Gallaghers and the effect on the workers and citizens of France of the students' lighthearted rejection of their government.

Two central features of Samantha's character are her childishness and her narcissism. Her delight in candy bars and willingness to lie on the floor for hours reading comic books like McKenna demonstrate the childishness that is apparent again and again in her readiness to use people like toys and cast them away when they no longer give her pleasure. Samantha's self-absorption is revealed when she dances by herself, becoming so self-involved that she loses awareness of everyone around her. Because her narcissism can be easily related to her childishness, the combination could be deemed a sufficient cause for her destructiveness.

Another force in her character that may be more fundamental, however, is the desire to make her identity felt by others, the same reason Jack ascribes to the assassination of Robert Kennedy by Sirhan Sirhan, a "silly little Arab immigrant boy . . . whom society stares through like a plateglass window" and who "tries to prove his existence in the only idiot way he knows how" (300-301). After developing his assassination theory, Jack tells Samantha that he thinks she would be capable of doing what Sirhan did, and she admits she could. The implication is that she would have a similar reason for acting like Sirhan. This motivation is also indicated when she tells Jack that "all of you white motherfuckers are out after my little old black ass. . . . And then you'll go away, go home, and pretend you didn't do it" (273). Samantha intends to let no one walk away untouched and thinks that the surest way to make someone remember her is to injure him—or her. Certainly, neither the Gallaghers nor Weintraub will ever forget her.

Samantha's decision to tempt the Gallaghers to their destruction is her own choice, just as Harry's, Hill's, and Louisa's decision to respond to her lures is theirs. Nevertheless, Jack seems justified in asserting that Samantha's influence offers the three Gallaghers a chance to act in a way they might not have acted otherwise, and she is led to do so by the influence of Sirhan's deed. Although Samantha's and Sirhan's activities are horrifyingly vicious, however, their bloody, selfish behavior has had the beneficial effect of shaking the complacency of not only their victims but also of everyone else around them. If Jones's philosophy of spiritual evolution has validity, Robert Kennedy might have taken what he learned from his encounter with Sirhan into a new incarnation while the United States remained shocked by what had happened to him, and the Gallaghers and their acquaintances might follow a more promising path than their former comfortable existence had provided. Samantha argues that revolutions (and, presumably, other disastrous upheavals) change nothing and the world absorbs every-thing. Both statements are true in a material (and possibly spiritual) sense, yet it is also true that revolutions can lead many individuals to change them-selves—and that is their ultimate benefit.

An intriguing commentary on the students' revolution and society is suggested by Jones's description of the repair work being done on roads where students had ripped out paving stones to form barricades against the police. The removal of the stones seems equivalent to the students' attempt to remove themselves from a society unfit to live in, and against which they have used their bodies and lives. The stones' removal also represents the stu-dents' desire to force society to notice them as individuals, a desire similar to Samantha's and Sirhan's to make society see them. In contrast, the gov-ernment's decision to replace the paving stones with "the sticky in-the-heat, evil-smelling modernity of asphalt" indicates its desire to cover over the in-dividuality of its citizens in the interest of security and efficiency (145).

Given these opposing attitudes, clash between the students (along with the citizens) and their government is inevitable. A third approach, however, is implied by the way Italian master stone-layers replace the pavers the students have ripped up. They do not try to chip off parts of the stones and force them into tightly confined patterns, but instead examine five or six possible spots for each stone and choose that in which a stone seems most likely to fit. Some of the largest, most irregular stones are rejected, but most are placed alongside others with which they are "not at all that evenly matched" (144) and yet fit perfectly. Perhaps the stonework is a metaphor for what an ideal society would be like if citizens were allowed to express their individuality but relate it to a meaningful overall pattern so in-dividual actions would be helpful to society at large. That state of society can only be reached, however, when a sufficient number of people have learned compassionate understanding and moral self-control. Until then, society will continue to stimulate conflict among those who are still at a low spiritual level.

In the conflict between de Gaulle and the students of the Sorbonne, de Gaulle's "nineteenth century pride" is "hurt" by the necessity of interrupt-ing a state visit to deal with a nationwide strike (208), and the students' self-confidence is deflated by de Gaulle's shrewd victory. During a speech that the French leader makes after his return from Romania, Jack notes that de Gaulle's "old self-assurance seemed to be missing. For the first time since I had watched his talks, he gave the impression that he was not really sure his latest call would be heard by the people" (210). Even though he wins, the students' activities effectively educate de Gaulle.

The students, humbled by exposure of their inexperience and by their inadequacy in counteracting the government, have been similarly embarrassed by Harry, who confronts the cinema committee with the mistakes they made in their use of the camera while trying to film their version of the revolution. Harry points out that only the subjective vision of the cinema committee students could have made them think their film was any good, and he further punctures their egos by castigating the students for failing to perform the elementary task of using a light meter properly. By the time Harry finishes, even the usually cocky committee chair, Daniel, is subdued and willing to admit that he and the others may not have the ability to rescue themselves from their errors and perform the additional filming necessary to complete their task, although they still want to try.

Earlier, the cinema committee students had been forced to concede the limitations of their policy of democratic discussion. Certain situations, such as the need for direction in film-making, require the authoritative leadership of someone with experience and skill. Their willingness to accept Harry's condition that he be given dictatorial control over a student film shows recognition of the benefits of creative guidance and respect for professionalism. Ironically, they accord to Harry the kind of leadership they spurned from de Gaulle, another professional, because they need Harry in order to make their movie. Yet when the students depend upon Harry too fully, they become unable to make any further effort on their own when he abandons them. They bitterly find that they must learn to take care of themselves, and they have not discovered how to do that.

What Harry wants to teach the students, above all, is how naive and unrealistic their conceptions of portraying the truth about their revolution have been. He asserts that they cannot merely show pictures of students fighting police and expect an audience to share their view of those events. Moreover, they should not expect an audience to be interested in the activities of a mass of students who display no individual qualities. Because the point of their revolution is to make society acknowledge them as individuals, this last objection is a devastating comment on the students' approach to their task. Harry argues that what they should do instead is create an illusion and tell a false but meaningful story about two students with whom the audience can identify. Even using actual events as a background, they must work through a fictional plot and make-believe characters to convey truth. Harry is convinced, after all, that the students' ideal of absolute honesty is not only impossible but also in many cases, especially in relation to his way of film-making, undesirable.

The decline in the students' idealism and their gradual loss of control over the revolution are symbolically represented by Jones's description of the paving stone barricades. The "pure barricade" of paving stones suggests the original stage of the revolution, when students rebelled and were motivated strictly by their ideals and self-righteousness. Significantly, the only such barricade that remains during the latter stages of the rebellion is kept as a half-joking reminder of the purity of their original intentions. When Hill defends Dany Cohn-Bendit's use of rhetorical devices to arouse "that greater mass of students, which was where the needed power lay," Jack points out that the students are resorting "to the same bad methods which you hate and attack the Government for using" (66). Later, Jack similarly argues that the students' employment of a group of roughnecks poses a "philosophical discrepancy" that opposes what they declare to be the aims of their revolution (231).

Time and again, Chairman Daniel, the doctrinaire Anne-Marie, and other students assert that the government has forced such tactics upon them but that they consider any means justified because they are in the right. It is another example of how their karmic relationship with the government has begun to demonstrate the illusory nature of their superiority by revealing their similarity to the enemy, supporting the theory of the "circle of *politique*" that Lucky Videndi had studied at school and suggesting once more the impossibility of shunning the cloak of evil when it is thrust upon you. Their tolerance of any expedient method, in addition to the entrance into their struggle of "bums and riff-raff" who "apparently were in all the fighting just for the hell of it," is equivalent to "the crates and rubbish the garbage collectors had not collected" that students begin to pile on their barricades (209). Finally, the placement of the barricades, made of beautiful wrought-iron fences and iron grilles that had surrounded old trees, stands for the revolution's destruction of much that was charming and valuable.

Because revolutions, even student revolutions, are nothing new, Jones includes many pointed indications of the relation between present events and the past. He describes Notre Dame, for example, as an "old stone barn raised to tribal blood gods" (99) and notes that the Odeon "was burned in the Revolution and later restored" (151) and that the Place du Notre Dame de Paris "just in front of Notre Dame . . . is where they used to pull people apart with horses for having committed some crime or other" (326). Granting Jones's philosophical premises, such recurrence of patterns of violence from generation to generation conveys how slowly the evolution of individual souls takes place and what an important role clashes play in the process. Because different souls learn at different rates, and political, social, military, and quasi-military conflicts provide some of the largest classrooms in which pain teaches, it can be expected that bloodletting rituals will continue until a majority of souls has moved beyond that stage of development. Evolution operates so gradually that the world can only change through the eyes of a few individuals at a time. To put it differently, some individuals change their worldview while the world remains outwardly the same so others may have a similar opportunity to change their worldviews—and themselves.

In a karmic relationship, each person involved arouses a strong feeling of love or hate in the others and brings about a collision between their subjective views of reality. The result of this collision is that all in the relationship, to varying degrees, lose part of their illusions and become aware of the inevitability of their personal isolation and everyone else's. Hence, even though a karmic relationship is a painful, binding force, a person can and should try to get free from it by abandoning the pride and illusions that have kept him or her captive. In gaining this release from a karmic attachment, a person will stop placing the blame for misfortunes on others and acknowledge personal responsibility in full.

In the four story-beads from *The Ice-Cream Headache and Other Stories* that I have chosen to represent the theme of individual, social, and karmic responsibility threaded through all of Jones's works, some characters free themselves from their karmic relationships and others remain firmly bound by them. Like Hill Gallagher in *The Merry Month of May*, for example, the three characters in "Two Legs for the Two of Us" still blame outside forces for the shape their lives have taken. The greatest danger facing all three is the trap of a self-pity based on the idea that their lives would have been happier if the war had not interfered with them. George, however, at least avoids the snare of a renewed karmic relationship with his former wife, Sandy, that would be founded on the pity that his lost leg inspires in her. At the same time, though, he chooses to continue his dangerous relationship with a fellow veteran who also feels bitter about the loss of a leg in the war. Finally, Sandy appears to succumb to self-pity by lamenting that her misfortunes are not her fault. In a similar manner, Sidney Greene in "Sunday Allergy," blames her allergy on her cat rather than seeing its source in her misery over failing to achieve her desire to be married. It is obvious that her illness will continue until she realizes that she alone is responsible for her suffering.

Sylvanus Merrick in "None Sing so Wildly" has also been bound by a subjective worldview. His karmic relationship with Norma Fry, however, brings him to a point where he can begin to release himself from many illusions. He has been forced to recognize that Norma's subjective picture of society is so different from his own that there is no possibility of their forming a lasting relationship. Yet even though he could have chosen to flee from his pain at her loss or to place all the responsibility for their separation on her, he has avoided both pitfalls. Instead, he finds a new inner strength through his effort to understand the reasons for their differences and come to terms with his subjectivity. Similarly, the bar-owner narrator of "A Bottle of Cream" accepts the fact that everyone's worldview, including his own, is subjective, and the ability to touch the life of another person in a significant way is extremely limited.

The title "Two Legs for the Two of Us" points to the dependent relationship formed between two men who have each lost a leg in the war and implies that the subject of dependence will be as fundamental to this story as that of wartime injury. It is not surprising, therefore, that the chief danger confronting the two, George and Tom, is self-pity. Their frequent attempts to joke about their missing legs seem neither casual nor convincing, and their heavy drinking further indicates weakness in response to their loss. Their decision to stick together is hazardous; each has allowed himself to become a mirror-image of the other's distress and to think it is safe to feel sorry for what they see in that mirror.

Nevertheless, George's relationship with Tom Hornney is healthier than the one he might form with his former wife, Sandy, who pities him too openly and is inhibited by her rigid morality from accepting him in the passionate way he desires. Before George leaves, Sandy overcomes her moralistic outlook enough to offer him a bottle of liquor to take with him. Yet once he is gone, she reflects that the failure in their relationship came because the world would not let them alone, and "it was not her fault" (Jones, "Two Legs" 54). Hence, her self-pity is as strong as George's and Tom's, and she blames the same convenient scapegoat: the war.

As Jones notes in his introduction to "Two Legs for the Two of Us," the character of George, based on one of Jones's friends who had lost a leg in the Pacific, is also one of the "major characters" in "They Shall Inherit the Laughter," and the story itself "much less well written and with almost no dialogue, formed part of a chapter of that novel" ("Two Legs" 43). In the novel, the story and the character of George serve as warnings to the protagonist, Johnny Carter (Jones himself), about the dangers of self-pity, one of Johnny's most glaring, karmically binding weaknesses, from which he frees himself only at the end.

In apparent contrast to George's and Sandy's self-pitying failure to attain mutual understanding, "Sunday Allergy" offers the rare spectacle of two women (obvious reincarnations of Lucky Videndi and her roommate Leslie in *Go to the Widow-Maker*) who share the same subjective worldview: "each knew fully as much about the other as she knew about herself, so that in effect each was living the lives of both" (Jones, "Sunday Allergy" 187). Yet the basis for Elena ("Cott") Cotrelli's and Sidney Greene's shared viewpoint is a mutual goal—escaping their unexciting careers by finding men for whom they can care—and mutual failure in achieving that goal. Unfortunately, each has suffered from the collapse of her affairs (and hopes) on many occasions, and they have taken turns comforting each other. The day one of them finally gets the kind of man she wants, however, their combined image-picture of the world will probably fall apart.

Because Sidney's distress is the more aggravated of the two, she is the one who fears the end of their shared life more. Certainly, her allergy attacks coincide, revealingly, with her roommate's more serious dates and later with her married lover's weekly departure to spend the weekend with his family. At the end of the story, Sidney, unlike Cott, who has taken the advice of their "spiritual father and nurse" Doc Bernstein to always keep a "stud around" (190), is preparing to open herself to further anguish by ending an affair without having a new man waiting. Even under these circumstances, she clings to her illusion that the allergy is caused by their castrated cat rather than her inner turmoil.

In the context of *Go to the Widow-Maker*, Cott's final advice to Sidney ("you have to believe there's a man somewhere. With your name on him") and her confession that she has to believe that, too (194) seem to foreshadow Cott's karmically destined encounter with a man such as Ron Grant. With such a man she will be able to form a more meaningful single viewpoint than she had with Sidney, because that viewpoint will be based on mutual shedding of pride and illusions added to mystical, unifying sex rather than on shared weaknesses. Seen in light of Sidney's problems of excessive dependency and the way most karmic relationships between men and women function, however, the advice can only seem, in a personal and a cosmic sense, "komic" (to conflate the words *karmic* and *comic*).

Like Sidney Greene, Sylvanus Merrick in "None Sings so Wildly" also loses a lover, yet he is better equipped to face that loss than she because he is far more honest about his emotions, a key to unlocking the bonds of karma. He neither hides what he feels from himself nor seeks to blame others for his circumstances. Although he, too, suffers from an external situation, he chooses to accept the pain and derive as much insight from it as he can because he has learned that it is better to remain open to life than build a growth-inhibiting wall around his emotions.

"None Sing so Wildly" focuses on the combination of puritanism, security-seeking, and materialism that seems so common in the Midwest and on the karmic clash between the subjective worlds of Sylvanus Merrick and his fiancée, Norma Fry. At odds with what he believes to be the values of the Midwest, Merrick is pleased to go camping with Norma because the outing appeals to his thirst for adventure and his wish that all of life be exciting. Yet she is satisfied that the state park has only a "little patch of woods hemmed in by the fields" (89), committed to a view of maturity as living within the restrictions that guard against the terrors of an open confrontation with life, and takes as few risks as possible. The distance between his inner world and hers is even more evident in the contrast between his assertion that the men ogling her on the beach are aroused by her body and her claims that they simply appreciate the fashionable design of her bathing suit.

Norma's pride is revealed in her irritation at Sylvanus for having made them both appear foolish by championing a couple caught necking, whom she felt had courted their punishment, and by her refusal to call him back after insisting he choose between her and the boy he wants to help. Such pride can be seen as a sixth-generation descendent of the pride that motivated "the grim Bible-toting fathers, who knew their rights God owed them and were prepared to take them—so that they might bequeath us, their offspring, their heritage of mordant Protestantism; out of their lust for salvation, sometimes called security" (101).

Of course, Merrick's pride is as great as Norma's, even though he does not share her Protestant ethics or beliefs, and she is probably right in saying that he, too, wants to convert his beloved to his way of looking at life. Their impasse is that Norma will never be able to make Sylvanus take a secure job, and he will never convince her to accept the life of roving and contact with disreputable persons that he views as valuable for his writing. Yet their break comes because of the unbending stance each takes on whether a boy on the beach should be defended from that law, because each believes that surrender on that side issue would mean capitulating to the other's entire outlook on life.

Knowing when he sets out to help the boy that he will not be able to accomplish much because "life was all compromise anyway" (114), Merrick is neither surprised nor upset that the boy has paid his fine and left, and he hurries back to Norma once he no longer risks injuring his pride or surrendering his way of life. The fact that she has departed while he was gone makes his decision irrevocable and his separation from her final if he wants to retain integrity and freedom. His subsequent movement from bounded Fandalack, where he has been staying with Norma, to lawless Lake Lawler,

where he finishes his vacation, is an attempt to escape not only from a reminder of Norma but also from the midwestern, middle-class way of life in
which she believes. It would be easy for Merrick to let the break with
Norma cause him to hate everything she has come to represent. Yet he feels
no more comfortable with the noisy, undisciplined life at Lake Lawler than
he had with his confined existence in Fandalack, or with the sniggering,
antipuritanical widow than he had with Norma. He most wants a sense of
balance between these opposite poles of midwestern culture so he can have
a clear enough vision to write about what he has experienced without ran-
cor or juvenile sarcasm.

As in "None Sing so Wildly," truth and balance are central issues in "A
Bottle of Cream." At the beginning of the story, the bar-owner narrator
poses a moral conundrum to himself concerning the difficulty and ques-
tionable value of telling the truth, offering a key to the tone and attitude of
everything that will follow. When he was a child, the bar-owner discovered
that telling the truth and being believed are two different matters and that
the best way for a story to be believed is to tell a listener what he or she
wants to hear. It is a discovery that has led him both to recognize the subjectivity of everyone's vision of truth, the central element in karmic clashes,
and to refuse to view life in terms of absolutes. Thus, he tends to accept the
world as he sees it and believe that nothing would be gained through an extensive effort to change it. During his early boyhood, the narrator had
shared his parents' feeling of being "angry at life" (Jones, "A Bottle of
Cream" 178), and he still has an occasionally irritated sense of the injustice
of much that happens in the world. Yet he cannot make any large statements
or wishes about justice, and his typical reflection is likely to be, "So these
things happen, what then?"

Although he feels that whatever moral distinction can be made between
the criminal Chet Poore and the smug deputy sheriff who arrested a friend
of the bar-owner will be in Chet's favor and he dislikes the deputy as a man,
the narrator intends to keep on good terms with him. Moreover, he toler-
ates the irony that the judge who sentences his friend for reckless driving
while fining him for drunken driving and the sheriff who escorts the friend
to pay the fine are both drinking companions of the friend and himself.

Even though the bar-owner admits that drunken driving can be a problem and tries with little success to keep his customers from drinking so
much that they will become hazards on the road, he regards the propaganda
against drunken driving as simple-minded and the penalties for it as overly
stiff. The bar-owner argues in favor of a more complex view of life that affirms that sometimes drunken drivers may be the victims of youngsters who

run in front of them to show off to friends or old people who want to use a car as a means of committing suicide, and that, more often than not, drunken drivers may be frightened individuals trying to get home safely without injuring anyone. The bar-owner remembers that he, too, has been drunk and does not allow himself to become self-righteous about the drunkenness of others. He compromises with the issue of drunkenness in continuing to run his bar and is resigned to the idea that "people will always drink" (176). Neither can he feel superior as the deputy and the lawyer do about Chet Poore's thefts, because he has also stolen in the past. The only thing that matters to him about Chet is that once he stopped to help the narrator.

Implicitly recognizing the small effect that anyone has on another person's life, the bar-owner states that he "would like to be able to say Chet Poore and the episode of the bottle changed [his] life in some way or another," but he does "not honestly think it did" (182). Although he wishes that things were different so such concern and intervention would matter, and he would like to become more involved with his sons, he accepts the fact that they will not let him any further into their lives than he let his parents into his. In the same way, he "hungers" to know more about Chet but is resigned to being able to obtain only limited information about him and never fully understanding his way of life. He vaguely comprehends that Chet's wildness and the physical and mental punishment he received for it enabled him to respond to the narrator's boyhood terror at a situation that seemed impossible to escape and allowed Chet to act to end the terror. He knows, however, that he will never be able to get close to Chet's—or anyone else's—soul and perceive it as a whole. The moment that meant so much to him—Chet purchases a bottle of cream to replace the one the narrator has broken—meant nothing to Chet. The narrator is left to ponder how little we know about the inner worlds of others or our own. Yet he is also left with an image of Chet's kindly smile, which hints at the peace that may come with compassionate understanding.

Jones's seventh published novel, *A Touch of Danger,* not only adheres to the conventional patterns of hard-boiled detective fiction but also remains true to the patterns of his philosophy, including those which relate to his views on individual responsibility and karmic relationships. This is a difficult technical achievement, because even the hard-boiled version of the detective novel is an extremely rigid form of fiction and does not readily permit the introduction of serious content. For example, the bulk of the type of detective novel Jones chose to write must concern the investigation of a crime, and the criminal's identity must be hidden until near the end. (Although some forms of the detective novel, such as the inverted mystery, do reveal the criminal's identity early, Jones adhered to the more traditional format.) In addition, most of the suspects should have something to conceal and maintain false fronts that the detective must cleverly pierce before discovering who performed the crime.

These requirements force mystery writers to devote a great deal of effort to devising an intellectual puzzle founded upon deceptive appearances, and under such conditions it is far from easy to develop complex characters or complicated, meaningful themes. Only a few remarkable writers, such as Dashiell Hammett, Raymond Chandler, Chester Himes, Ross MacDonald, John le Carre, Ngugi wa Thiong'o, P. D. James, and Ruth Rendell, have devised plots that satisfy both a mystery reader's demand for an intellectually stimulating game and the desire of readers of serious novels for substantial psychological, social, and philosophical content. Thus, George Garrett is right in emphasizing that "probably the most interesting fact about *A Touch of Danger* is the pure skill of it," because "as entertainment, as a genre piece, it holds up with the best of them and proves (if it needed proving) that Jones had the craft and the capacity to write economically and well within the strict limits of the thriller" and "that he was a more versatile writer than at least some of his critics had imagined" (*James Jones* 154).

Jones accomplishes a large part of his difficult task of blending puzzle and philosophy by making the investigation a learning experience for his detective, Frank "Lobo" Davies. In a letter dated August 23, 1972, to Helen Meyer, president of the Dell Publishing Company, Jones argued that *A Touch of Danger* was "a symbolic novel couched in a 'mystery' form. One big symbol of the crisis in ethics of America today" (Hendrick, ed., *To Reach Eternity* 340). The symbolism begins with Davies's nickname, which suggests both his starting position on the animal level of spiritual evolution and the detective's traditional role as a lone wolf. Lobo's efforts to function socially and ethically as a lone wolf, however, are ironically complicated by the karmic relationships he forms with suspects who compel him to face several of his strongest illusions and accept responsibility for some painful mistakes. Most obviously, his involvement with both Chantal and Marie teaches him that he can never escape the isolation he had once eagerly welcomed but, in response to aging, would now like to deny, and his relationship with Freddy Tarkoff, the boss of a drug ring, disturbs his confidence in his judgment and values. At the end of the novel, Lobo is still a long way from attaining the level of spiritual man, but he has at least started to question his belief in the virtue of acting responsibly and to achieve momentary glimmers of compassionate understanding.

Jones's major technical feat, however, is his double surprise ending, because the hardest task for a serious mystery writer is to create a single ending that provides the answer to a puzzle and also illuminates a theme. Jones does so twice in the same book. He prepares the way for the revelation of Sonny Duval's motive for murder by calling attention to the parallel case of Chuck, who claims to believe in free love and finds that he has begun to feel a possessive love for Diane. Yet Jones also uses that motive as a springboard for social commentary on the hippies' desire to reconstruct society along freer lines and philosophical commentary on the folly of attempting to shun the cloak of evil. In addition, Jones prepares readers to accept the discovery that Freddy Tarkoff is the boss of a drug ring by making it clear that Leonid Kronitis seems too weak to hold such an operation together and stressing Kronitis's acquaintance with Tarkoff. Then Jones points out how this discovery moves both Lobo and Tarkoff toward the humility necessary for spiritual progress by forcing them to admit that they, too, have performed the evil they shun.

As expected, the character in *A Touch of Danger* who has reached a higher level than the others and comes closest to being Jones's spokesman is the detective-narrator Lobo Davies, who has a sense of failure almost as acute as Jack Hartley's. Although he had once gloried in his acclaim as a hero for killing the murderer of his detective partner, he has come to regard that shoot-out as a blunder and admits he would now handle the situation differently. Davies feels similarly ashamed of the job he did for Tarkoff in which he terrified a Greek into returning embezzled but legally untouchable money by breaking his finger and threatening his children's lives. Lobo's pride is hurt even more by the discovery that Tarkoff has used part of the recovered money to mastermind a heroin operation. Although there is little chance to see how that discovery will effect Lobo's development, it can only move him further along the path of spiritual growth through ego-reduction.

Several observable changes do occur in Lobo as a result of his experiences, including the alteration in his attitude toward vengeance. When his partner died, Lobo had set things up so that he could shoot the murderer. As he tells Chantal, however, if the same thing happened now, he would place the murderer in the hands of the law, even though "six months later he would be back on the Street, terrorizing and extorting other black people, and bragging about how he fooled us whiteys" (293). Moreover, he proves that he means this by his handling of Sonny Duval, a man who murdered someone who mattered more to Lobo than his partner had. He not only turns Sonny over to the law but is also willing to let him be confined to a mental institution because he "didn't really want to see Sonny executed" (Jones, *A Touch of Danger* 425).

The deal Lobo makes with Tarkoff and Kronitis about Sonny's punishment and their heroin ring reflects the same change in attitude Lobo had shown in his treatment of Sonny. Although Lobo may wish to hurt Tarkoff, he reins himself in out of concern for Chantal, whom he no longer loves but still wants to help. He could let his idealism or anger induce him to turn over his information about the heroin operation to Inspector Pekoris and ignore the consequences but chooses instead to accept the compromise Tarkoff and Kronitis offer him. Moreover, he does not try to make his desires paramount, but rather enters into what he calls "horse trading" and proffers only modest demands in return for letting the men go free. He fulfills the promise he made Chantal to obtain her release from the heroin operation and succeeds in his main goal of halting the operation. The two concessions are sufficient to satisfy him about the solution, and the spirit of compromise they represent now frees him to seize back the money his idealism had made him return to Kronitis. Money is all he allows himself to gain, and it is likely that he will use most of it to meet what he considers his responsibilities to his former wife and two daughters.

A related change in Lobo occurs in his attitude toward violence. Even though physical force is a form of assertiveness and Lobo is highly competitive, he has reached a point where he strives to limit the bodily damage he does to others. Like the "fifth-graders" in *Viet Journal*, he will not let anyone dominate him and is ready to fight for any number of reasons, yet he has come to regard killing as wrong and the more extreme forms of violence as destructive. After hippies beat him, Lobo reflects, "In all, I was in pretty good shape. They hadn't chest-stomped me. Hadn't kicked in my jaw. I felt a kind of liking for them. No maiming; just good, clean old American fun" (248).

Presumably, Lobo's remorse over shooting his partner's killer and terrorizing the Greek embezzler have helped give him the insight to appreciate the control they exerted while venting their hostility. When he subsequently battles with Chuck, who appears to be Marie's murderer and has kicked him twice in the testicles, Lobo limits the damage he inflicts. The moment he is about to break Chuck's jaw, Lobo finds that "something" stops him and shakes him back and forth instead. Afterward, he almost grinds Chuck's glasses under the heel of his shoe but then contents himself with snapping the bridge of the glasses. Moreover, Lobo begins to feel dissatisfied about his part in the fight and asks himself, "Was I feeling a little sorry for goofy Chuck?" (325). Although Lobo has a long way to go to reach the level Dave Hirsh attained, he is advancing toward it. It is an achievement for him to restrict the harm he does to others and experience sympathy for those whom he does hurt.

Another feature of Lobo's character that perhaps undergoes modification is his sense of responsibility, and in that he resembles Jack Hartley. When he takes on an obligation, Lobo feels bound to carry it through, no matter what it costs him mentally, physically, or spiritually. Part of the reason he agreed to terrorize the Greek, for example, was to obtain money for his former wife, Joanie, and for his daughters' support payments, and part of the reason he takes back Kronitis's retainer is to help them maintain their social life. Such consequences of his aid to Joanie are something he will have to think about before accepting other "responsibilities."

Working out some of his other karmic relationships provides Lobo with an area of responsibility that will undergo major change. The most powerful relationships are those with Tarkoff, Chantal, and Marie. That with Tarkoff is especially important because it precipitates this adventure and is likely to have the most lasting effect on him. When he and Tarkoff meet, Lobo believes that "as long as you worked for him and took his money, the client was right" (35) and that Tarkoff is correct in assuming that it is justifiable to ignore decency with the Greek embezzler because the Greek seems to be "depending on human decency to let him off the hook" (36). Discovering how hard it is to live with his actions against the Greek not only moves him toward belief in behaving decently but also, even more significantly, undermines his confidence in the ability to judge right and wrong, forcing him to view human behavior from a more complex perspective. He still has sufficient conviction in his responsibility for the results of everything in which he involves himself to be hurt by the knowledge that Tarkoff has used money he regained through Lobo's efforts for a purpose Lobo considers evil. He will eventually learn, however, that he can only be responsible for his own actions and not for the use others make of them. Perhaps he will then see irony in the fact that Tarkoff had gotten the idea of starting a heroin ring by after seeing Lobo's efforts to assist hippies damaged by the misuse of drugs and thus observing that a large drug market exists.

This painful encounter with Lobo is also a learning experience for Tarkoff, who thinks that he has winningly combined the roles of shrewd businessman and good citizen, yet the furious Lobo forces him to admit that both parts of his self-image are illusions. As Lobo points out, Tarkoff's cleverness is suspect because he let his partner Kronitis hire irresponsible thieves and also a Narcotics Bureau agent to run the drug operation. Hurling the worst insult he knows, Lobo calls both Tarkoff and Kronitis "amateurs," and Tarkoff is compelled to admit the accuracy of that accusation. The angry detective also challenges the fact that Tarkoff is a member of the City Anti-Drug Commission as well as a heroin smuggler. It is possible, however, that Tarkoff sent Lobo to the island of Tsatsos because he subconsciously wished to be caught, just as Edith Barclay in *Some Came Running* arranges to have herself exposed as Frank Hirsh's mistress and exorcize the guilt of having called her dead grandmother a whore. Tarkoff is in a position where, willingly or not, he must abandon his idealized self-image and confront realities that he had been sidestepping.

Lobo's affair with Chantal is equally a source of uncomfortable illumination for both, relating to their increasing mutual concerns about aging and the restrictions and self-doubts it entails. Perhaps the main reason Lobo is so pugnacious is that he is eager to test himself in physical combat and prove that he is still strong, skillful, and able to endure abuse. He is also testing himself in the bedroom with Chantal, especially at those times he comes to her after having been in a fight. He has reached some acceptance of time's ravages, however, because his response to Chantal's distress over growing old is to tell her "softly" that "there's nothing anybody can do about that" (342). He has also come to terms with the knowledge that he cannot get outside himself through loving Chantal. He bids her farewell with "a medium-light, passionless kiss" in recognition of their past relationship and mutual failure to achieve anything more substantial (431).

Chantal's affair with Lobo similarly focuses attention on her age—and on her foremost illusions. Her primary asset has been her appearance, and she knows that asset is losing value. Moreover, Lobo has wounded her ego by his lack of interest in her much of the time and his indirect pity of the effect of aging on her. She is especially vulnerable to rejection because she has centered her life on pride in her beauty, title, and social position. She has been a social butterfly like Lobo's former wife, and her similarity with Joanie is probably what both attracts and repels him in their relationship. Lobo exposes the emptiness of Chantal's social life, however, and confronts her with her impecuniousness and the vapidity of her "friends"—ugly realities underlying her illusion of social prominence. He also forces her to admit to herself that she has been a petty, greedy carrier of drugs and to face getting out of that business. At the end of the novel, Chantal has the strength to joke about her situation and ask, "What will I do now? . . . I guess I can sell my hot body to a rich old Greek. But I'm getting a little too old even for that" (431). She is willing to be honest about the story she had told Lobo concerning Girgis's imaginary attempt to blackmail her and reveal that she had told it because she was attracted to the detective and wanted to gain his attention. In making this admission, she faces the implication that little else in her life can interest a man like him.

Age also plays a significant role in the relationship between Lobo and Marie. Although Lobo desires her as much as he has ever desired any woman, he learns that there are other considerations more important to him than sexual excitement. In particular, he is disturbed by the ways in which she reminds him of his daughters and he reminds her of her father, so his primary feeling toward her becomes one of protectiveness rather than lust. When he is about to accompany her to her apartment to accept an obvious invitation for sex, he finds that he dislikes the hard look he sees on his face in the mirror and the "whorish" look he had previously observed on her face when she was striving to be seductive. He senses that the overtones of incest and kinkiness that would be involved in any sexual act between them would be damaging to Marie as well as to himself, and he is willing to sacrifice whatever pleasure the act might give him to help her remain youthfully open to life rather than become jaded and self-enclosed. Yet he does have a powerful sympathy for her that is at least part of the motivating force behind his actions. In this and other ways, he shows concern about her growth as a person and does what he can to promote it.

Marie is an apt pupil because she has reached a stage in her life where she recognizes the folly of the direction she has taken and is looking for a way out. In a 1973 interview Jones stated, "I have found the overpermissive liberalism of today somewhat a dead end and wanted to explore the feeling that the young of today are only seeking to reestablish the ancient virtues of honor, honesty, personal integrity, etc. The concept of moral self-discipline seems to be getting lost in today's rush for 'absolute' freedom" (Bannon, "Story behind the Book" 38). Marie is obviously an example of a youth making this kind of search, and Lobo significantly refers to her as "the only bit of true gentility and integrity I'd found here" (Jones, *A Touch of Danger* 292). She is candid not only about the extent of her sexual life but also about her realizations that its effect on her has been disastrous and that her present anguish is the result of her bad choices. Marie's biggest mistake has been allowing people to make use of her; she has never displayed the vicious self-concern of Jane Duval or Jim Kirk. Beyond that, she has demonstrated courage in spear-fishing by herself and spending the winter on Tsatsos (something Chantal was unwilling to do). Thus, it is little wonder that Lobo becomes interested in her welfare.

Even though he has not advanced enough to give her more than elementary spiritual advice, Lobo can oversee Marie's growth toward his level, and their relationship is that of master-disciple. Significantly, the first time Lobo notices her, Marie is alone in the water, which indicates to him that she has progressed further than her hippie comrades who bunch together most of the time. Then, once he takes her in tow, he notices that he can quickly lead her "over the psychological hurdle" in skin diving so she can go forty-five feet underwater without panicking at the heaving of her diaphragm (200).

Although there is no hint that Lobo has any comprehension of Jones's theory of reincarnation, it is possible that he dimly senses its meaning, which is why he becomes so interested in the question of what level Marie had attained at the time she was forced to abandon this incarnation. It comforts him to learn that she did not surrender to despair when she realized that Sonny was trying to kill her, but rather took measures to preserve her life and had the fortitude not to scream or plead, because such a response implies that she was ready to move on to a new stage of development.

In addition to Lobo's karmic relationships, there appears to be a three-way karmic bond developed among Sonny Duval, Jane Duval, and Jim Kirk. The essence of a typical karmic relationship is that each of its members acts in a way that exposes the illusion of the other or others and allows his or her own to be exposed. Sonny's involvement with Jane and her lover Kirk reveals to him that underneath his overpermissive attitudes is a childish desire to have everything go his way and all his wishes fulfilled. Given his self-image, it is a hard truth for him to accept. Similarly, in their turn, Jane and Kirk must learn that they are not the superior beings they consider themselves to be.

Sonny Duval is an overage hippie who violates every one of his ideals. He is a millionaire who believes in working and living strictly on what he earns, but he hires men to clean his boat and spends money he cannot afford from his earnings to travel throughout Europe to retrieve his wife Jane whenever she runs off with a lover. Moreover, when Lobo exposes his crimes, Sonny tells him, "When you've got the money, nobody can touch you. . . . And I've got it" (393-94). Like Steve and Chuck, Sonny professes to be a pacifist, an ideal he betrays through his murders. He also claims to be opposed in principle to marriage, yet he is legally married to Jane, although he usually denies that. Above all, he asserts that he respects Jane's "free spirit" and would not wish to hold her down by preventing her from having as many love affairs as she wants, when in reality he is so upset by her promiscuity that he is driven to kill her lovers. Sonny's one redeeming trait is his suffering; he has been hurt by her indifference to him in the past and will be hurt even more by her decision to confine him to a mental institution to obtain his money. It is undoubtedly this capacity for pain that prompts Lobo to agree to shake his hand.

In contrast, neither Jane nor Kirk is capable at the moment of the kind of intense suffering that Sonny undergoes, although they are both vulnerable to being hurt and can be educated about specific points. Jane's weak spots are her sexual vanity and pride in her independence. Like Samantha-Marie Everton in *The Merry Month of May*, who thinks only of herself and is heedless about what her pursuit of pleasure does to others, Jane not only is confident about the appeal of her body, having no doubt she can attract any man or woman after whom she lusts, but also is convinced that she can get away with anything. Thus, she is stunned to learn that her husband Sonny has been killing her lovers and, even worse, that her fate now seems to be in his hands. Jane is also disturbed by the knowledge that Lobo has been immune to her charms and has manipulated her into a humiliating position as bait in a trap for Sonny. Lobo notices that when she appears on the balcony clad in a towel concealing almost nothing that she has "a big broad sexy smile on her face. A fake one. I guessed for the first time since I'd met her anyway, she wasn't looking superior and self-confident" (391). Following Sonny's capture, Jane begins to lean on Kirk for support and acknowledge her dependence on him. Because Kirk is untrustworthy, however, Jane's attachment may well further her spiritual education, particularly because she will have Sonny's money, and that will provoke Kirk's cutthroat tendencies and likely lead him to view her as an obstacle in getting it.

Kirk's own education is simple and profound. When he first meets Kirk, Lobo has the impression that he "would just bull ahead and do anything, anything that came in his head and that he wanted to do. He would talk or fight his way out of it afterward. And had complete confidence that he could" (123). Kirk has no discernible scruples and deals casually in hashish and heroin; he also does not hesitate at shooting at Lobo or threatening him with a knife. Furthermore, he shows no more fear when Lobo has him at gunpoint than he did when he held the gun on Lobo. It is an edifying experience for him when Sonny points a gun at him and pulls the trigger. Because Lobo did not forewarn him that the gun contains blanks, Kirk believes that he is about to die, and there is nothing he can do to prevent that. His sense of helplessness shakes him to the core of his being. After he learns that he is safe, he sobs and screams that he wants to kill Sonny. Even though he later recovers much of his outward confidence, it is clear that he will never again be able to believe so profoundly in his indestructibility. It is comforting to reflect that the ego of even a man such as Kirk can be dented and that he can be moved along a path toward spiritual growth through his karmic relationships.

6

The Last Lesson:
Whistling in the Dark

Outwardly, *Whistle*, the final volume of Jones's army trilogy, is his most depressing book, drawing painful attention to the plight of the returning wounded after World War II and discussing the self-destructive slide of all four major characters: Mart Winch, John Strange, Bobby Prell, and Marion Landers. Moreover, Frank MacShane has recorded that the aging author "once jotted down on the back of an envelope" a message to his brother, Jeff: what he wanted in *Whistle* was "to make everybody in the world groan with the inevitability of sorrow" (*Into Eternity* 305). In any case, Jones, who wrote much of the book while suffering from congestive heart failure, inevitably infused it with his increasing knowledge of the restrictions that arise from advancing age, prolonged illness, and approaching death—the last lessons to be learned.

Although all of the main characters are relatively young (at the beginning of the novel, Winch is forty-two, Strange, twenty-seven, Prell, twenty-three or twenty-four, and Landers, twenty-one), their war experiences have aged them, and they are all aware of new limitations on their physical abilities. They cannot do many things the way they did them before the war: cannot walk the same, cannot drink, cannot make love (at least not without breathlessness or pain and sometimes not at all), or cannot even sleep for fear of having nightmares of dead friends. They also experience a weakening of their mental powers, frighteningly diminishing their comprehension, enthusiasm, and decisiveness.

The saddest case, the one that demonstrates the difference between this book and those that preceded it, is Mart Winch. In his previous incarnations as Milt Warden in *From Here to Eternity* and Eddie Welsh in *The Thin Red Line* (the other two books in the trilogy), the character revived as Winch is a master manipulator. True, he is also a bit eccentric by choice, even gleefully and calculatingly crazy at times, but he seems both wise and wily, a top sergeant on top of every situation. *The Thin Red Line* even implies that his resourcefulness and durability might win him a state of permanent bliss through permanent combat numbness.

As Winch, however, he begins with the same wiliness but ends as certifiable, screaming his head off because he could not save the men for whom he felt responsible. His loss of reason and control is perhaps the most disturbing event in Jones's fiction. If Warden/Welsh/Winch can become a self-destructive fuckup like Prewitt, then how can the rest of us hope to maintain a firm hold on our lives? Moreover, his greatest talent, a profound understanding of human nature and ability to predict behavior, is revealed to be a major reason for his crack-up. His friend John Strange reflects that "it must be hard on the sanity, seeing things ahead of time like Winch. Seeing. And knowing. And telling people. Who never listened. Damned hard on the sanity" (Jones, *Whistle* 417).

Yet the basic patterns of spiritual evolution are still present in *Whistle*, making it clear that all this pain and apparent futility (including the futility of knowledge) have the same purpose as they do throughout the rest of Jones's writing: to reduce the ego. That suggests that the novel's overwhelming darkness is but the dark half of the circle of yin and yang and cannot be viewed properly apart from the all-embracing whole. The thumbscrew of salvation has simply been given one additional turn. Winch, Prell, Landers, and Strange all lose self-confidence and feel guilty over the knowledge that because of physical problems from their wounds they can grasp some good fortune at home while others of their former company who are equally meritorious must remain at war. Further, they all destroy themselves because of their awareness of not deserving to be happy while others like them must continue to endure intolerable tension and misery. Like so many of Jones's other characters, their compassion expands as their ability to cope contracts.

The character who exhibits this trait most clearly is John Strange (Maylon Stark in *From Here to Eternity* and Maynard Storm in *The Thin Red Line*). Strange decides to commit suicide because he cannot bear to stand by again as a cook in a "safe" position and watch a company of inexperienced men go off to be maimed and killed in battle. Because of his previous experience with combat, he knows what will happen to them but cannot prepare them for it. Like Winch, he learns that knowledge offers only a different way to suffer; it is not a defense. The final lesson is that there is no way to prepare for pain or avoid ego reduction.

That lesson is reinforced by the fate of Marion Landers, who, although not included among the reincarnating characters in "A Note by the Author" at the beginning of *Whistle*, bears a close resemblance to Geoffrey Fife in

The Thin Red Line, Richard Mast in *The Pistol*, and Jones himself, which is likely the reason Jones did not include him. Landers, a college-educated company clerk, shares much of Prewitt's idealism and rage against injustice, as well as his inability to get along with authority. He (as Jones did) gets all the breaks Prewitt failed to get, however. Every time Landers has a fight or goes AWOL, he is excused, not only because of Winch's behind-the-scenes manipulations but also because of Colonel Steven's conscience. Unlike Prewitt, Landers has a commanding officer who is fair. Moreover, the second time he is arrested for going AWOL, he is given what he says he wants: a discharge. Prewitt, however, is railroaded into the stockade.

In a letter to his brother Jeff, written on June 3, 1944, from the psychiatric ward in the hospital at Camp Campbell, Kentucky, where he had been placed after going AWOL, Jones wrote that he had informed the psychiatrists that "if they attempt to send me overseas again I'll commit suicide; that if I don't get out of the army I'll either go mad or turn into a criminal" (Hendrick, ed., *To Reach Eternity* 44). The result for Landers is the same as for his imprisoned predecessor: self-destruction. When authorities refuse to do it for him, as they so kindly did for Prewitt, Landers must mete out his own punishment by throwing himself in front of an oncoming car. Part of his reason for doing so is that he has been haunted by the memory of how, after being wounded, he chose to drink the water in his canteen rather than offer it to the men around him. In his dreams, "the men of his platoon wanted his water, looking at him silently with beseeching eyes" (Jones, *Whistle* 32).

The importance of the canteen incident may be underscored by Jones's account in *WW II* of his own contrasting experience with being wounded: "As soon as I found I wasn't dead or dying, I was pleased to get out of there as fast as I could. . . . The thing I was most proud of was that I remembered to toss my full canteen of water to one of the men from the company headquarters lying there" (53). Landers's remorse over his selfishness has rendered any offer of advantage or assistance an anathema to him and increased his need to do penance, even unto death. More important, the difference between the treatment Prewitt and Landers receive and the similarity of their fates, taken jointly, imply that the end is what matters; whether a person has good luck or bad luck ultimately has little meaning, because both may lead in the same direction.

Another familiar pattern in *Whistle* is that of characters unsuccessfully attempting to shun the cloak of evil. Winch's girlfriend, Carol Firebaugh, admits, "I don't want to be a Southern Belle. . . . But I'm afraid I'm a Southern Belle, anyway" (Jones, *Whistle* 300). For this pattern to operate, it does not matter what other people consider to be evil; it only matters what you regard as evil. John Strange, who abhors cunnilingus although delighting in fellatio by women, must learn to reject his selfishness in sex and enjoy using this means of giving pleasure. His change in attitude toward cunnilingus mirrors a change in the way he sees women—as equals rather than as sexual servants. Bobby Prell (Prewitt in *From Here to Eternity* and Witt in *The Thin Red Line*) must likewise learn not to view others with contempt. When Marion Landers kills himself by stepping in front of a car, Prell feels little concern: "his first natural reaction had been to think it was some drunken fight. In some poolhall or bar" (402). When his guilt over trading on the Medal of Honor, an award he feels nobody still living deserves, becomes unbearable, however, he chooses to kill himself in the way he expected Landers to die, a drunken fight in a bar. In this way, responding like Edith Barclay, who had let herself be publicly labeled a whore as penance for having said that about Old Jane Staley, Prell can atone to Landers for having thought so little of him by similarly destroying his own reputation.

What is new in *Whistle*, at least new since *From Here to Eternity*, is the inclusion of several overtly mystical experiences. All four of the major characters experience at least one such encounter, and in a few cases the experience is recurrent. While Jones, as in previous works of magic realism, offers the literal-minded a rational explanation for these fantasy episodes, implying that they may be dreams, visions, or semihallucinations, he also leaves signs so more spiritually open-minded readers can regard the scenes on a symbolic or metaphysical level. All of the episodes are suggestive rather than pointedly allegorical, although all may be interpreted in terms of spiritual evolution.

The setting of the novel in the mythical city of Luxor, Tennessee, gives a preliminary hint of the mystical experiences awaiting readers. The Egyptian name *Luxor* (evoked in Jones's mind no doubt by the equally Egyptian name *Memphis*, where the army sent him) is reminiscent of the fact that ancient Egyptians were among the first believers in reincarnation. The name seems well chosen because *lux* (Latin for "light") suggests in this context the yang-like light of reincarnation and spiritual evolution amid the yin-like darkness of dissolution and death in *Whistle*. It seems probable that Jones learned about Egyptian religion through his interest in Paul Brunton, author of *A Search in Secret Egypt*, but his fascination with reincarnation may also have led him to the *Egyptian Book of the Dead*. When Norman Mailer finally expressed his Jones-inspired belief in reincarnation several years later, he chose to do so in an Egyptian setting in *Ancient Evenings*.

Landers's mystical experience, which occurs on the way to Luxor, is that of being lifted out of his body to a position above the hospital ship in which he is a passenger. From that lofty viewpoint, he can observe an "unpeopled mysterious blue continent" that is "the most beautiful and serene and peaceful, and *right*, sight he had ever seen" (34). He has no idea what the continent represents or what his ability to get outside his body means, and all too abruptly and uncomprehendingly he returns to his "normal" life of conflict. The experience remains in the back of his mind, however, and at the moment of his death Landers again sees the hospital ship with a red cross on top (the cross of Christ? of blood and pain? of a spiritual organization akin to the planetary one with that sign and dedicated to the curing of the unhealthy in soul?) and the mysterious continent it can never touch: "Far off, the great blue continent still stood. Uninhabited. Green with the silent, unpeopled forests and soft grasses. The breakers clashing on the white, unpeopled sands. And the silence of home" (395). Although the "great blue continent" is identified on one level as the "American landfall" that the ship approaches (455), the facts that it is "unpeopled" and filled with "the silence of home" suggest that it may represent, on another level, a place—or state—where humans are not separate beings but parts of a beautiful, peaceful whole and will eventually return and be absorbed. The suffering (the hospital ship?) that brings humans near so that they may be reintegrated into the continent is only a means; it will not remain at a destination where only tranquility and harmony exist.

Winch also has an out-of-body experience, although his is less dramatic. While suffering from acute edema, he feels as if he were no longer "inside himself" and as if there were "another him" (140-41). He wonders whether he is dying but is in no way disturbed by that thought. "At the same time, it was not as if he were *actually* outside himself, and could 'see' himself from some other place. In other words, he could in fact 'see' nothing" (141). Later, he wonders if there might be "another him outside somewhere waiting to be rejoined to this part" (195). Although the question is highly suggestive, it is unclear what this "other him" may consist of or what its relation may be to the tranquil continent. It does not appear to be as individualized as the embodied Winch, however, and that seems appropriate; the goal of spiritual evolution is to break down the ego so humanity may be reunited with God. Moreover, both Emerson and Madame Blavatsky, as well as Jones himself in "They Shall Inherit the Laughter," have indicated their belief in a divine spark of spirit within. The theosophists consider the divine spark as the reincarnating part of the human soul, which is different from the soul-part that remains attached to the body and the body's needs and perishes at each death.

Prell's encounter with the unknown is equally unindividualized. Although he describes it as a "religious experience," he "might as easily have said mystical" (56). During the train ride from San Francisco to Luxor, the pain in Prell's legs turns him inward, sealing "him off from other awareness." In the midst of this inward contemplation, he discovers that "somebody or some thing was in there with him" (56). Significantly, the mysterious presence "was not a personality" and "did not do anything. It was not an added strength. . . . Nor was it a detriment. It was just there" (56). Is this presence God, or another Prell, or a master from the world of bodiless souls surrounding the material world? We do not know. But it seems clear from this experience, as it had been in Jones's other works, that we must find salvation on our own without the aid or interference of any other being. Or must we?

Strange's experiences are the most readily interpretable. On two occasions when he is under anesthesia he enters a great, Romanesque hall, where lights flash and a shrouded judge informs him that he cannot remain. It is almost certainly the world of bodiless souls that Bob French described to Dave Hirsh, and the judge's verdict means that Strange has not yet learned enough to gain entry, a sentence that may be reversed after his additional experience in the mystical final scene of the novel when Strange is dying. After his first visit to this world, Strange reflects that he felt a "new compassion" there and that "included everything in God's created universe" (184). Underneath this compassion, however, is a pocket of rebelliousness "over the fact that things must be the way they were" (184). That suggests why he must return to the material world with its embodied souls. In addition, he feels an increased sense of rebelliousness toward his wife, Linda, and a heightened sexuality that prods him to desire affairs with other women, an area in which he must decrease his selfishness. Shortly after his vision, he meets Frances Highsmith, who asks him to "make her come by licking her pussy" (185), and thus an obsession begins that will teach Strange not to fear the cloak of evil or try to thrust it aside.

The implication that the world of bodiless souls may be inducing Strange's new sexuality and rebelliousness toward his wife to educate him further is reinforced by one of the epigraphs, the supposed "Ancient French Jingle" that Jones created, as he told me in 1972. He also said that he created one of the epigraphs for *The Thin Red Line*, the "Old Middlewestern

Saying": "There's only a thin red line between the sane and the mad." The chilling "Ancient French Jingle" reads:

> Bounce, and dance; bounce, and dance;
> Jiggle on your strings.
> Whistle toward the graveyard.
> Nobody knows who or what moves your batten.
> You'll not find out.

The idea that unseen forces direct us is unavoidable and perhaps a significant flaw in the novel—or maybe a modification in the system or a last-minute, important question. Although nearly everything else in the novel, including Prell's mystical experience, affirms the typically Jonesian insistence on each person's responsibility for his or her own salvation, Strange's experience and the jingle argue that each person's destiny is decided by a spiritual puppet master or puppet masters. It may be possible to reconcile the two views, to some extent, by positing that the spiritual masters only make use of psychological forces already existing within each man and woman, but that does not fully overcome the sense of interference by outside forces that appeared to be denied in Prell's encounter. It suggests a possible conflict in Jones's thinking that he might not have worked out or perhaps did not want to work out, preferring to leave the issue open.

Thus, far from occasioning any serious harm to the novel, this discrepancy may even have added useful and intriguing ambivalence to its overall emphasis on uncertainty. The uncertainty in *Whistle* begins with the title's ambiguity. The first epigraph, taken from the memoirs of R. J. Blessing, states, "There was an almost standard remark the night medic on duty would make to the newly arrived patients at the hospital. He said, 'If you want anything, just whistle for it.'" Yet the implication of the comfort and benefits to be derived from whistling is immediately canceled—or at least cast in doubt—by the second epigraph, the "Ancient French Jingle," which counsels that whistling is futile and a useless attempt to keep up courage on the way to death. In a letter to his brother Jeff on March 22, 1942, concerning their father's suicide, Jones had significantly noted with similar bleakness that there is "no final whistle" in life, and the game "ends only when you quit or cannot fight some more" (Hendrick, ed., *To Reach Eternity* 18).

Uncertainty over the meaning and value of whistling is part of every aspect of the novel. The men in the hospital are simultaneously ashamed and arrogant about their wounds and think of those still in combat zones as "lucky-unlucky" (Jones, *Whistle* 5). They are half glad to be home and no worse off than they are and half remorseful that they are not with their still-endangered former comrades. They do not know whether to take part in the home-front prosperity or seek to return to the war they love as well as hate. The minute they start enjoying themselves, they envision the past or future agonies of these comrades, and they are not sure how they should re-act toward what they envision.

Strange theorizes that the reason Landers killed himself after receiving a discharge for which he whistled was that he wanted to remain in the army and be discharged "equally." That "unsolvable position" became unbear-able for him (428). Strange himself, after receiving the posting for which he whistled to an infantry company (making the opposite choice from Lan-ders), finds that he also wants equally to be near and away from combat and chooses the same way as Landers of dealing with his dilemma. In the final line of the novel, Strange, in the midst of committing suicide by remaining alone in the ocean, senses his ultimate isolation and continuing connection to those he has abandoned rather than face another time the kind of hurt he knows war will inflict, and he reflects with a dreadful lack of certainty that he does not know whether he will "drown first or freeze" (457).

Much of the power and fascination of *Whistle* come from the tensions of such uncertainties, especially from the finely honed balance between the horror instilled by the tragic fates of these highly sympathetic characters and the hope induced by the mystical episodes. As always, Jones puts hope—his system of beliefs—foremost, but he also puts many of his pro-foundest fears and questions about the great unknown of death into the book. The perennial tension between faith and doubt must surely have evoked its most personally passionate response here, and it gives Jones's last novel—his last lesson—a haunting quality that is not easily dispelled.

Technically, as well as emotionally, *Whistle* is one of Jones's finest achieve-ments. Its pattern is one of dissolution. The company dwindles into a core of four men who return to the United States together, and the core breaks down into four individuals who meet destruction separately. In *The Thin Red Line*, Jones had skillfully portrayed an infantry company as a "single animal," and he provides a subtle continuation of that concept at the beginning of *Whistle*. He also permits John Strange later to imply that he had been part of such a unit with the observation that "the fire and the strains of combat" can "combine" men and "squeeze" them into "one big self" (417).

The novel begins, appropriately, with the word *we*, as the unidentified representative of all the hospitalized men of the company speaks of their unified reaction to the news that Winch, Prell, Landers, and Strange are being returned to the United States for treatment. The representative continues to describe the common feelings of the wounded men for several pages and uses "we" throughout. Later, Winch thinks to himself, "We all of us feel the same way at some point" (10), and Landers reflects, "All of us were burdened with the same thing, at one point" (23). Gradually, however, as loyalty to the old company begins to fade, "we" is used less and less, and its meaning is narrowed to the group of four. By the end of the novel, the word has virtually disappeared.

Another striking device for conveying the impression of dissolution is the extensive use of sentence fragments. Consider the scene in which Landers is killed:

> Landers heard the wild squeal of the brakes. And perhaps a cry. And then the crash of glass and tear of headlight metal And a loud thumping thud.
>
> He saw or thought he saw the look of horror that came across her face in back of the windshield. Because she thought she was doing something wrong, and he wanted to laugh. The mouth a wildly spread O of lipstick. Eyebrows arched up. Eyes staring. (395)

In effect, the language shatters. As Landers shatters. Other fragments abound throughout, more so than in any of Jones's other books.

Even Jones's inability to finish the novel because of congestive heart failure helps create a sense of dissolution. In spite of desperate, almost superhuman, efforts, he was unable to write the last three and a half chapters, but he left sufficiently detailed notes for outlines to be made of them. Those outlines give a sense of completion to the work and are a sad reminder of the fact that the author was dying at the time he was so poignantly envisioning—and coming to terms with—the deaths of his characters. The outlines, whether primarily in the words of Jones himself or of his editor and friend Willie Morris, who worked from detailed commentaries Jones made to him in the hospital or talked into a tape recorder from his deathbed, demonstrate the care Jones took in foreshadowing. In chapter 33, for example, is the reminder that "we have already seen the signs of Winch's imminent crackup: the night he saw the image of one of the platoon's dead infantrymen on the windshield of his car and skidded off the road; his urge to pinch the Gray Lady at Prell's wedding; his wild poker game at the Claridge and later his burning Jack Alexander's IOU; etc." (452).

Whistle concludes with a brilliant and memorable image: the dying Strange's vision of a soldier in uniform swelling "until he's bigger than the galaxy" and then shrinking "until he seems to be only the size of a seahorse, and then an amoeba, then finally an atom" (456, 457). The pain Strange had known through his personal experience of war becomes universalized, because, like a black hole, he absorbs all the "anguish and sorrow and misery that is the lot of all soldiers" and carries it with him in his expansion into the galaxy and beyond (456). The vision may represent the absorption of the individual into the "one big self" of a combat company (expanding man's capacity for violence and his concomitant suffering) and his inevitable return to being an individual.

Strange's uncanny augmentation and diminution also provides the perfect depiction of the spiritual involution-evolution process: parting from God, the subsequent swelling and shrinking of the ego, and reinstatement as one of the multitudinous atoms making up God's being. Moreover, it appears that Strange is wholeheartedly willing that his reincarnations cease here and that he be released to become part of the Over-Soul. If the bodyless puppet masters sitting in judgment on him have decided that he has learned enough to do so—and he has greatly advanced beyond the point when they last debated what to do with him—then he will finally be merged into the wholeness symbolized by the circle of yin and yang. Either way, as expanding slaughterer or divinely absorbed atom, this strange and haunting image is one of Jones's finest legacies and a fitting end to his final lesson.

CONCLUSION:
THE MANIFOLD ACHIEVEMENTS
OF AN AMERICAN LITERARY
ORIENTALIST MASTER

Although *Whistle* stresses the darker side of the yin-yang symbol and demonstrates the doubts Jones always felt about his system of belief or any other, it also, perhaps in response to Emerson's Law of Compensation, brings back more of the mystical underpinnings of his philosophy, including the world of bodyless souls that had been discussed in *Some Came Running* but actually appeared in the final book. But whether presented openly through Jack Malloy, Milt Warden, and Bob French or suggestively through the mystical encounters of John Bell, Ron Grant, and all four protagonists of *Whistle*, Jones's reincarnationist philosophy is the unsevered thread that ties all of his work together.

There were, of course, shifts in emphasis along the way, which could be expected over a period of more than thirty years. His Lowney Handy–inspired temporary passion for yoga, for example, apparently gave way to Zen Buddhism, because Jones's final house in Sagaponack, Long Island, contained a "Zen meditation room with a straw mat floor," and his ashes were placed on a "Buddhist shawl" (MacShane, *Into Eternity* 302). His belief in the solitude of all souls became modified by his experiences with his wife Gloria to an admission or hope that perhaps two individuals could achieve a single outlook and experience life as a unit, at least at times. He insisted that people can only take responsibility for their own lives and that the highest level of insight is a compassionate understanding of the role suffering plays. Such insight leads to noninterference (although Bob French's attempt to live in accordance with that insight was seen as his principal error). At the end of his life, Jones's original belief became altered, and he suggested that perhaps the masters, far from adhering to this principle, are actively involved in the lives of everyone and pull strings to direct our every gesture toward increasing illumination and the healing of sickly, expanded egos. Yet throughout the modifications, the thread remained constant and firm. Old beads could lose their former positions of prominence as new ones were added (like Blavatsky's beads of the incarnated personalities on the thread of the reincarnating ego), and maybe an occasional strand might have to be replaced with another of a slightly different hue, but the thread held, wonderfully withstanding the weight of changes.

This unsevered thread of reincarnation and spiritual evolution places all of Jones's writing within the steadily developing tradition of American literary Orientalism that stretches from the transcendentalists to the present. As Beongcheon Yu notes about the beginnings of this tradition:

> Emerson, Alcott, Thoreau, and Whitman all shared one thing in common: an openness toward the Orient.... What was unique about their response ... was the total absence of literary exoticism and cultural dilettantism. At once existential and mythical, they responded to the Orient as a mandate of history, as a matter of birthright. ... By translating Columbus's passage to the Orient into a symbolic return to the source of light, the source of life, they all set a singularly American pattern of Orientalism for ensuing generations to follow. (*The Great Circle* 22)

Having derived his Eastern conception of life primarily through the Western filters of transcendentalism and theosophy, Jones produced works that reified, amplified, and elaborated on Yu's concept of American literary Orientalism. Far from treating reincarnation and spiritual evolution exotically or as a dilettante, he embodied them as the essence of human existence in substantially detailed, convincing American settings and also among Americans abroad, whether citizens or soldiers. His frequent use of war as a background for spiritual education recalls the the *Bhagavad-Ghita*, similarly a paean to reincarnation and spiritual growth amid massed, armed combat, and confirms Joan Didion's perception that "James Jones had known a great simple truth: the Army was nothing more or less than life itself" ("Goodbye, Gentleman-Ranker" 64). He also applied his reincarnationist values and system to events in his life (*Go to the Widow-Maker*), Robert Kennedy's assassination and an eyewitness view of the Paris student rebellion (*The Merry Month of May*), and the Vietnam War (*Viet Journal*). In doing all this, he not only notably extended the contexts in which such supposedly exotic, mystical subject matter may be treated but also emphatically and positively "Americanized" them.

One key to Jones's American literary Orientalism is the approach to character implicit in the rubric he used in *From Here to Eternity* from Ralph Waldo Emerson's essay on "History": "The Sphinx must solve her own riddle. If the whole of history is in one man, it is all to be explained from individual experience." Significantly, in a later part of this same passage

Emerson further illuminates the individual through affirmations that "of the universal mind each individual man is one more incarnation" and that "all its properties consist in him" (Emerson, *Selected Essays* 128). Hence, given his Emersonian linkage between the individual and the Over-Soul, Jones always put individual characters and their spiritual growth first, no matter how much time and care he might spend on plotting or constructing images of entire societies and large groups such as student rebels and army companies. Added to the predilection for focusing on character was a belief he discussed in a letter to Maxwell Perkins on August 1, 1946: "It ought to be a universal requirement of all writing, as ironbound a requirement as a plot, that every character should be handled with sympathetic understanding—even the worst son of a bitch—because it is in him" (Hendrick, ed., *To Reach Eternity* 76).

As a result of these predilections and beliefs, each of Jones's novels was essentially a bildungsroman in which all of the characters, even the minor ones, were being educated, growing, and taking long or short strides from morally blind selfishness toward clear-sighted compassion. Maylon Stark, for example, a minor figure in *From Here to Eternity* although his later incarnations as Maynard Storm in *The Thin Red Line* and John Strange in *Whistle* assume greater roles in their respective novels, starts out as "a regular bragging kid who made a pass at [Karen Holmes] as a matter of pride" (Jones, *From Here to Eternity* 334) and ends as a man who can extend sympathy and aid to both Karen and Warden, whom he had resented for a while. His penalty for his cruelty to Karen is that he becomes unable to function "in any whorehouse unless he was properly liquored up" (225). After Stark learns compassion, however, he discovers that he has become free from his previous hang-up: "Something's happened to me. I'm not drunk at all. I used to have to be drunk as hell" (849). In his more important role as Storm in *The Thin Red Line* he shares many of Welsh's perceptions about the absurd, gamelike quality of war, but, in contrast to Welsh, he intensely and vocally dislikes being shot at, watching bestial behavior in combat, and finding himself turned into an animal capable of finding amusement in mistreating a Japanese prisoner.

Even though Storm blames his behavior on combat numbness, his conception of himself as a humane, civilized person is shattered, and he is forced to confront his folly as well as that of others he had once longed to serve. Although he compromises for a while by returning to his job as mess sergeant, which he had temporarily forsaken for his view of combat, and by trying to serve his company and others away from the battlefield, in the end he, like Stein and Fife, goes off to work out his salvation alone. As Strange, of course, his ego is even more greatly reduced and his compassionate understanding immensely expanded, so he seems on the brink of achieving the union with God that lies at the end of spiritual evolution.

Similarly, Dave Weintraub, an indisputably minor character in *The Merry Month of May*, changes from a man with "animal cunning" (21) who sponges off film celebrities by playing court jester for them to a man who can display "sudden sympathy and sensitivity on his small tough ageing Jewish face" (352). Moreover, he learns not only to handle his ego-deflation by Samantha-Marie Everton "really well" (227) but also to commiserate with his rival, Hill Gallagher.

Central to Jones's portrayal of the sexual relationships between male and female characters, a key topic in his novels and short stories, is a yin-yang-based view that the "masculine" yang and the "feminine" yin are never as far apart or as disparate as popularly conceived. Clashes between the sexes, like all other social conflicts, are part of the spiritual education of each soul that forces that soul to relinquish deeply held illusions and private, interior worlds often inspired (but never wholly shaped) by public opinion.

Although many reviewers and critics have noted the adolescent behavior of males trying to score in Jones's novels, they have often failed to observe that he, too, was aware of this puerility and that he attacked it. Jones, more than most of the male authors of his time, had long pondered the dangers involved in trying to live according to the traditional American stereotype of a male as aggressive, efficient, ruthless, work-oriented, and sexually athletic. His views on the need for men to be sensitive rather than brutal, tender rather than domineering, compassionate rather than strict, and flexible rather than rigid fit in well with the views expressed in such contemporary sociological work as Myron Brenton's *The American Male* and Karl Bednarik's *The Male in Crisis*.

At the same time, Jones understood the effects of sexual politics on women, and as Lucky Videndi's theory of the circle of the sexes in *Go to the Widow-Maker* spells out, he saw their problems and personalities as being parallel to, if not the same as, men's. One reason that *Go to the Widow-Maker* is more realistic and compelling than most love stories is that it stressed the tortuous, torturing, multilevel adaptive process that a man and a woman who have similar personalities and beliefs must nevertheless go through in order to sustain their relationship.

Even before *Go to the Widow-Maker*, however, Jones indicated the need for his female characters (Karen Holmes in *From Here to Eternity*, Gwen French and Edith Barclay in *Some Came Running*, Sandy Thomas in "Two Legs for the Two of Us," Mona Patterson in "Secondhand Man," and

Norma Fry in "None Sing so Wildly") to break free from internalized American images of women as dependent, emotional, materialistic, security-loving, and publicly self-sacrificing martyrs. It was important, he felt, that women admit and expand their supposedly masculine opposite traits that would lead them to greater independence as well as more equal relationships with men. Moreover, Karen, Gwen, Edith, and Mona show signs, in varying degrees, of joining Lucky Videndi in making this self-transformation, which was both a social and a spiritual improvement.

Jones once admitted that he believed he had "a knack . . . for structural organization" (Interview 243), and that knack also aided his American literary Orientalism. Certainly, he had a talent for making the smallest details count and for using structure to help convey ideas. For example, in *Some Came Running*, he presents both Old Jane Staley's and Raymond Cole's deaths by first having people talk about them after they are dead, then jumping back to their final moments of life, and then moving forward to the deliberations of those affected by their deaths. This succession not only provides a variation on the traditional flashback sequence but also, subtly and more significantly, suggests Jones's theme of reincarnation by keeping Janie and Raymond alive after they have been treated as dead. It also implies the lingering effects of their karmic relationships with those who remember them.

In *From Here to Eternity* Jones skillfully develops the theme that every aspect of life is permeated by unexpectedness, rendering all human effort to attain security utterly futile and leaving souls bruisably bare before the shocks that induce spiritual awareness. It is a theme that is especially appropriate to a novel climaxing with the Japan's attack on Pearl Harbor, but it is also apparent elsewhere, such as in Prewitt's discovery that the delightfully named Lorene is really Alma Schmidt and Bloom's justifiable astonishment that his attempt to thank Prewitt for helping his dog immediately provokes a fight. Even Warden's small effort to outmaneuver fate by avoiding the hotel where he first took Karen is promptly repaid by Stark's observation of Warden and Karen at a different hotel, which in turn leads to Stark's surprising drunken confrontation with Warden during the field problem.

Jones's use of construction to heighten social and spiritual insight can also be seen in some of the small details of *The Merry Month of May*, wherein the quiet local color provided by Jack Hartley's visits to Parisian bars and restaurants affords a counterpoint to the destructive breakdown of the Gallagher family and the revolutionary attitudes of the students in the main part of the story. At the Brasserie of the Red Bridge on the Isle St. Louis, for example, Jack finds a family relationship among the proprietors in which conflicts occur in the context of an affection so strong that they become converted into warm, mutually shared jokes, unlike the abrasive conflicts among the Gallaghers. Moreover, the daughter accepts the mother's decisions as final, even when she disagrees with them, and the mother respects the daughter's attitudes, even when she feels the need to oppose them. Later, at the Brasserie Lipp, Jack observes a rigid hierarchy among the waiters that seems satisfactory to everyone concerned. Younger waiters cheerfully help the waiter designated as Number One because he is too old to do much by himself, and special respect is offered to writers and film people. Because all these things—family relationships with parents firmly in charge, hierarchies, and traditions—are social patterns that the students find too confining and have made prime targets of their revolt, it is unlikely that they are presented as remedies for conflicts. Instead, they imply that people can get along under almost any social pattern, depending upon their attitude toward it, and that there is some value in the way of life the young are ready to reject, even though it may have serious drawbacks. They also hint once again at an individual emphasis in Jones's reincarnationist viewpoint, which always aims at individual salvation rather than mass-minded remedies or massive revolution.

Probably Jones's greatest structural achievement, however, lies in the complicated strategy he developed for portraying a group simultaneously as a single personality and a collection of individuals. The approach is most evident in *The Thin Red Line*, wherein the viewpoint shifts constantly from soldier to soldier without losing sight of Charlie Company as a single entity, and it also underlies *The Merry Month of May*, *Whistle* and other work. With this approach, Jones could stress how some groups are educated through encounters with other groups: soldiers from one country with soldiers from another, student rebels with government officials, passively resisting prisoners in a stockade with their warders, middle-class haves with working-class have nots, men with women at a singles' bar or mating dance, Catholics with Protestants, and Moslems with Hindus. At the same time, he is free to explore the ever-present diversity within this apparent unity, the vast variety of individual experience that always underlies the shimmering, disturbingly worn smoothness and unreliable connectedness of the social fabric. He never loses sight of—or fails to hint at—the insubstantiality of the physical and social world, the web of maya that awaits the unwary soul and traps it with deception only to sting it back into spiritual awareness. Time after time, he describes towns like Parkman, military units like Charlie Company, typical "happy American families" like the Gallaghers, collectively radical comrades like the students of the Sorbonne, and courting couples like Sylvanus Merrick and Norma Fry suddenly and irreversibly splintering into individuals who must then pursue their solitary, ego-shattering paths to reabsorption into Brahma, anima mundi, or the Over-Soul—not exotic but fundamental. It is the essence of Jones's American literary Orientalism.

What he did so successfully with structure, he also accomplished with language. As George Garrett, Terry Southern, Tom Carson, and John Thompson perceptively noted, and Jones discussed in a letter to me on September 24, 1973, he consciously introduced into the third-person narrative the speech and thought patterns of his characters, creating a composite narrative voice that was neither wholly his own nor that of the characters. The narrative often deliberately reflects the verbal tics and inadequacies of many of the characters, implying that this difficulty in expressing thoughts is at least part of the reason for their loneliness and constant failure to make lasting, meaningful contacts. Thus, the narrative is frequently cacophonous, reflecting the inescapable and feuding relationship between its components. As Thompson emphasizes in relation to *Go to the Widow-Maker,* the heavy use of obscenity by male characters reflects their aggressiveness toward, and insecurity with, women, which accounts for their brutish inability to reach beyond or comprehend people outside their small circle of like-minded males.

That point could have been made about most of Jones's other novels as well. The language of the majority of Jones's characters and most of his narratives relentlessly exhibit the privateness and subjectiveness of each man's and woman's interior world and the difficulty of communicating meaningfully with others, let alone genuinely touching or being touched by another's soul. Although the use of language to indicate its inability to break through personal barriers or make sure people understand each other can be found in works as disparate as Sherwood Anderson's *Winesburg, Ohio* and Samuel Beckett's *Waiting for Godot,* it is a central tenet in Buddhism (particularly Zen Buddhism), Hinduism, Taoism, and Oriental religion in general that the final, important understandings are beyond logic and words. As the four primary characters in *Whistle* approach the dissolution of their current incarnations and, by implication, the ultimate dissolution that prepares them to be reabsorbed into God, it is by no means accidental or a lucky coincidence that their language shatters into fragments. Jones's use of language is another innovative, imaginative strategy for presenting his American literary Orientalist perspective.

In a discussion of *A Touch of Danger,* George Garrett emphasizes how Jones's skillful handling of the entertaining, rigidly prescribed, detective novel format indicates his versatility. That seems especially true when we consider that Jones was successfully able to adapt his mystical reincarnationist subject matter to a form that had hitherto applauded logic and hard-boiled social realism, an achievement equivalent to Claude McKay's introduction of fierce, controlled protests against oppression and racism into sonnets in "If We Must Die" and "The White House." That he could apply this subject matter with similar and often even greater skill to the formally written and formally structured *The Pistol* and the prissy, even comically worded and heavily symbolic *The Merry Month of May*, as well as to such colloquially experimental, technically innovative, and strikingly diverse works as the army trilogy, *Some Came Running, Go to the Widow-Maker,* and several of the short stories suggests that his range was unusually wide and that his contributions to American literary Orientalism may be viewed as multifaceted and profound. They appeal as models or inspirations to writers in this tradition at every point of its formalistic/imaginative, materialistic/spiritual, intensely sexy/undesiring, and conventionally grounded/idol-busting spectrum.

Apart from the various writings of the transcendentalists, probably Jones's closest American spiritual literary precursor was John Steinbeck's *The Grapes of Wrath*. Steinbeck's Joad family is moved from selfishness (first for their individual selves, then for the still-limited larger self of the family) to concern for others by a series of misfortunes and injustices. As the general situation and living conditions of the family steadily decline, forcing the once united members to split up against their will, the understanding, compassion, and ability to embrace the whole of humanity of each of them increases. An important minor character, the doubting preacher Jim Casy, even talks of God in a way reminiscent of the Emersonian Over-Soul ("maybe all men got one big soul ever'body's a part of") and argues that what we consider to be sins are really mistakes, two of the basic tenets of Jones's system of spiritual evolution. Moreover, the combination of painstakingly detailed realism in depicting American society with spiritual and symbolic overtones (such as the turtle carrying the seed and, fortunately, being knocked off the road by a truck so the seed could be planted) is also reminiscent of Jones's writing, although without the Jonesian implication of maya.

Frederick I. Carpenter notes that early reviewers had "condemned" the novel's "mystical ideas and the moralizing interpretations intruded by the author between the narrative chapters" but, arguing against them, affirms that "all important novels—especially American novels—have clearly suggested an abstract idea of life" and that *The Grapes of Wrath* "goes beyond" such works as *The Scarlet Letter, Moby-Dick,* and *The Adventures of Huckleberry Finn* "to preach a positive philosophy of life and to damn that blind conservatism that fears ideas" ("The Philosophical Joads" 80). It is an argument that could be made equally well in favor of Jones's entire body of fiction.

In addition to analyzing Steinbeck's "consummate" skill in integrating Jim Casy's essentially Emersonian philosophy "with the action of the story, until it motivates and gives significance to the lives of Tom Joad, and Ma, and Rose of Sharon," Carpenter also points to the role of Whitman's "earthy democracy" in the *The Grapes of Wrath* (81), another important link to Jones. As Carpenter observes, while "in Whitman's time almost everyone deprecated this physiological realism, and in our own many readers and critics still deprecate it, . . . Whitman himself had suggested the necessity of it: just as the literature of democracy must describe all sorts of people, 'en masse,' so it must describe all of the life of the people. To exclude the common or low elements of individual life would be as false as to exclude the common or low elements of society. . . . Therefore, along with the dust-driven Joads, we must have Grandpa's dirty drawers" (85). And in Jones's writing, we must have Bead attacked while having a bowel movement, the incessant obscenities of soldiers and large numbers of civilians, and numerous other "low or common" antics. Coupled with this justification, however, should be Casy's Emersonian spiritual rationale: we are all truly part of "one big soul" high and low—to put it another way, spiritual man, mental man, and animal man alike.

Finally, Carpenter wryly comments that even though "throughout [Steinbeck's] turbulent novel an almost traditional reticence concerning the details [of sex] is observed," an accusation that could never be made against Jones's writing, disbelief in its sinfulness "converts Jim Casy from a preacher of the old morality to a practitioner of the new" (85). Carpenter defines this "new morality" as that of Whitman, which challenges our guilt about sex, suggesting, in Casy's words, that "maybe we been whippin' the hell out of ourselves for nothin'" and "uses sex to symbolize the love of man for his fellows" (86). Both are concepts that Jones, much freer in his approach to sex than Steinbeck ever was, fully appreciated, although Jones would probably have added that sex at its most mystical approached the wholeness of reunion with God.

Appropriately, Beongcheon Yu had considered Steinbeck for analysis in his book on American Orientalism but ultimately eliminated him from his "original list" (as he similarly deleted Edwin Arlington Robinson, Amy Lowell, Kenneth Rexroth, and Allen Ginsberg) in favor of such writers as

Eugene O'Neill, T. S. Eliot, Ezra Pound, Jack Kerouac, and J. D. Salinger because he wanted to concentrate "on those writers who responded intensely to the Orient, matured significantly in the process and thereby contributed to the furtherance of this particular tradition" (*The Great Circle* 12). The probable reason Yu considered Steinbeck less representative than the others is that *The Grapes of Wrath* is a singleton among Steinbeck's writings and fails to link with the bulk of his work, which is more strictly realistic and, in later years, more politically and socially conservative.

Jones's writing, on the other hand, is emphatically representative in Yu's terms because the entire body of his work, like that of Emerson, Thoreau, and Whitman before him, reflects his intense response to Oriental thought and his considerable maturation in the process. He grew as an artist and a man from a lifelong struggle, and intense doubts, with the basic concerns of the Orient about reincarnation, karma, maya, and the illusory personal world in which we each live, the unity of Brahma or the Over-Soul, the absolute rejection of dualistic thinking conceptualized in the yin-yang symbol, master-disciple relationships, and, most of all, the path of spiritual evolution through ego reduction and unattached, compassionate understanding in preparation for reabsorption into God. Peter Matthiessen, who "was impressed by Jones's seriousness as an artist and by the reading he had done on his own," believes that "he tried to work out everything for himself" and "approached existential problems with a freshness others lacked." On the basis of both his freshness and thoroughness, Matthiessen has argued that Jones "did the deep thinking for all of us" (MacShane, *Into Eternity* 285). Like any creative artist, Jones's thinking was not exclusively, or even primarily, concerned with abstract ideas but rather embodied ones, and in intricately and innovatively realizing and elaborating on his ever-developing philosophy in new or renovated forms he masterfully expanded and enriched the tradition of American literary Orientalism.

WORKS CITED

Adams, Richard P. "A Second Look at *From Here to Eternity*." *College English* 17 (1956): 205-10.

Ardrey, Robert. *African Genesis*. New York: Atheneum, 1963.

Bannon, Barbara A. "Story behind the Book: *A Touch of Danger*." *Publishers Weekly*, May 7, 1973, 38-39.

Bednarik, Karl. *The Male in Crisis*. New York: Alfred A. Knopf, 1970.

Besant, Annie. *Reincarnation*. Adyar, India: Theosophical Publishing House, 1985.

————. *The Spiritual Life*. Wheaton: Theosophical Publishing House, 1991.

Blavatsky, H. P. *An Abridgement of the Secret Doctrine*. Edited by Elizabeth Preston and Christmas Humphreys. Wheaton: Theosophical Publishing House, 1967.

————. *The Key to Theosophy*. Los Angeles: Theosophy Company, 1987.

Bowers, John. *The Colony*. New York: E. P. Dutton, 1971.

Brenton, Myron. *The American Male*. New York: Fawcett, 1967.

Brunton, Paul. *A Search in Secret Egypt*. York Beach, Me.: Samuel Weiser, 1984.

————. *The Secret Path*. York Beach, Me.: Samuel Weiser, 1991.

Burress, Lee A. Jr., "James Jones on Folklore and Ballad." *College English* 21 (Dec. 1959): 161, 165.

Cantwell, Robert E. "James Jones: Another Eternity?" *Newsweek*, Nov. 23, 1953, 102-4+.

Carpenter, Frederick Ives. *Emerson and Asia*. Cambridge: Harvard University Press, 1930.

————. "The Philosophical Joads." In *A Casebook on* The Grapes of Wrath, edited by Agnes McNeill Donohue. New York: Thomas Y. Crowell, 1968.

Carson, Tom. "To Hell with Literature: James Jones's Unvarnished Truths." *Village Voice Literary Supplement*, Sept. 28, 1984, 1, 18-20.

Carter, Steven R. "James Jones, an American Master: A Study of His Mystical, Philosophical, Social, and Artistic Views." Ph.D. diss., Ohio State University, 1975.

Christy, Arthur. *The Orient in American Transcendentalism*. New York: Octagon, 1978.

Collins, Mabel, ed. *Light on the Path: A Treatise*. Los Angeles: Theosophy Company, 1975.

Didion, Joan. "Goodbye, Gentleman-Ranker." *Esquire* 88 (Oct. 1977): 50, 60-61, 62, 64.

Dolbier, Maurice. "Writing Is an Unnatural Pursuit." *New York Herald Tribune Book Review*, Feb. 25, 1962, 5.

Emerson, Ralph Waldo. *Selected Essays, Lectures and Poems*. Edited by Robert D. Richardson, Jr. New York: Bantam, 1990.

Emmons, Marlene M. "*Some Came Running:* A Reappraisal of James Jones's Misjudged Masterpiece." Unpublished typescript of master's thesis, 1996. Handy Writers' Colony Collection, University of Illinois at Springfield.

Garrett, George. *James Jones*. San Diego: Harcourt Brace Jovanovich, 1984.

Giles, James R. *James Jones*. Boston: Twayne Publishers, 1981.

Giles, James R., and J. Michael Lennon, eds. *The James Jones Reader: Outstanding Selections from His War Writings*. New York: Birch Lane, 1991.

Griffith, Ben W., Jr. "Rear Rank Robin Hood: James Jones's Folk Hero." *Georgia Review* 10 (1956): 41-46.

Handy, Lowney. Letters and notes to students. Unpublished typescript, Handy Colony Collection, University of Illinois at Springfield.

Head, Joseph, and S. L. Cranston, eds. *Reincarnation: An East-West Anthology*. Wheaton: Theosophical Publishing House, 1990.

———. *Reincarnation: The Phoenix Fire Mystery*. New York: Crown Publishers, 1977.

Hendrick, George, ed. *To Reach Eternity: The Letters of James Jones*. New York: Random House, 1989.

Hills, Rust, ed. *Writer's Choice*. New York: David MacKay, 1974.

Hopkins, John R., comp. *James Jones: A Checklist*. Detroit: Gale Research, 1974.

Jones, James. "A Bottle of Cream." In *The Ice-Cream Headache and Other Stories*, 169-82. New York: Delacorte Press, 1968.

———. *From Here to Eternity*. New York: Scribner's, 1951.

———. *Go to the Widow-Maker*. New York: Delacorte Press, 1967.

———. "Greater Love." In *The Ice-Cream Headache and Other Stories*, 123-40. New York: Delacorte Press, 1968.

———. "The Ice-Cream Headache." In *The Ice-Cream Headache and Other Stories*, 213-40. New York: Delacorte Press, 1968.

———. Interview with Nelson W. Aldrich. In *Writers at Work:* The Paris Review *Interviews, Third Series*, edited by George Plimpton. New York: Viking Press, 1967.

———. "Just Like the Girl" In *The Ice-Cream Headache and Other Stories*, 13-24. New York: Delacorte Press, 1968.

———. "The King." In *The Ice-Cream Headache and Other Stories*, 141-54. New York: Delacorte Press, 1968.

———. "Letter Home." *Esquire* 60 (Dec. 1963): 28, 30, 34, 40, 44.

———. *The Merry Month of May*. New York: Delacorte Press, 1971.

———. "None Sing so Wildly." In *The Ice-Cream Headache and Other Stories*, 81-121. New York: Delacorte Press, 1971.

————. "Phony War Films." *Saturday Evening Post*, March 30, 1963, 64-67.

————. *The Pistol*. New York: Scribner's, 1959.

————. "Secondhand Man." In *The Ice-Cream Headache and Other Stories*, 55-79. New York: Delacorte Press, 1971.

————. *Some Came Running*. New York: Scribner's 1957.

————. "Sunday Allergy." In *The Ice-Cream Headache and Other Stories*, 183-94. New York: Delacorte Press, 1971.

————. "The Temper of Steel." In *The Ice-Cream Headache and Other Stories*, 1-11. New York: Delacorte Press, 1971.

————. "The Tennis Game." In *The Ice-Cream Headache and Other Stories*, 195-211. New York: Delacorte Press, 1971.

————. "They Shall Inherit the Laughter." Unpublished typescript, Handy Writers' Colony Collection, University of Illinois at Springfield.

————. *The Thin Red Line*. New York: Scribner's, 1962.

————. "Too Much Symbolism." *The Nation*, May 2, 1953, 369.

————. *A Touch of Danger*. Garden City: Doubleday, 1973.

————. "Two Legs for the Two of Us." In *The Ice-Cream Headache and Other Stories*, 43-54. New York: Delacorte Press, 1971.

————. Unpublished letters to Lowney Handy. Typescript, Handy Writers' Colony Collection, University of Illinois at Springfield.

————. "The Valentine." In *The Ice-Cream Headache and Other Stories*, 154-68. New York: Delacorte Press, 1971.

————. *Viet Journal*. New York: Delacorte Press, 1974.

————. "The Way It Is." In *The Ice-Cream Headache and Other Stories*, 25-41. New York: Delacorte Press, 1971.

————. *Whistle*. New York: Delacorte Press, 1978.

————. *WW II: A Chronicle of Soldiering*. New York: Grosset and Dunlap, 1975.

Judge, William Q. *The Ocean of Theosophy*. Los Angeles: Theosophy Company, 1987.

Kipling, Rudyard. "Harp Song of the Dane Women." In James Jones, *Go to the Widow-Maker*. New York: Delacorte Press, 1967.

Lennon, J. Michael. "Glimpses: James Jones." *Paris Review* 29 (Summer 1987): 205-36.

Lennon, J. Michael, and Jeffrey Van Davis, producers. "James Jones: Reveille to Taps." Sangamon State University, 1984. PBS Television documentary.

Lydon, Michael. "A Voice against Anonymous Death." *Atlantic Monthly* 268 (Sept. 1991): 119-22.

MacShane, Frank. *Into Eternity: The Life of James Jones, American Writer*. Boston: Houghton Mifflin, 1985.

Mailer, Norman. *Ancient Evenings*. Boston: Little, Brown, 1983.

————. Unpublished interview with J. Michael Lennon, June 14, 1983, New York City. Used in part in the television documentary "James Jones: Reveille to Taps." Typescript. Complete videotaped interview on file in Handy Writers' Colony Collection, University of Illinois at Springfield.

Maugham, W. Somerset. *The Razor's Edge*. New York: Pocket Books, 1972.

McKay, Claude. "If We Must Die." In *Selected Poems of Claude McKay*, p. 36. New York: Harcourt Brace and World, 1953.

———. "The White House." In *Selected Poems of Claude McKay*, p. 78. New York: Harcourt Brace and World, 1953.

Michel-Michot, Paulette, "Jones's *The Thin Red Line:* The End of Innocence." *Revue des Langues Vivantes* 30 (1964): 15-26.

Morris, Willie. *James Jones: A Friendship*. Garden City: Doubleday, 1978.

Randle, Greg. "James Jones's First Romance: An Examination of 'They Shall Inherit the Laughter.'" Unpublished typescript of master's thesis, 1989. Handy Colony Collection, University of Illinois at Springfield.

Ray, David. "Mrs. Handy's Writing Mill." *London Magazine* 5 (1958): 35-41.

Remarque, Erich Maria. *All Quiet on the Western Front*. New York: Fawcett, 1975.

Said, Edward W. *Orientalism*. New York: Vintage, 1979.

The Song of God: Bhagavad-Gita. Translated by Swami Prabhavananda and Christopher Isherwood. New York: New American Library, 1972.

Southern, Terry. "Recent Fiction, Part 1: 'When Film Gets Good.'" *The Nation*, Nov. 17, 1962, 330-32.

Steinbeck, John. *The Grapes of Wrath*. New York: Penguin, 1976.

Styron, William. Foreword. In *To Reach Eternity: The Letters of James Jones*, edited by George Hendrick. New York: Random House, 1959.

Thompson, John. "The Professionals." *New York Review of Books*, June 15, 1967, 14-17.

Thoreau, Henry David. *Walden and "Civil Disobedience."* New York: New American Library, 1960.

Walker, Benjamin. *The Hindu World: An Encyclopedic Survey of Hinduism*. Volume 2. New York: Praeger Publishers, 1968.

Whipple, A. B. C. "James Jones and His Angel." *Life*, May 7, 1951, 142-44, 147, 149-50, 152, 154, 157.

Whitman, Walt. *Complete Poetry and Collected Prose*. New York: Library of America, 1982.

Wood, Thomas J., and Meredith Keating, eds. *James Jones in Illinois: A Guide to the Handy Writers' Colony Collection*. Springfield: Sangamon State University, 1989.

Yu, Beongcheon. *The Great Circle: American Writers and the Orient*. Detroit: Wayne State University Press, 1983.

INDEX

STEVEN R. CARTER is an associate professor at Salem State College in Salem, Massachusetts. He has also taught at the University of Puerto Rico, the University of North Carolina at Wilmington, and the University of Sassari in Italy. He is the author of *Hansberry's Drama: Commitment amid Complexity* and has published articles on contemporary American, African American, African Caribbean, and popular literature.